Philosophy in Philosophical Counseling

Philosophical Practice

Series Editor: Lydia Amir, Tufts University

The last decades have witnessed a renewed interest in the power of philosophy to address everyday problems, on both an individual and a social scale. The outcome has been a theoretical and practical field called "philosophical practice," an original approach that highlights the timely and perennial need for philosophy. This series aims to bring to the academic public the best reflections that bear on the relation of philosophy to everyday life and to the contemporary world, as grounded in experience or arguments or both. It honors the founders of this innovative field while calling for new ways of empowering philosophy by demonstrating its relevance to individual and social concerns both inside and outside academia. It thus hopes to strengthen philosophy by bringing its potency to the attention of philosophers and scholars from other disciplines, as well as to students and the general public.

Titles in the Series

Philosophy in Philosophical Counseling: Unasked Questions, Open Answers, by Ora Gruengard

Wonder, Silence, and Human Flourishing: Toward a Rehumanization of Health, Education, and Welfare, edited by Finn Thorbjørn Hansen, Solveig Eide Botnen, and Carlo Leget

The Philosophy of Practical Affairs: An Introduction, by Joseph Agassi

Philosophy in Philosophical Counseling

Unasked Questions, Open Answers

Ora Gruengard

LEXINGTON BOOKS
Lanham • Boulder • New York • London

Published by Lexington Books
An imprint of The Rowman & Littlefield Publishing Group, Inc.
4501 Forbes Boulevard, Suite 200, Lanham, Maryland 20706
www.rowman.com

86-90 Paul Street, London EC2A 4NE

British Library Cataloguing in Publication Information Available

Library of Congress Cataloging-in-Publication Data

Names: Gruengard, Ora, author.
Title: Philosophy in philosophical counseling : unasked questions, open answers / Ora Gruengard.
Description: Lanham : Lexington Books, [2023] | Series: Philosophical practice | Includes bibliographical references and index.
Identifiers: LCCN 2023021134 (print) | LCCN 2023021135 (ebook) | ISBN 9781793649096 (cloth) | ISBN 9781793649102 (ebook)
Subjects: LCSH: Philosophical couseling. | Philosophy—Therapeutic use.
Classification: LCC BJ1595.5 .G78 2023 (print) | LCC BJ1595.5 (ebook) | DDC 100—dc23/eng/20230602
LC record available at https://lccn.loc.gov/2023021134
LC ebook record available at https://lccn.loc.gov/2023021135

To the memory of Petra von Morstein

Contents

Acknowledgments

First of all, I would like to praise Professor Lydia Amir for her wonderful initiative in creating a special series of books on practical philosophy, representing, among other things, the variety of approaches in the emerging field of philosophical counseling. I thank Lydia for inviting me to participate in this important project.

I would like to compliment Lexington Books for its readiness to be the publisher and thank Jana Hodges-Kluck and Sydney Wedbush for their patience and help.

A wise man once said, "I have learned a lot from my teachers, still more from my study mates but the most—from my students." I would like to thank my counselees for helping me realize how relevant theoretical philosophy can be to issues that trouble people, and how discussing philosophical problems on a practical level can be relevant to a better understanding of theoretical philosophy.

I never studied philosophical counseling, but I owe to many teachers my arrival at that occupation. My philosophy teachers taught me, by their disagreements and polemics, the paths of controversies and the advantages of debates. My teachers in psychology and the social sciences paved my way to a philosophical interest in the practical application of theoretical insights. Many psychiatrists, clinical psychologists, family therapists, movement therapists, and art therapists, as well as clinical social workers, helped me develop my thoughts and work. Some enabled me to realize the relevance of philosophy in psychotherapeutic treatments. Others demonstrated how philosophical conceptions can be misinterpreted. Still others helped me identify incorrect applications of both philosophical and psychological insights. I am grateful to the patients who shared with me their good and bad experiences and to all the professionals who were ready to discuss with me my impressions, experiences, and mistakes. I am thankful to my parents, who taught me that I may learn from my own mistakes and from those of others.

I thank my colleagues, scholars of philosophy and philosophical counselors, for the long hours they dedicated to conversations about the relevance of philosophy to human life and about ways to apply it properly in counseling. I am grateful for their encouragement and critiques. They brought to my attention aspects which I tend to neglect, and sometimes illustrated to me approaches which I try to avoid.

I am indebted to the late Professor Petra Von Morstein, to whose memory I dedicate this book. She was a pioneer philosophical counselor and brilliantly demonstrated the possibility of combining abstract scholarship with concern for the concrete counselee. She had a remarkable ability to integrate and wisely interpret divergent philosophical traditions in ways that were relevant to the problems of the people who sought her counseling assistance. I am grateful for her intelligent listening and friendly support. I admire her brave coping with her terminal disease.

I am also indebted to the late Dr. Shlomit Schuster, from whom I first heard about the philosophical counseling movement. Her modest yet determined promotion of the emerging field won recognition even among those who preferred different conceptions of philosophy and other practical approaches. I, myself, had in fact started, as Molière would say, to "speak prose" before I knew that it was "prose," but she enabled me to become aware of my style and develop it into my own "poetry."

I am obliged to both Professor Lou Marinoff and Dr. Ran Lahav for giving me my first opportunity to participate in international conferences of practical philosophy and meet inspiring practitioners.

I am grateful to my colleagues from philosophy and philosophical counseling who read the manuscript and helped me to improve it with their wise comments, especially Professor Elhanan Yakira, Professor Peter Raab, and Ms. Alexandra Konoplyanik.

I am obliged to Ms. Linda Goldenberg for her wise editorial advice and cautious linguistic editing.

I alone am responsible for the errors, omissions, or mistakes.

I am grateful to the good friends, Dr. Michael Marcus, Dr. Nurit Markus, and Dr. Petra Zinser, among others, who encouraged me to develop my own way of counseling, and helped me cope with difficulties and confusions.

I am grateful, above all, to my spouse, Emanuel, my sons, Avishai and Iddo, and their families, for their help, encouragement, and patience.

Introduction

The Relevance of Philosophy

Philosophical counseling in its present forms is a recent phenomenon. It is part of a wider movement that fosters the idea of practical philosophy, which insists that philosophy can be relevant to everybody, and that philosophizing can be practiced by nonphilosophers. This seems to challenge academic philosophy. Philosophical counselors go a step further and claim that philosophy can help people to cope better with their personal problems. In saying this, they seem to challenge two other groups: the heterogeneous group of professionals who are supposed to be experts in psychological issues and the even more heterogeneous group of religious guides who are supposed to be authorities in spiritual matters. Philosophers, however, recognize neither professional expertise nor spiritual authority in philosophical questions, and the group of philosophical counselors is, in consequence, still more diverse.

Diversity of opinion, perspective, and approaches has been typical of philosophy since its earliest days. The ingenious and influential attempts of some great philosophers to put an end to controversies gave birth to new ones. I therefore do not offer here an approach that represents a common element in the emerging field of philosophical counseling; neither do I make claims about the efficacy or efficiency of one approach to philosophical counseling relative to others, or that of any kind of philosophical counseling to other forms of attempts to assist people cope with their personal problems. My aim is to explain and demonstrate how philosophy can be relevant even when the problems that bother people do not seem, initially, to be philosophical, and to show how philosophical counseling can be helpful precisely because philosophy is a domain of diversity and debate. I believe it may interest theoretical as well as practical philosophers, counselees no less than counselors, and induce challenged psy-professionals and spiritual authorities to join the philosophical dialogue.

Philosophical opinions are neither necessarily nor contingently true. They are possible answers to philosophical questions, and as such, they are neither true nor false, but like any answer to any question they are more or less *relevant* to the question in the context in which it is asked, and, unlike many surprising answers to empirical questions, more or less *reasonable*. Indeed, some theologians claim to believe in a certain religious dogma precisely because it is absurd, and some philosophers, religious in their own way, insist that one arrives at deep or meaningful answers thanks to intuition or insight rather than intellectual analysis. Yet even philosophers who claim to be nonrationalist *argue* for the acceptance of—or at least a preference for—their proposed answers to their philosophical questions and try to *justify by reasoning* the rejection of alternative answers, whether they seem to be intuitively obvious or call the obvious into question, whether they are a matter of insight or logical reasoning. Briefly, philosophical opinions are reasonable or unreasonable answers to possible philosophical questions in their relevant context. As such, they may have alternatives that are also reasonable. I say *possible* rather than actual, philosophical questions, because people hold many philosophical positions tacitly, having learned them unknowingly from others, and simply take them for granted.

Philosophical counseling is helpful when it challenges the philosophical positions that obstruct the counselee's capacity to solve or dissolve the problem. When this cannot be done, it may help the counselee accept the possibility that, at least for the time being, the problem is insoluble. It can challenge "troublemaking" philosophical opinions because philosophical opinions are replaceable by others; alternatives may seem more reasonable and become more acceptable when the context is changed. This can be done by criticizing and reformulating questions, examining prior assumptions, exploring implications of answers, or, alternatively, by adding perspectives and widening horizons.

That is what philosophers try to do in their academic debates about theories, approaches, or principles, and that is what philosophical counselors try to do—even when they do not conceive of their counseling in my terms—in dialogues with their counselees about the latters' concerns. This is not an attempt to discern the common element of philosophical counseling, as such an activity is not specific to philosophers. It is done spontaneously, knowingly or unknowingly, by neighbors and spouses when their disagreements involve tacit philosophical positions. It also happens, though perhaps less spontaneously, by salespersons and politicians, lawyers and pedagogues, religious guides and psychotherapists in their attempts to change opinions, behavior, feelings, or attitudes. It is philosophical not because philosophers do it, but because it is done in philosophically proper ways: when the challenged person and the challenger are aware that what is called into question is a philosophical opinion or attitude (whether as an explicit position or tacit presupposition) and neither participant attempts to hinder the philosophical dialogue. Such hindrance can be done by an appeal to an irrelevant authority or to expertise. It can also be done using threats, attempts to reduce the other's capacity to think critically or express his opinion, by explaining-away his philosophical claims as if they were "really" something else—symptoms, cognitive biases, defensive resistance, rationalizations, gender caprices, ethnocultural dispositions, and last but not least—blindness, disobedience or disloyalty.

Counseling is philosophical, to my mind, when the counselee's concerns are addressed, when his, rather than the counselor's, *philosophical questions* are identified and discussed, and when his obstructive philosophical opinions are challenged *in philosophically proper ways*. In the present book (in chapters 1 through 4) I try to explain and demonstrate what I mean by counseling in philosophically proper ways, and I argue that philosophy can be relevant even when the initial concerns of the counselee do not seem to be philosophical, when the counselee is not attuned to abstractions and generalities, when he insists on relevance to his concerns. In that context I also deal with the possible biases of the counselor, with ethical questions and with the issues of training.

In response to some readers who might find my approach too analytic or too rationalistic, I discuss in Appendix A some issues related to rationality and the apparently nonrational aspects of life. It is not "the" final answer, but an invitation to join the conversation. Readers who are not interested should nevertheless be aware of the main points. For one thing, the place of rationality on the meta-level, where one talks *about* philosophy and philosophical counseling, may be as different from its place on the level of a *philosophical conversation with the counselees about their problems* as the latter is different from its place on the level on which the counselees *experience* their problematic concerns. They should also be aware that the *decision* of the counselor as well as those of the counselees, about the place to give, in the conversation, and in life, to nonrational aspects—from faith, creativity and intuitive cleverness to feelings, moods, and emotions—can be rational. Such decisions are a matter of wisdom, which, I suggest, is not an alternative to rationality. Rather, wisdom is the ability to move back and forth, in the appropriate context, between different levels and domains of discourse and rationality, with the skill to administer that activity prudently and responsibly.

I also argue that academic philosophy, that is, the acquaintance of the counselor with a variety of philosophical theories and approaches, and his experience in participating in philosophical debates about theoretical issues, is necessary, although not sufficient, for fruitful and ethically proper counseling. I therefore critically examine some notions of "alternative" philosophy, proposed by practical philosophers who claim that academic philosophy is irrelevant. In this context I examine with particular attention the claim that philosophical counseling can be conceived as a philosophical cure of "philosophical thinking pathologies" (chapter 5). I also discuss the psychotherapeutic pretension of replacing philosophy along with the unjustified claims of some philosophical counselors against psychotherapy. I do it by distinguishing between psychological treatments that challenge the patient's beliefs and attitudes but do not deal with his philosophical positions, and treatments that do; and by explaining which of the latter are practiced in philosophically improper ways (chapter 6).

The other appendixes are also an integral part of the book, although for continuity of argument, they are presented separately. Appendix B deals with various attempts to put an end to philosophical controversies. I seek to justify, in some detail, my general claim that philosophy is a domain of controversies, and my conviction that philosophical debates, by widening horizons and changing perspectives, enable better dealings with unsolved problems. I seek, in particular, to justify claims about the benefits of inviting the counselee to a debate concerning alternative answers to his personal philosophical questions. Appendix C deals with some of the philosophical influences on Freud, Jung, and Adler. I seek to elaborate some claims (made in chapters one and five) about the attempts of some psychotherapeutic approaches to replace philosophy with what I consider the pretentious task of "the education of humanity," and with the still more pretentious claim to knowing the developmental failures and the unconscious causes of a person's "psychological difficulties" in dealing with the problems of life. With due respect for the contributions of those pioneers in the understanding of human psychology—their *personal philosophical opinions*, which are embedded in their therapeutic approach and sometimes unknowingly preached by their followers as "sanity," "maturity," or "authenticity," are still just opinions. From my philosophical perspective, imposing them on the patient as psychological goals is as disrespectful of his ability to consolidate his own philosophical position as the demand of some philosophers to impose "spiritual exercises" on students in an attempt to "form their character" according to the convictions of somebody else.

People sometimes have difficulties coping with their problems—the practical and the theoretical, the philosophical and the professional, the moral and the existential—for a variety of reasons. Having such difficulty is a psychological inconvenience, but the problem is not necessarily psychological and the obstacles are not necessarily due to developmental failures or character weaknesses. Sometimes difficulties are due to conceptual confusions or obstructive presuppositions. These might prevent, even in the case of great scientists and brilliant philosophers, the finding of a satisfactory solution (or realizing that under existing conditions there is no such solution). I am convinced that not only philosophical counselees, but also many among those who seek psychological or religious assistance, are in the same boat, stuck on a reef. They might get off the reef and sail to new destinations thanks to philosophical debates with people who have other perspectives. I believe that a proper academic philosophical background, which instills the habit of exploration from a variety of perspectives and approaches, can enable counselors to be more helpful than the decipherers of unconscious messages and the interpreters of divine announcements. It is therefore a pity that some graduates of philosophical studies who want to be philosophical counselors but do not know how, seek inspiration in the wrong places, or present the personal convictions of a specific philosopher as "the" philosophy, and the way to everybody's salvation.

In my references to anonymous persons, I have decided to use only masculine pronouns so long as it does not create problems of unclear reference. Yet, I want to avoid any unintentional impression about the distribution of roles in counseling between genders. In contrast, I intentionally refer mainly to Western philosophical traditions. I realize that philosophical texts about Western philosophy written by critical Western authors are sometimes misunderstood by philosophical counselors with non-Western backgrounds, who are not directly acquainted with Western philosophy (see, in Appendix B, an example for misunderstanding of a postmodernist text). I have no doubt that scholars with non-Western backgrounds can understand such texts, criticize them correctly, and add new perspectives to their interpretation, but the possibility of such misunderstanding made we aware that my own notions about other philosophical traditions, with which I am acquainted only indirectly, might be based on parallel confusions.

Being loyal to my conception of philosophy, my approach is polemical. I hardly mention philosophical counselors whose general approach is close to mine, and instead give room to a sampling of others, with whom I disagree in one or more points.

CHAPTER ONE

Philosophical Questions

The Possibility of Alternative Answers

Philosophical Counselors and Other Challengers

Philosophical counselors, whatever their orientation, assume that the concerns motivating counselees to seek their assistance are due, at least in part, to some of the counselee's beliefs or attitudes. They therefore encourage counselees to reexamine and explore possible alternative to beliefs and attitudes that may interfere with their ability to deal satisfactorily with their concerns.

They are not the only ones who challenge peoples' beliefs and attitudes. Pedagogues, advisors, psychotherapists, religious guides, missionaries, political propagandists, salespersons, lawyers (and, occasionally, spouses, offspring, and in-laws as well as colleagues and friends) also challenge the beliefs or attitudes of other persons. What is, then, the difference between philosophical counselors and the other challengers?

Some distinctions are easy to make: philosophical counselors are, or should be, among those who do it *for the sake of the challenged other* rather than those who do it for the sake of somebody else or some general cause. This distinction separates them not only from those who are not interested in the well-being of the challenged person, but also from people who are supposed to act for the latter's sake, but are actually trying, like some family members and friends (as well as some pedagogues and psychotherapists), to adapt them to prevalent norms, assumed needs, tacit requirements or the declared aims of their common group (and in the case of professionals, also those of their employing institutes).

Moreover, philosophical counselors are, or should be, among those who try to *do it by rational dialogues* with the challenged person rather than by persuasion, which aims at "bypassing" the latter's rational critical thinking, considering such thinking as "resistance to change." This distinction separates philosophical counselors not only from political demagogues and sophistic educators, but also from some psychotherapists and religious preachers who *do* care about the well-being of the challenged person but do not sufficiently respect his *rationality*.

Philosophical counselors, furthermore, are not, or should not be, advice givers. They are *conducting philosophical dialogues* with *partners who are, or could be, philosophers*. That distinction separates them not only from professional advisors, but also from philosophers who claim to have already "come out of the cave" of fallacious and confused beliefs and are therefore capable of guiding the perplexed "cave dwellers." That is, unlike some philosophers, for example, Plato's accomplished philosopher (Plato, *Republic*, book VII) or Maimonides's perfect sage,[1] philosophical counselors encourage the challenged person to explore and *arrive rationally*, through the dialogue, at *his own conclusions*, which may be different from those of the counselor. The long history of philosophical controversies has taught contemporary philosophers some modesty and a tolerant readiness to accept such possibility.[2]

Philosophical counselors, finally, *deal with the philosophical positions* of the challenged person. They do it even when the initial beliefs that are called into question are about matters of fact or taste, affect, mood, or context, or, as Karl Popper would put it (Popper, 1957), even when the "problem situation" is practical or "mundane" rather than theoretical or "spiritual." In other words, philosophical counselors deal *not only with the explicit philosophical positions* of the counselees and their practical *implications*, but also, and perhaps mainly, with their *philosophical presuppositions*. That distinction, which is not easy to make, separates philosophical counselors from not only family members, colleagues, and friends in most of their nonphilosophical arguments, but also from religious guides and psychotherapists, who *are* often challenging *philosophical* presuppositions, *but doing it unknowingly*. They assume that the challenged positions are just blind, sinful, or infantile ways of thinking or are a matter of instincts, prejudices or stubborn habits rather than contestable philosophical positions.

Philosophical Presuppositions

The latter assumption is, to my mind, a widespread error that is reflected, for example, in the identification of a mistaken mathematical answer as nonmathematical.[3] The philosophical presuppositions that are called into question in some philosophical counseling dialogues—from the sophisticated but tacit philosophical positions (like those that are challenged in debates among the most erudite and experienced philosophers) to the most naïve unexamined philosophical assumptions (of the least philosophically sophisticated, legendary "man of the street" or "peasant")—are *philosophical answers* that the challenged person *would* give (in his terms) to *philosophical questions* (expressed in terms that are comprehensible to him). As I shall explain later, philosophical answers are, in principle, a matter of debate. There is, however, no debate when the questions are not asked, and the possible answers are taken for granted rather than explicitly stated. Yet they are a matter of debate.

Some of those presuppositions may be based on personal inferences, but whether such processes were originally done consciously or not, their conclusions are not reexamined considering new information. Most of our presuppositions have, however, been learned from others, whether explicitly or as tacit positions that are embedded in various forms of sociocultural beliefs. They may be transmitted not only by explicit statements, but also through ways of speaking and thinking, as well as through the unexamined adoption of customs, values and norms or the concerns and anxieties of meaningful others. As they are transmitted in tacit ways, their holders may not be fully aware of holding them. Together with other, nonphilosophical, presuppositions they may form the *shared taken-for-granted background of a discipline* in one of its phases, the *dominant "spirit" of an era, the "episteme" of a given civilization*, or the *tradition of a specific sub-group*. It may be a *personal tacit worldview* that reflects both personal inferences or habits and sociocultural influences. It is philosophy, to the extent that it can be explicated as providing answers to philosophical questions, but it is *philosophy on its first level*: taken-for-granted and unexamined.

Levels of Philosophy

I distinguish between different levels of philosophy to clarify my approach and explain why academic philosophy sometimes seems irrelevant to life issues although it *is*, indirectly, very relevant. In the *actual* philosophizing activity of academic philosophers there is most often no such distinction, as elements that belong to different levels are frequently interwoven.

The first level of philosophy is, as said, the level of taken-for-granted and unexamined philosophical beliefs and perspectives, attitudes, and values. They have different sources and are ambiguous, non-systematic, and not entirely coherent. The assumptions on which they rest are unclear, their implications are unexplored. Philosophy on higher levels is linked to the *activity* of *philosophizing*.

On the second level, philosophical positions are called into question. In particular, the *adherence to presuppositions* that are taken for granted is challenged. Although the holder of those positions is criticized, the challenger is not necessarily less dogmatic or more coherent than the one who is challenged. Yet he is, at least, aware of himself as philosophizing, as performing an activity of examination of alternative answers to philosophical questions. It is not necessarily the activity of an acknowledged philosopher. It is not necessarily done for the purpose of philosophical expansion. People challenge the positions of other people for a variety of reasons, and sometimes it fits their purposes to challenge their philosophical positions.

Philosophy on the third level is also an activity that calls philosophical positions, tacit or explicit, into question, but it is done not only with awareness of the possibility of alternative possibilities, but also with the purpose of critically examining *one's own as well as the other's positions*. As such, it is, or should be, part of a decent philosophical education.

Several kinds of practical philosophy activities, such as the so-called Café-Philo or Socratic Dialogues, aim at the acquaintance of the participants with a variety of alternative positions. In the former, debates are permissible and mutual criticism is welcome; in the latter arguing is against the rule. Instead, the participants are invited to elaborate their positions, listen, and understand the positions of others. They are encouraged to rethink their initial positions considering the other options and to agree about common elements in their initially different positions.

Similar processes sometimes take place, not necessarily verbally, in psychological workshops where participants are invited, for example to imagine being in each situation and to demonstrate their interpretation and response by speaking, dancing, dramatic acting or drawing. It is expected that they will reflect about the position underlying their interpretation and response considering the demonstrated alternatives (and perhaps change it to a "more functional" option).

In modern academic philosophical education, the confrontation of students with a variety of answers (or approaches) to a given philosophical question is not meant to reduce disagreements or change "non-functional" positions. Modern universities, unlike some ancient schools of philosophizing and institutes for religious formation, aim (at least officially) neither at similarity of opinions nor corrected personalities. Modern philosophical ideals, perhaps the result of failures to obtain the old ideals of absolute truths, have demonstrated, at least under liberal democratic regimes, a preference for freedom, openness and therefore *plurality of opinions and practical choices*. This has been especially true in departments of philosophy. The aim, beside the sharpening of the students' reasoning, is to familiarize them with a variety of philosophical options and the theories in which they are embedded. The students are, at least theoretically, encouraged to use their own reason and arrive at their own conclusions, independently of the opinions of their teachers.[4] I believe that a philosophical counselor should have reasoning skills and an acquaintance with philosophical theories that are acquired on *that* level even if his counseling does not consist in improving the counselee's intellectual capacities or widening his theoretical knowledge.

Such skills and knowledge may, of course, be acquired in other frameworks, but third-level philosophizing expertise is philosophical even if it was taught in, say, the department of pedagogy, theology, or law, or in some nonacademic setting.[5]

Dealing with philosophical texts—creating, interpreting, and criticizing them, and taking part in debates about their meaning and worth—is philosophizing on a fourth level. Such studies whether they deal with a single philosophical question or present a theory that is supposed to provide answers for many queries, often refer to a variety of preexisting theories and contain the author's arguments for or against them, as well as a presentation of what the author's contribution is supposed to make. Thus, even when the creation of the text or its interpretative and critical reading is done by somebody who is not keen to participate in live philosophical dialogues, his philosophical activity is performed in *a context of debate* with other philosophers. Whoever has experience in philosophizing on the fourth level is aware that *philosophy is a domain of controversies*.

A still higher level of philosophizing is a meta-level on which philosophizing itself is discussed: Its principles and criteria, its meaningfulness and importance, etc. It is also the level on which one deals with the question of what a philosophical question is, whether it can have a definite answer, or whether and how to choose among alternative answers. It is also the level on which changes of so-called philosophical paradigms and perspectives are explored.

My personal approach to philosophical counseling was inspired by ideas that I have met on that level. Other counselors may have been inspired by discussions on other levels. In any case, one of the tasks of the philosophical counselor is to respect the counselee as a partner in a philosophical dialogue on the third level and adapt his ideas to the background of the counselee, adopt a level of generality and abstraction that is "tolerable" to him and translate it into a language in which he feels comfortable.

Philosophical Questions

There is, of course, no agreement among erudite philosophers about the questions that a "real philosopher" should ask. See, for example, the question "Why is there something rather than nothing?" which was originally a theological question. Leibnitz raised it to explain the principle of sufficient reason (Leibnitz, 1976, Article 7).[6] The Big Bang theorists, who are nowadays asking it as a scientific question,[7] consider Leibnitz's reason ("God willed that the world exists") insufficient and irrelevant. Some past philosophers shared the opinion that Leibnitz's "reason" was insufficient but agreed with him that it was a metaphysical question. Some of them, for example Kant, said that although our Reason is asking such questions, the *answers are beyond the reach of our Intellect* (Kant, 1999a, The antinomy of pure reason, sec II: 396–402, sec III: 422–29). It was supposed to be an answer not only to metaphysicians but also to their opponents, who, like Locke, insisted that metaphysical questions in general reflect *confusions that are caused by "unnatural associations of ideas"* and in this respect are just like "other follies," such as teatime gossip, speeches in parliament, and madness (Locke, 1975, Book II, Ch. XXXIII). More recent philosophers use other terms and perspectives. Some, like Russell, may consider the existence of the universe as a "*brute fact*" that just *is* and cannot be explained (Russell, 1948), while their opponents, for example, Wittgenstein, insist that although such a question does not refer to a state of affairs that can be talked about meaningfully, it is nevertheless a matter of *mystical wonder* (Wittgenstein, 1922, 6.44). Heidegger discovered it somewhere in Schelling's attempts to distinguish between questions about *essence* and questions about *existence* (Schelling, 2008), and translated it into an "*ontological*" *question*. He blamed the whole tradition of Western philosophy for failing to ask it in that sense (Heidegger, 2014 pp. 7–8). Some of his contemporaries, such as Ayer, maintain that it is a *pseudo-question* (Ayer, 1973). Philosophy, which is, according to some philosophers of language, "*the battle against the bewitchment of our intelligence by means of language*" (Wittgenstein, 1958, pt. 1 sec. 109), should expose the futility of such questions.

The example shows, briefly, that what is considered by a philosopher as a philosophical question depends on his conception of philosophy and philosophical ways of inquiry.[8] Most philosophers would nevertheless agree that there is a difference between questions such as "What is truth?" on the one hand, and questions such as "Is the witness telling the truth?," "Is it true that it never rains in the Sahara Desert?," "Is 2×2=5 true?," "Are those stones true diamonds?" on the other hand. The difference I have in mind is *not* that philosophers ask, as Socrates believed they should, about *general* concepts while judges (or journalists), geographers (or tourists), mathematicians (or shopkeepers), gemologists (or thieves) are apparently thinking of a variety of *instances* of the same concept. The belief that all philosophers and only philosophers are interested in general concepts is however wrong; and the idea that philosophers should deal with concepts, or at least have a clear *concept* of what a concept is, has been called into question by contemporary philosophers as well as linguists and psychologists.[9]

Yet, although some philosophers would suggest that we distinguish between, say, truth in science, truth in court, and truth in art or literature, and others would say that we should ask for *criteria* for truth or for the *uses* of the word 'truth' rather than its *meaning*, there is an agreement about the difference between the first and the other factual or mathematical questions in my example.[10]

Of course, not all the questions that have been asked by philosophers are nowadays considered to be philosophical. Ancient philosophers dealt with everything, from "spiritual" themes (such as the immortality of the soul and the nature of metaphysical justice), to moral or ethical issues (such as the good life of the virtuous man), political subjects (such as the stability of political regimes and the expertise of good politicians), biological questions (concerning the classification of insects etc.) and astronomical questions (about the behavior of heavenly bodies). They left to others only questions concerning "technical" expertise, such as building, sculpting, shipping, cooking, and healing.

During the Middle Ages philosophers left decisions about legal or conventional norms in the hands of jurists and abandoned theoretical as well as practical medicine to the physicians. Gradually, however, philosophers were "robbed" by natural scientists of the other factual questions that can be dealt with by observations of "data" (or explanatory theories whose hypotheses are empirically testable) but continued to speculate about the principles of nature and of science. Later, for the same reasons, they lost the checking and interpreting of documents and other kinds of evidence for assumed historical, cultural, linguistic, social, and political states of affairs, and were left with meditations about their principles or criteria.[11] Matters of mathematical calculations, demonstrations, or analyses, to which some philosophers have made important contributions, are also outside their present territory.

Psychologists and sociologists have also taken "their" share, although in those fields philosophers do not surrender so easily. They still insist that questions of rationality, sanity, knowledge, and meaningfulness, just like those of happiness, freedom, and morality, are not reducible to themes that are dealt with by the human and social sciences. They therefore collaborate with the professionals in some areas and criticize their theories and practices in others. Philosophical counselors are mainly among the critics, and some of them blame psychotherapists for attempting to reduce philosophical considerations and confusions to the apparently empirical facts of "malfunctions" and "disturbances." I believe, as I shall argue later (in chapter 6), that they fail to see how much psychotherapists as well as sociologists have "invaded" philosophical terrain, and, under the guise of clinically or empirically based knowledge, are making philosophical claims.

Briefly, contemporary philosophers deal with questions that cannot be answered by empirically testable answers, whether by observation or interpretation of documents; nor can they be answered by pure logic. From the contemporary philosophical perspective, even in the discourse of past philosophers only such questions are philosophical. (Those who deal nowadays with linguistic and cultural phenomena, and seem, like Foucault, to have returned to the mixed analyses of past philosophers of history, do it in the context of *meta-philosophical questions* about the possibility of arriving at universally valid and unbiased philosophical positions (Gutting and Oksala, 2018). Similarly, those who seem to deal nowadays with the ancient questions of virtue and the good life try, unlike ancient philosophers, to detach their analyses from metaphysical and religious issues, such as the "essence" of good or virtue or the immortality of the soul. They simply believe that dealing with questions from the perspective of virtue and the good life can contribute more sensitivity to a variety of moral aspects and thus enrich the *contemporary moral discourse*, which is about the *criteria* for moral *behavior*, or, on the fifth level, the *criteria for such criteria* (Hursthouse and Pettigrove, 2016).

Philosophical counselors, who differ from each other in many philosophical respects, may also differ in their conceptions of philosophical questions, and even disagree that their mission is to deal with such questions. (In chapter 5 I deal with some radical approaches that are opposed to mine.) Most philosophical counselors, however, are not radical. They challenge philosophical preconceptions not only to clarify misunderstandings with regards to their own mission, but also (and mainly) they challenge presuppositions that interfere with the counselee's ability to *cope better with the issues that interest—or disturb—him*. To the extent that they seek to help the counselee, they must call into question some of his *philosophical* presuppositions as well. They may have different approaches to counseling than mine and sometimes disagree with me about some questions, yet they normally have, for all practical purposes, a sufficiently clear notion of latent philosophical positions and they know to which questions there could be possible answers. They can therefore invite the counselees to take part in personally relevant philosophical dialogue.

In doing that they introduce the counselee to the realm of philosophical controversies, for, as philosophers believe nowadays more than ever before, the *answers* to philosophical questions are *a matter of debate*, and the philosophical counselor is not supposed to dictate his opinion but rather encourage the counselee to "take part in a philosophical debate," i.e., explore alternatives and arrive at his own conclusions.

To do this, they may sometimes suggest that a question the counselee raises is philosophically unanswerable or even meaningless. They therefore need to have some idea of the debates about the meaningfulness of general, abstract, detached, and confusing questions such as in the above-mentioned example ("Why does something exist rather than nothing?"). They may also, as I demonstrate in chapter 2, use the various positions toward such questions as strategies in the counseling dialogue. The presuppositions that they find appropriate to challenge are normally less abstract and general than a Parmenidean tacit conviction that "something, rather than nothing, exists."

Philosophical Controversies

Controversies, of course, are not specific to philosophy, and philosophers are not the only ones who get involved in philosophical debates. As Kuhn's study of scientific revolutions has shown, theories are considered "scientific" by scientists (in the relevant discipline) thanks to a shared background of philosophical presuppositions. Those presuppositions are about the nature of the subject matter as well as the adequate ways to investigate it—from the questions that are considered "scientifically" meaningful to the "scientific" relevance of observations and experimentations. According to Kuhn's theory, in times of "normal science" scientists take the background assumptions for granted and may be unaware of the philosophical basis of their scientific activity. However, they become aware of it in times of crisis, when theories that fit the existent scientific "paradigm" get entangled in difficulties, and an alternative approach, which seems to cope better with those difficulties, is proposed. When the new approach is "revolutionary," that is, when the philosophical assumptions upon which it rests are incompatible with the exiting shared philosophical background, and the existing criteria for judging the scientific validity of an approach do not apply, even positivist scientists and philosophers of science, who are normally convinced that philosophy is irrelevant, get involved in philosophical debates. A "paradigm shift," the acceptance of the new "paradigm" by the relevant community, is enabled thanks to such debates. This happens in other domains as well, and to the extent that there are "normal science" periods in certain fields of philosophical inquiry, they happen in philosophy too. Although the subject matter of philosophical research and debates is explicitly philosophical, the consideration of their themes as "philosophical" and their ways of dealing with them as "philosophically" appropriate are based on other philosophical assumptions (Kuhn, 1962).

Philosophy, even if one limits that term to Western mainstream philosophical history, was, however, never a single discipline with a shared "paradigm." Since the pre-Socratic times, there are always some philosophers who claim that it "fails" to do what is "really" important, while others point to different philosophical convictions in different periods or places. Moreover, even the tacit agreements within groups—in and outside the mainstream—does not enable a totally "normal" activity without debates on tacit assumptions. There have been many attempts to propose an approach that would put an end to philosophical controversies, but they were always criticized by opponents with alternative proposals and by sceptics, relativists, pluralists, and others who preferred practical wisdom to theoretical analyses. This applies even to some contemporary attempts to put an end to controversies by alleged proofs of inevitable plurality or relativity.[12]

Kuhn's book is an attempt of the last kind: It claims to have proven that the validity of "paradigms" is relative and that the "incommensurability" of "paradigms,"—the impossibility of judging the adequacy of one "paradigm" by rules that are part of another "paradigm"—necessarily implies pluralism of approaches and a skeptical attitude to sciences. Although some prominent philosophers of science disagree with parts of his conclusion, and insist that scientific studies bring us gradually closer to the real world or to the basic rules of human ways of describing and exploring it (Bird, 2018), the present impact of Kuhn's analyses seems to be much greater: His onslaught on the logical positivists' basic assumptions—that scientific activity can be free of philosophical assumptions, and that methodological criteria can be discussed independently of theories and observational data—challenged the last "heroic" attempt to put an end to metaphysical and epistemological controversies by proving, from a methodological point of view, their alleged futility and irrelevance to science, His concentration on the natural sciences challenged the illusion that at least in the "hard sciences" there is no room for debate. It amplified the fact that since the end of the nineteenth century dogmas regarding truth in mathematics and physics were called into question. Kuhn's conclusions seemed, moreover, to be paralleled and supported by some philosophers of language, who claimed to be following the alleged relativism of Wittgenstein's idea of variety of incommensurable "language games." Poststructuralists and their followers considered his conclusions as supporting their ways of using the structuralist assumption that linguistic "elements" have no "meaning" independently of their "differences" from other "elements" in the whole "structure" (Smith and West, 2008). Over and above the changes of attitudes in those fields, Kuhn's relativism and pluralism appealed to philosophers who opposed the belief in the possibility or desirability of non-relative knowledge, and the predominance that is attributed to scientific approaches, for other reasons: Neo-Marxists and Nietzscheans, reinterpreters of Hegel's universalism and admirers of Herder's national particularism, religious conservatives and seekers of romantic ideals, followers of Heidegger or other existentialists, and thinkers who believe in the specific "voices" and "identities" of the "others"—those who, according to their respective claims, were ignored or misrepresented in Western scientific studies or philosophical investigations. In fact, even philosophers who oppose the current relativistic and pluralistic tendencies and disagree with Kuhn's conclusions admit that we have not arrived at the stage where controversies are ended.

I believe that the history of philosophical controversies demonstrates neither their futility nor avoidability.[13] Philosophers learn from the polemic process about unjustified assumptions and alternative points of view even when they do not come to agreement. They also learn from other evolving domains. Therefore, at least in certain respects, later philosophers may be wiser than their predecessors. For this reason, I believe that philosophical counselors who ignore the present "state of the art" and present their views as "the" philosophical truth or approach, rather than philosophical options that are not beyond doubts and debates are deceiving the counselees.

Counseling, however, is not a course in philosophy or a training for critical reasoning. The counselee comes to the session with concerns and difficulties. The counselors are supposed to assist them in the search for solutions. The approach that is described in the present book is inspired by Kuhn's belief that philosophical debates enable "paradigm shifts" that open new horizons. However, unlike the "revolutions" that he describes where the new approach has already been proposed and debates have enabled its acceptance, the "shifts" in counseling occur thanks to philosophical challenging of the counselees' tacit beliefs, which enables him to realize that alternative approaches are possible. The approach that the counselee finally adopts is a matter of his choice among discussed alternatives or his discovery or creation of new options.

The Relevance to Philosophical Counseling

Keeping Deceptions at Bay

The purpose of my insisting on the inevitability of philosophical controversies (which are due to the fact that answers to philosophical questions, however plausible and reasonable they may sound, are neither *necessary* truths nor "*brute facts*") is not to promote a relativistic approach. I want, first, to prevent *deceptive* presentations of philosophy to the counselees: Some counselors present their *specific* philosophical *position* as "philosophy" while discarding alternative positions, which are held by other philosophers, as "not philosophical." Socrates could, perhaps, allow himself to distinguish between his "philosophical" approach and that of the "sophists," discarding thereby not only the charlatans but also some serious thinkers who were too pluralistic, skeptical, or relativistic for his philosophical taste. He was among the mythical inventors of the term 'philosopher'—"lover of wisdom"—and could try to impose his understanding of it on others. A contemporary philosopher, however, has no reserved rights on the term, even if some Heideggerian groupies may claim that "thinking" did not occur before Heidegger told us what it "really" is, and some more recent innovators reveal to us when philosophy is "really" deep. A contemporary philosophical counselor should not *mislead* the counselee into believing that, say, "spiritual" values are philosophical while "non-spiritual" ones are not; or that asking, "What is a good life?" is philosophy while responding that "What is important is the morality of actions and not the quality of life of the moral agent" is not.

I do not think that counselors who mislead in these ways are necessarily mischievous; they may simply be philosophically ignorant. As such they would, perhaps, fail to understand my two other reasons for mentioning the controversial nature of philosophy. One of them, already mentioned, is my conviction that philosophical counseling consists in inviting the counselee to take part in a philosophical dialogue where some philosophical positions or presuppositions are called into question and alternatives are explored in a way that enables the counselee to arrive at his own conclusions. I believe that *the counselor's initial awareness of the inevitability of philosophical controversies is a pre-condition for his real tolerance and respect for the counselee's freedom of thought.* The other reason is that such awareness justifies the counselor's attempt to *call into question positions that may hinder a better coping with the issues*. It is up to the counselee to choose his preferred positions, but he can do it more freely when he realizes that they are neither necessary truths nor self-evident intuitions.

That conviction is based, as already said, on a lesson that can be learned from the history of philosophy, science, and many other domains. Controversies come to the fore when it is difficult to cope with a problem and the solution offered by one group is incompatible with some of the basic assumptions of the other group. Philosophical discussions of those assumptions may give birth to new approaches that overcome the relevant controversy and enable the solution of the problem in its specific context.

Historical controversies that seemed to have been overcome may indeed reappear later in new versions. Yet the temporary overcoming enabled the solution of some actual difficulties. The new problems that might reevoke the old controversy belong to another level of knowledge and understanding. The new version of the disagreement does not bring them back to the initial level of debate, because some philosophical assumptions have changed in the meantime.

Philosophy, which has contributed to such processes in other domains of theoretical knowledge and pragmatic activity, is relevant to life not because it offers ultimate solutions (although sometimes it seems to); but rather because it can make a parallel contribution to coping with the problems that individuals face in their personal life. Philosophical counseling can help persons who are apparently "stuck" in their issues by helping them make a beneficial "paradigm shift." It does this by inviting the counselee to philosophize about other questions and may thereby help him or her overcome those dilemmas and other problems and confusions. That is how philosophy can be relevant to the lives even of people who are not particularly interested in abstract philosophical theories.

Philosophical Counseling Is Not Forming Philosophers

I believe accordingly that philosophical counseling, unlike the grand plans of some seemingly inexperienced philosophical counselors, does not normally turn philosophical counselees into philosophers. I therefore do not adopt Fayerabend's (1975) approach, according to which one should encourage the creation of alternative scientific and metaphysical theories even in times of crisis-free "normal science," to encourage elasticity and openness of mind. I do not presuppose that the counselee is necessarily more dogmatic and rigid than the counselor, and I do not conceive of counseling as education. Moreover, I am convinced that philosophical teaching or counseling *should not* resemble a religious conversion. I would not try to shatter the counselee's "hard-core" philosophical convictions (Lakatos, 1970) just because they are different from my "hard-core" convictions (as I would occasionally do in arguments with philosophical colleagues), if they are irrelevant to dealing with his difficulties in coping with the issues that concern him. Moreover, if the counselee is not a philosopher, I would not try to turn him into one.[14] At best, I would try to enable him to experience *the relevance of philosophy for a while*, which is very different from a nonbeliever's experiencing the relevance of a specific religious faith, although in both cases "paradigm shifts" occur.

My counseling experience suggests that the issues that engage counselees are not necessarily "the" philosophical questions that occur to philosophers talking in the abstract about "the relevance of philosophy to life." "The" questions that occur to those philosophers may, indeed, be compared, in some respects, to those that lead to conversion to a new religion. They are supposed to lead one to change, not only one's entire attitude to life, but also one's daily behavior. But even if contemporary philosophical counselor were asking "the" philosophical questions according to the ancient Greco-Roman conceptions of philosophy, they are not living in the Greco-Roman era, and, as philosophers have learnt since those remote times, they should not pretend to know "the" answers. They therefore should not try to prepare their counselees to join any philosophical sect. Nor should they pretend to be teaching the *idiōtēs* [idiotes]—the Greek term for laypeople—who would not be admitted to an elitist sect of "true" philosophers, to live "somewhat more philosophically": Sometimes it may make sense—the "true" philosopher may choose, like Diogenes, to live in a barrel—the "layman" can live in a modest apartment; but what should those "simple humans," who are not idiots, do "a little bit more philosophically" in circumstances under which the "true" Stoic philosopher, listening to Epictetus, would choose to commit suicide? Hamlet, a student of philosophy, has already remind us (see next chapter) that ancient "philosophical ways of life" are incompatible with values that have since become more important in the eyes of most philosophers—and laypeople. However, not only values (and metaphysical beliefs), but some ancient philosophical beliefs also concerning "ordinary people" and "philosophers" are surely contradicted by what we have learned in the meantime. For instance, we know that some *idiōtēs* may be more loyal not only to their unsophisticated and unexamined life-philosophy than some "true" philosophers are to their grand theories, but also live closer to some ideals of the latter. We also know that counselees do not come nowadays to a philosopher because they want to learn from him how to become, "like him," wise, virtuous, and happy. . . . So why return blindly to the ancient conceptions? Why replace them blindly by more recent conceptions that distinguish "true" philosophers from *idiōtēs*? Some groups of Jewish *Hasidim* perhaps still believe that their rabbi, the *tzaddik*(lit. a just man, pious observant of God's instructions) with his special connections to the "upper worlds," is "truly" embodying, in the "lower worlds," the philosopher and the prophet, the intellectual and the mystic, the saint and the miracles-maker. There are probably similar groups in some other cultures. But I do not know of any group of contemporary people who take philosophy seriously that would agree about "the" philosopher who truly and fully embodies contemporary philosophical ideals, be it "authenticity," "critical rationality," or any standard for being a "true philosopher" that occurs nowadays to postmodern philosophical minds.

Personal Problems and Philosophical Counseling

My reason for mentioning the historical and sociological studies that expose *philosophers* and scientists as "simple humans," thinking and acting under the impact of unexamined preconceptions, is not a wish to point to their apparent failure to be critical. I do it to save the "simply human" counselee from accusations of such a failure. Socrates, Descartes, Locke, and the logical positivists, each in his time, tried to convince us that we should be purged of all our false or nonsensical beliefs and dubious concepts. Their opponents noted that their methods, however radical, had left them with many unexamined assumptions. What we understand nowadays is, however, more radical. No method has sense nor can be meaningfully applied without prior assumptions that are taken for granted by the community of discourse, and there is, in principle, neither the possibility nor a need to examine them all. The meaningfulness of the question "Why is there something rather than nothing?" is so controversial because we normally take for granted the existence of many things when we doubt the existence of certain kinds of things or look for an explanation for a specific thing or event (Strawson, 1959). So, if the erudite and sophisticated, shrewd or wise, do not (and cannot) cast in doubt all their beliefs, the philosophical counselor should not presuppose that the counselee's problem is due to the latter's *failure* to check his beliefs and his living, as some say, an "*unexamined* life."

Moreover, the case of philosophers, scientists, and other wise people who "get stuck" in dilemmas or confusions calls into question a wider presupposition that seems to be shared by religious converters as well as dominant schools of psychotherapy: The presupposition that *false beliefs* and *defective ways of thinking*, whether in the theoretical or religious sphere and whether in practical or emotional life, are a necessary condition for having such difficulties. A philosopher or scientist who is aware of some difficulties in his conception but does not know how to solve it, is not necessarily holding wrong beliefs. In addition, the fact that an alternative approach, which could have enabled him to overcome those difficulties, did not occur to him, does not mean that his thinking processes were defective. Philosophers who were aware that it is not a perceptive or logical problem, but something else, spoke of "intuition" (Bergson, 1992) or distinguished between two kinds of "reason" (Whitehead, 1997b). Both meant a way of thinking that does not make deductions, inductions, or—according to Peirce—"abductions," that is, conjecturing explanatory hypotheses (Peirce, 1935, 172), within a given metaphysical or conceptual scheme, but creates instead a new conception. Under their influence some philosophers of science suggest introducing discussions of metaphysical alternatives to the syllabus of scientific studies and some psychologists try to foster "creativity" in general. Yet nobody knows how innovative conceptions that are both relevant and fruitful are created. We know that when they have been created, they enable thinking of possibilities that were beyond the horizon determined by the prior conception. Such changes, which are involved with reexamining and discarding some philosophical presuppositions, show how background philosophical ideas and attitudes as well as the philosophizing that helps to change them are relevant to issues beyond the domain of philosophy.

The counselee that is "stuck" in his personal dilemmas and confusions may, similarly, have plausible beliefs and normal cognitive capacities. He may be open to metaphysical speculations and capable of "creative" thinking. There is, furthermore, no reason to assume a priori that his difficulty is due to the allegedly impaired thinking of the "neurotic" (and otherwise "mentally disturbed") or the "sinner" (and otherwise "spiritually deprived"). Yet no idea that may enable his breakthrough has occurred to him: Like many good scientists and philosophers, his preconceptions limit his horizon.

A philosophical counselor can help him although philosophers are normally not as innovative in the domain of life problems as Darwin, Einstein, Kant, Peirce, Wittgenstein, or other revolutionary thinkers were in their respective academic fields. In fact, sometimes a philosophical conversation with a friend (or a stranger) may help a "stuck" person, just because the latter, whose background and perspective are somewhat different, may think of possibilities that are beyond that person's horizon. And indeed, in the nineteenth and the early twentieth centuries, when people, at least in some parts of the world, were less inclined to rely on religious guidance but were still without the new faith in psychological treatment, such dialogues (which appear in novels, dramas, and personal correspondence) were probably rather frequent. Dialogues with a philosophical counselor may be more effective.

I say, "may," as I am not sure whether among all those who define themselves as philosophical counselors there are no preachers and catechism-teachers. I mean counselors that are trying, unphilosophically, to persuade the counselee to adopt their specific ideas about life or their attitude to it (rather than enable him to make his own choices), ignoring thereby his concerns (rather than responding to them) and disrespecting his initial convictions (rather than encouraging their reexamination). I guess that what they do is not more effective than the attempts of religious guides to persuade resistant sinners or heretics. But philosophical counselors with a sufficient philosophical background, who are acquainted with a variety of philosophical theories, approaches, and debates and have experienced participation in philosophical dialogues, *can* be more effective. Philosophical debates consist not only of arguing against the opponent's positions and their possible implications; they also call into question their supposed tacit assumptions. Therefore, the experienced philosopher can detect more easily presuppositions that limit the counselee's horizon, offer a variety of alternatives—not only those that have occurred to him personally, but also those that have occurred to a variety of other philosophers, and induce the counselee to take part in a virtual debate with any of them.[15]

A philosophical counselor with a sufficient background can, moreover, relate more specifically to the counselee's issues and to the presuppositions that interfere with his ability to cope with them. He can "diagnose" more correctly whether they are preconceptions about the "good life," "self-realization," "authenticity," and other so-called "spiritual" questions, or, as is often the case, about other philosophical themes, such as knowledge or truth, uncertainty and risk, rationality and meaningfulness, obligations and duties, responsibility and guilt, fairness and justice.

To sum everything up: Philosophy matters, and acquaintance with academic philosophy is relevant to the philosophical counselor's ability to do the job. However, it is a necessary condition, not a sufficient one. In order to do his job honestly the counselor has to *believe* that philosophy matters and be aware of cases in which *it mattered to him personally*.[16] In order to do his job with responsibility, he should also be aware that the counselee is *another person*, with different background, perspectives, and concerns, and be ready to learn, in a patient and prudent process of trial and error, how it can matter *to him*.

Notes

1. Maimonides, a Jewish Mediaeval Aristotelian rabbi, believed that humans are unable to reach the Greek ideal of perfect knowledge, as the knowing and understanding of God is beyond the reach of human intellect. Yet he compared the wisdom of the philosopher to that of the prophet, and considered himself capable, qua philosopher, to "guide the perplexed" to philosophical and theological clarity, and, qua rabbi and *possek* ["decision maker" in matters of practical application of the law], put an end to controversies in the interpretation of the Mosaic law. While many Orthodox Jews admire him, he is also widely contested, whether because of his opposition to mystical readings of the Scriptures or because of his disrespect for the rabbinical tradition of *ongoing theoretical interpretative debates* and the rule of accepting the opinion of most rabbis participating in the discussion in decisions about practical application of laws in specific situations (*cf*. Goodman, 2015).

2. Unfortunately, some contemporary practical philosophers are not updated.

3. See Socrates's interrogation of the ignorant slave, who answers '2' to the question "How many squares of the size nXn are needed in order to cover the area of a square of the size 2nX2n?" (Plato, *Meno*, 644–52). A contemporary philosopher would not even say that it is necessarily a *wrong* mathematical answer; he may argue, following Wittgenstein (1958, IIxi, 226–27), that the *question* has no meaning in the mathematical "language game" of creatures who have only one-dimensional geometry.

4. Practically, however, it does not guarantee that independent thinkers will always get the notes or jobs that they deserve.

5. Such expertise is, of course, not acquired in courses on the "philosophy of" some discipline, profession, or art, if what is presented there is only the dogmatic citation of slogans borrowed from the discourse of some fashionable philosophers and the sorting out of ideas, persons, institutes, artifacts, states of affairs or processes to "good" or "bad" according to their criteria. Some of their graduates apply their "philosophical" expertise for a social or political cause, and sometimes they try to help individuals become, as they sometimes say, a "subject" (which is better than being just an "object"). However, such expertise is not sufficient for philosophical counseling that is fully philosophical.

6. As my colleague Elhanan Yakira has noted in a personal communication, Leibnitz's interest in that question is related to his conception of the existing world as the best among all the possible worlds. As such it is not just a theological question but also a metaphysical, and more importantly, moral one.

7. In fact, they are not asking precisely that question, for they presuppose the prior existence of something: the "singular point," "energy," et cetera.

8. See Appendix A.

9. See Margolis and Laurence (2021). With regards to the status of 'concept' in the analytic camp. The debates are even deeper in the camps of the so-called continental and postmodern thinkers.

10. Naturalist philosophers like Quine may insist that even such a question, which is not only abstract and general but also seems to depend on values rather than sheer facts, is ultimately empirical (Hylton et al. 2019). His claim assumes that statements about philosophical matters as well as value judgments are translatable to purely empirical statements that refer to the same things: observable facts. The latter include human behaviors that are, to his analytic-behaviorist mind and those of his followers, the real reference, "in any possible world." of statements about beliefs, wishes, attitudes, criteria, principles, meanings, and rules. They have developed a heavy logical artillery to protect their claims and still must define the theory in whose context it is an empirically testable hypothesis. Some philosophers would disagree that the protection is efficient; Wittgenstein, for example, would say (compare Wittgenstein, 1958, IIxi, 226–27) that the mathematical statement "Is '2+2=4' true?" is not reducible to "Do people believe that '2+2=4' is true?," "Do the behavior of people show that they believe that '2+2=4' is true?," or "Is it always true that when

two observable objects are added to two observable objects four observable objects are actually observable?" I propose, accordingly, a rule of thumb: When heavy logical artillery is needed to prove that a seemingly philosophical question is ultimately empirical, it is practically philosophical.

11. Nowadays however, some claim that interpretation, or hermeneutics, is a philosophical issue.

12. See Appendix B for a detailed discussion.

13. Some Western philosophers claim that Indian philosophers considered the impossibility of solving a controversy a sufficient reason to stop intellectual philosophizing (Biderman, 1980). I also heard opposite opinions. I do not know enough about that tradition, its sources, or influences, and cannot say whether it was relevant to the popularity of Zen Buddhism or Taoism in Eastern Asia, or whether their alleged popularity indicates that there were no traditions of intellectual philosophizing in that part of the world.

14. An aim that is shared by some philosophical counselors, each with his specific vague notion of "being a philosopher," but equally pretentious, especially considering the average number of conversations that they hold with their counselees.

15. Of course, religious guides do other things besides preaching and rote teaching. When they are studying among themselves how to interpret sanctified texts and apply their messages in specific life situations, they may be confronted, as in the Jewish Talmudic studies, with a great variety of different approaches and the debates among them, which are interwoven with philosophical issues of all kinds. But in the religious institutes in which such studying takes place, there are authoritarian interventions, explicit or tacit, and there are hierarchies of texts' importance, and the authoritarian status of interpretations and teachers. There is therefore a great difference between the degree of liberty that a contemporary nonbeliever or a "non-orthodox" religious reader takes in considering the variety of possibilities and the liberty taken by an "orthodox" student. In any case, in his counseling to the "non-initiated" the orthodox religious guide tends to bring only authorized conclusions.

16. See Gruengard, 2018.

CHAPTER TWO

Coping with the Questions of the Counselees

Informal philosophical discussions with a friend about one's personal worries are quite common in fiction and drama. Tacit philosophical dialogues between authors and readers, where opposing philosophical views are concretized in the author's presentation of his protagonist's problems, are even more common. Professional philosophical counseling is, in contrast, a recent phenomenon.

Some philosophers assume that philosophy cannot be relevant to the lives of "ordinary people" that is, nonphilosophers, unless it deals, as in the Greco-Roman world, with general questions like "What is a good life?" or "What is happiness?" or, like the old author of *Ecclesiastes* and the young Kierkegaard and some famous Shakespearean protagonists in between, "What is the meaning of life?" Some believe that answers to such questions cannot make a difference in the lives of "ordinary people" unless professional philosophers prepare them with special exercises. Others are less radical and assume that even "ordinary people" who do not aspire to become philosophers may sometimes want to know what the "really important" things in life are. These philosophers believe that philosophical analysis can be adapted to "ordinary people" and can provide satisfactory answers. Some assume that "ordinary people" need philosophy (sometimes in the guise of religious precepts, sometimes in the tenets of an allegedly freer secular alternative) to give them reliable principles or rules for reasonable thinking and wise, or moral, conduct. Others believe, in contrast, that philosophers should give them a lesson in reflective thinking about their thinking or feeling. Some believe that "ordinary people" need philosophy as consolation when they are suffering. As the usual answers of monotheistic religions cannot satisfy skeptical modern persons, philosophizing is, in their mind, the answer. It can alleviate the pain. It can divert the sufferer's attention from the issue that is bothering him to something else, allegedly more important, or more meaningful. It can, alternatively, foster a change of orientation or mood. Paying attention to awe-inspiring nature, self-absorption in contemplation, or ego-forgetfulness in meditation are among the more spiritual philosophizing options offered to "ordinary, non-religious people."[1]

Many books deal with these themes.[2] They raise many objections. As in all philosophical positions, there is room for debate. I, for instance, disagree with at least one of the common assumptions of these philosophers—the assumption that, as philosophers, they *know* what bothers "ordinary people" and therefore they *know* why and how philosophy is relevant to their concerns. I believe that philosophers cannot know how philosophy can be relevant to "ordinary people" without knowing the *particular* concerns of those people, "ordinary" or not, in concrete life situations.

The Concerns of the Counselees

Counselees are individuals of various backgrounds. Some have studied philosophy at a university, and some were not interested in philosophy at all; some never went to college, and some did not finish high school. Some come to philosophical counseling with no idea about philosophy, they just know that they do not want "psychotherapy." Some come after several attempts to be helped by psychologists or religious guides.

They come to counseling for a great variety of reasons. Some are intrigued by an explicit philosophical question and seek a partner for a philosophical discussion. Some have already made up their mind and come with the hope of getting the approval of "a philosopher." Some think a philosophical counselor is a kind of coach and expect the counselor to help them achieve their ambitions. Some come to dissipate their religious conflicts. Some have moral dilemmas or more mundane ones—personal or professional, conjugal or familial. Some are confused about themselves—their emotions and moods, their identity, and worth. Some are bothered by inner obstacles, such as shyness or shame, which they believe block them from realizing their goals and ideals. Some want to deal with their existential anxieties or find a reason to live on after a major loss.

Counselees describe themselves in different ways. However, whatever they are trying to cope with, they surely share the feeling that their coping is not fully satisfactory. That is why they seek the counselor's assistance.

Philosophy, or rather, dialogues about philosophical conceptions that are relevant to the specific issues that bother a specific person, may help him to cope better. The relevance of philosophy in the case of any counselee is therefore a subjective matter and an intersubjective challenge.

The Counselees' Questions

Counselees do not necessarily come with explicit questions, and when they do, their questions are not necessarily the most adequate way to express their concerns. Nor do they necessarily come with explicit concerns. The counselor needs patience and attentive listening skills while trying to discern the issues that bother the counselee. Sometimes the latter avoid talking directly about the problem that troubles them. Often, they are confused and not clearly aware of the issues at stake. The counselor, attempting to understand what is problematic from the point of view of the counselee, may need to ask for clarification. At the initial stage, he should be especially tactful and cautious, and take into consideration the still unknown sensitivities of the counselee. He needs, moreover, to get acquainted with the perspective of the counselee and the way in which he perceives his problem, and therefore should be careful, and avoid not only explicit imposition of his own categories but also the implicit suggestion of "the correct" approach. The counselor may also ask for information to improve his understanding of the problematic situation and its personal, social, and cultural background. He may discover that the counselee conceives his case as a cluster of problems and ask him to sort it out or choose his order of priorities.

Although this "verstehende"—understanding—attitude is inspired by the Verstehen approach of some German historians and sociologists (Dilthey, 2002; Weber, 2010), it may seem too "psychological" to some philosophers. Their famous predecessors, from Socrates and Epicurus to Nietzsche and Heidegger, did not "descend" to that level, and even those, like Epictetus or Spinoza, who meant to teach rather than provoke and criticize, invited the readers to raise themselves toward their own level.[3] However, they were not, nor pretended to be, counselors. To know how they would have proceeded if they had chosen to become counselors, one should know many things about them; for example, how they behaved when personal friends tried to talk with them about concrete personal problems. I do not know, and therefore it would not be fair for me to warn potential counselees against their contemporary equivalents (if there are any). Yet I would not recommend people with genuine problems to seek "treatment" from counselors who are eager to point out seeming contradictions and other fallacies in reasoning (or, with a different orientation, a seemingly faulty attitude to Self, Other, Life, God,

Being and so on) as soon as the counselees open their mouths.[4] The "verstehende" attitude may, in contrast, appeal to counselors with some background in phenomenology and are therefore attuned to looking at things from subjective perspectives. Such counselors might think of Husserl's method of *epoche*—putting "in brackets" some doubts or judgments (with regards, for example, to the reality, rationality, or morality of the counselee's presentation) in order to explore other aspects.

The "verstehende" attitude does not mean, however, that a philosophical counselor should deceive himself or the counselee into believing that their dialogues are going to be what some blind psychotherapists call "nonjudgmental." Freud, who was probably, like Husserl, inspired by their common teacher, Brentano (Brentano, 1973), did indeed put "in brackets" some judgments when he was examining a patient's dream or listening to his free associations. Yet Freud, like Husserl, "opened the brackets" and offered his (critical) interpretation, as the critical audience usually does when the theater show is over. I therefore have difficulty understanding why some psychotherapists fail to see the "judgmental" elements in their diagnosis of a patient as suffering from this or that "disturbance," interpreting his behavior toward the analyst as a "transference of his unconscious infantile wish to kill his father," or describing his behavior as "sticking to habits that have stopped being functional" or having other imperfections that, according to their judgment, are the issues that *should* be treated. Psychotherapists as well as philosophical counselors, even when they believe that a client is fine as he is and needs no change, are making factual judgments about truth and reality, *and* value judgments about rationality, normativity, and morality.[5] Philosophical counselors, however "verstehende" is their initial approach, open "the brackets" at a certain point, just as psychotherapists do. Their wisdom is judged, however, by their ability to learn from the counselees and respect their critical reservations, and by their openness to the objections of colleagues or even "ordinary people."[6] Both counselees and counselors need to listen to the opinions of others as the others may see, from their different perspectives, what they themselves cannot.

Although the initial understanding of the counselee[7] is just a starting point for the philosophical dialogue, it might, in some cases, be a slow and long process.

A Case Study with Multiple Dilemmas

In the following paragraphs I will use the story of a famous though fictitious person as a case study. I choose a fictitious person, whom I know solely by the information that his author chose to convey, because that information is also accessible to the readers, and therefore they can judge the extent to which the counselor's approach depends on his interpretation of the counselee's case. The counselee is the main protagonist in a play, and as is often the case in classical drama, there are things the audience knows that the protagonist will learn, if ever, only later. This will help me to demonstrate the importance of understanding the relevant problems from the subjective perspective of the counselee.

The protagonist I chose, from one of Shakespeare's best-known plays, is not one of the "ordinary people." He is a prince who has studied philosophy. He is both self-aware and eloquent as only Shakespearean protagonists can be, and the dramatic dimensions of his dilemmas as well as the catastrophic consequences of his confusions are, fortunately, not typical of regular persons or counselees. Yet there is something in his questions and hesitations that is common to "ordinary people." I do not mean the Oedipal complex that Freud's disciple, Ernst Jones, "diagnosed" in our character (Jones, 1976), and that more sophisticated followers attributed to his creator. Nor do I mean the tendency to "procrastinate" that another psychologist, probably not well acquainted with the Shakespearean play, "discerned" in the indecisive man.[8] The protagonist is Hamlet, as the reader has surely guessed by now, and I imagine that he decides to seek philosophical counseling right after the end of Act IV. His initial questions are translatable to philosophical questions to which, at least according to Kant (Kant, 1885, 15), the whole of philosophy is reducible. I am not sure that all philosophers agree with Kant's opinion, but I am convinced that those questions, in one concrete form or another, concern "ordinary people" no less than philosophers.

I assume, for my purpose, that Hamlet was Shakespeare's contemporary, and shared his Renaissance background. Therefore, he could not be aware that he was asking Kantian questions. It is more probable that Shakespeare inspired Kant, or else that both were inspired by processes that started, perhaps, at Wittenberg, where Luther allegedly published his famous "theses" and started the Reformation—and the fictitious Hamlet studied philosophy (Shakespeare, 1993a, Act I, Scene 2). Hamlet's personal questions, in any case, did not stem from his theoretical learning, but from the personal circumstances in which he found himself when he had to interrupt his studies and return to the Danish court. They were personal questions that needed translation, with the help of the counselor, into general, philosophical, ones.

I skip the first imaginary stage, in which Hamlet the counselee, tense and angry, tells his confused narrative. Thanks to Shakespeare's (or Hamlet's) talents, I can start the analysis when he is able to formulate his questions and dilemmas.

To remind the readers, Hamlet's narrative is as follows: he was studying philosophy peacefully in Wittenberg when he got the message that his admired father, the king of Denmark, died of a serpent bite, and was ordered to return home. Once at home, he discovers that his father's brother, whom he despises and mistrusts, is now the king, married to his widowed mother. Shocked and depressed, suspicious of adultery and conspiracy, he unwillingly obeys their request that he stay in Denmark. Soon after that, he gets the message that the ghost of his father appeared several times to the guardians of the royal palace. He goes to meet the ghost, who tells him that his brother poisoned him and demands revenge. Hamlet shares the information with his friend Horatio but says nothing to anyone else. He is not sure whether the message of the ghost is true, imagined, or a demonic temptation to sin, and does not know what to do. He even considers suicide but is afraid of eternal damnation. He decides to fake madness, repudiates his beloved Ophelia as well as his childhood friends, and confuses the king and his accomplices. (The audience learns in the meantime that the king is suspicious of Hamlet and asks people to spy on him, while the king's counselor, Ophelia's father, who had advised his daughter to reject his courtship and is suspecting that Hamlet became mad because of his frustrated love, is spying on him for his own reasons.) Hamlet, however, is not aware of either of these developments. He has an opportunity to kill the king while the latter is alone, praying and confessing, but hesitates and postpones the act. When he learns that the prince of Norway is going to pass through Denmark with his army on his way to Poland, he says that he cannot understand why he himself is hesitating to kill a single wretched man while the other prince, without much consideration, is going to cause the death of at least twenty thousand innocents. When his childhood friends (who are also spying on him) tell him that a group of actors has arrived at the court, he asks the group to perform a play whose plot is the same as the ghost's description of his father's murder. He tells Horatio that the reactions of the king and queen to the performance will provide him, indirectly, with the needed evidence while their revived remorse will induce them to confess. As expected, the king reacts angrily to the show, orders it stopped, and leaves with the queen. Hamlet goes to the queen's apartment to get her confession, while Ophelia's father, still believing that Hamlet's state of mind is due to Ophelia's refusal, is hiding behind the curtain. His movement, while Hamlet is reproaching his mother, raises Hamlet's suspicion that the person from behind the curtain is the king, and he stabs him. He soon discovers that he killed the wrong man. His mother speaks excitedly, but the show did not achieve Hamlet's purpose. It is not clear what his mother is admitting, and his uncle does not share with him any feelings of remorse. Instead, the king decides to send Hamlet to England, accompanied by his childhood friends, allegedly to defend him from the people's wrath. (In fact, he wants to punish Hamlet right away in Denmark, but knowing that the people love the prince, he is sending him away.)

At this point, in our telling, Hamlet decides to try philosophical counseling (he does not know, of course, that after his departure Ophelia, already confused by his behavior, will lose her mind completely in her bereavement for her father, and will eventually be found drowned in a brook, perhaps by suicide and perhaps by an accidental fall).

Hamlet's Questions and Dilemmas

At that stage, it is already clear that Hamlet is intrigued by many questions: How did his father die? (Shakespeare, 1993a I, 5). Is the ghost's message reliable? (ibid., III, 2). How can he get evidence in the intrigue-laden court? Who is spying on him? How could his mother marry his uncle so soon after his father's death? (ibid., I, 2). Should he kill the uncle, the suspected murderer? (ibid., III, 3). When? Why cannot he decide whether to kill a single wicked man when other princes do not hesitate to cause the death of thousands? (ibid., IV, 4). Should he commit suicide? (ibid., III, 1). And what then? Will the reaction of the uncle to a show, whose plot is the same as the assumed murderous behavior of the uncle, would be a proof for the uncle's guilt? (ibid., III, 2). What is the meaning of human life when one cannot find the right equilibrium between emotion and reason? (ibid., V, 1).[9]

One can group those questions, perhaps with the help of the counselor, into several dilemmas. Some dilemmas regard the counselee's wish to know: Can he rely on the ghost's message and his own suspicion, or should he venture his life and look for evidence? Hamlet decides to look for evidence first by trying to collect evidence from people in the court, and then by observing the uncle's reaction to the show. His major dilemma is whether to consider the information he has as knowledge that the uncle killed his father.

Some dilemmas regard his wish to avenge his father's death: His eagerness to know indicates that he does not want to kill a man that did not kill his father. He is, moreover, not sure that killing a person is the right thing to do even if that person is a murderer. He is, finally, not sure that killing a person deserving death is justified when that man is praying (His dilemmas do not stop him from causing intentionally, in self-defense, the death of Ophelia's father, mistaken for the king. Yet they lead him to the third group of dilemmas).

That group of dilemmas regards life after death: When he considers suicide, he is not sure whether it is nobler than suffering and whether it will bring him peace or infernal tortures. When he considers killing the praying uncle, he seems to believe that what matters is the confession that the innocent father is in purgatory because he died without confession and that the murderer king will go straight to paradise, thanks to his confession.

The Counselee's Philosophical Questions

Hamlet's interrupted philosophical education helped him, perhaps, to be acquainted with various incompatible philosophical approaches, but did not give him the tools to decide between them or to decide between any of them and prevalent popular beliefs. He may be confused for other reasons as well, as both the events in his family (and his emotional ambivalence toward his mother and Ophelia) and the political events in the kingdom, where "something is rotten" and there is nobody that can be trusted, can "drive one crazy" even without assumed Oedipal conflicts. However, Hamlet does not speak about his feelings nor about politics; he is "obsessed" with the issue of revenge. If he had known Kant and had been in a theoretical mood, perhaps he would have said that to settle the issue he should know the answers to the three Kantian questions: What can I know? What should I do? For what may I hope? He is not, however, in a philosophical mood.

Here begins the job of the philosophical counselor. He can see that Hamlet's questions belong to three groups and that each group contains questions that are special, concrete cases of a general Kantian question. The counselor must, of course, check with Hamlet and see whether he agrees with him, and he must translate his proposed interpretation into a language that Hamlet is able to understand.

It is important to note that another philosophical counselor might understand the text differently and discern behind Hamlet's questions and dilemmas other philosophical questions. Hamlet's agreement with one of us does not mean that the other is wrong. A person's problems can be interpreted in more than one way, and the person himself can see it, in different moods, in different lights. Yet I do not think that "anything goes." An adequate interpretation should take into account what a person says, sometimes it is also relevant to speculate about what he does not say. In all cases, his cultural background should be considered. If we assume that Hamlet's background is that of Shakespeare, we may wonder why until Act V, Hamlet says nothing, about his uncle being a usurper while he himself is the legitimate heir.[10] I do not think, however, that he could be bothered at any point by the Greco-Roman question of the good life, or by Buddha's questions with regards to suffering in general, or by the controversial question with regards to the existence of something rather than nothing. In the time of Hamlet, when new approaches to knowledge clashed with both popular beliefs and the church's dogmas, when Catholic versions of Christianity clashed with Protestant ones and popular norms were challenged by humanist moral ideals, his dilemmas as I interpret them make sense. It is also reasonable to believe that a person with such a background cannot easily solve such dilemmas. The task of the philosophical counselor is to try to help Hamlet cope better with his dilemmas.

Dealing with the Counselee's Dilemmas

Philosophers deal with their dilemmas in various ways. I shall deal with the options in the next chapter. Here I propose one possible way: Hamlet cannot cope with his dilemmas because he cannot decide between several tacit and incompatible theories with regards to each of them.

He assumes three different conceptions of knowledge with regard to the question whether a certain act was committed by a certain person: unnatural—ghosts can reveal truth; juridical—only confessions, testimonies or empirical evidence are relevant criteria; and psychological—one can infer from a person's reaction to the behavior of others what the intentions or deeds of that person are. The three incompatible conceptions were acceptable in his time, while he has doubts with regards to each of them: he is not sure that visions of ghosts are reliable, he knows that he cannot trust anybody in in the intrigue-laden court, and he knows that playwrights and actors may manipulate the audience's reaction at will. He is therefore unable to prove his suspicions or decide whether the conceptions that apparently support those suspicions are valid or invalid.

In other words, he wants to answer the question "How can I know?" while being aware that practically speaking, he cannot get the wanted information. Moreover, philosophically, he cannot answer the general question "What can I know?" The philosophical confusion is due to his inability to decide between two different sources of knowledge about the afterlife: the Stoic conception and the Christian one. Both were considered legitimate sources in his time. As a philosophical counselor is not supposed to impose his own philosophical positions on the counselee but rather encourage the latter to explore and choose between possibilities that are intelligible to him, I would not teach him how Descartes, Locke, Kant, or later philosophers tried to clarify the meaning or limits of knowledge. I would rather suggest to him the possibility of accepting the fact that he cannot know what he wishes to know since he cannot get reliable evidence, and has no theoretical criteria for choosing among the prevalent incompatible beliefs of his cultural world.

Hamlet also tacitly assumes several incompatible moral conceptions: blood feuds—the idea that a son must revenge his father's murder; Christian—one should not kill nor commit suicide; Stoic—under some conditions one should kill oneself rather than continue suffering; retribution—one should not enable the wicked to gain better life conditions than the righteous. (Hamlet expands the last conception to include the afterlife.) He cannot behave according to the first conception, for he must be sure that the suspected indeed murdered the deceased. Regarding the second view, moreover, he is not precisely a good Christian. He is unable or unready to consider forgiveness, and even if a Christian is allowed to kill in self-defense, Hamlet is uneasy about a decision to kill those who might harm him. He cannot follow the Stoic position as he is not sure that in his situation suicide is nobler than bearing suffering with equanimity. In any case, his emotional state and his non-Stoic beliefs with regard to the afterlife prevent him from a rational Stoic choice of the "nobler" behavior. He postpones, finally, "just retribution" because he fears that the afterlife suffering of the wicked uncle (killed while praying) would be lesser than that of the righteous father (murdered without confession).

Hence, Hamlet cannot answer the question "What should I do?" When he tries to calculate his uncle's lot in the afterlife he seems to mistake himself for God and thereby reveals his scorn, or misunderstanding, of the competing dominant religious conceptions of his time: that of Erasmus (one's lot is decided by Divine rational justice and not by human mistaken calculations) and that of Luther (one's lot is determined by Grace, which depends on God's will, and not on rational considerations). On other occasions, he considers himself a doomed sinner, which is incompatible with the Stoic conception. I believe that his being in deep moral confusion is a better explanation for his "missing opportunities" to kill the hated uncle than having an Oedipal complex, or a tendency to "procrastinate." Although I do not share most of his moral conceptions, I would not hesitate to point to the contradictions in his considerations and the incompatibilities of the conventional conceptions. I might tell him that to my mind his generation is unable to settle moral controversies just as it is unable to settle epistemological ones. Yet I would not suggest that he ignore all those conventional conceptions, nor is this even possible, although there have been philosophers who rely on their imaginary ability to cast doubt on "all" their beliefs, and think only in terms of autonomous methodological and moral principles. Neither would I suggest that he think in classical terms of "the good life," "happiness" or "virtue"; his world is not the world of classical philosophers, and their ideals do not seem to speak to him. I believe that he might be helped by changing his perspective, but the counselor must take care that the possible new perspectives are intelligible to him.

Hamlet is also concerned with the afterlife, and here too his various conceptions are incompatible. While the Stoic in him expects "dreamless sleep," the Christian expects hellish tortures for everyone concerned: for himself for committing suicide or killing his uncle; for his father, for dying without confession, and so on. Yet if he kills his uncle while the latter is praying, the rascal murderer might escape punishment. Hamlet's reaction to the death of Ophelia and his remarks while holding the skull of Yorick express, in contrast, the view that death is neither sleep nor hell nor salvation; it is just a senseless end to a meaningless life. However, Hamlet of Act V is, to my mind, not the same person as Hamlet of the previous acts.

Finally, Hamlet who cannot answer the question "What may I hope for?" has no encouraging answer to the fourth Kantian question: "What is man?" If we can judge by what he says of his friend Horatio (ibid., III, 2), "being a man" meant to Hamlet and his intellectual friends, living through ambiguity and ambivalence yet searching for answers in an adequate equilibrium of reason and emotion. His generation was already intrigued by modern Kantian rather than Socratic, Platonic, or Stoic questions, but was still unable to cope with them.

What Can the Philosophical Counselor Do?

Psychologists might intervene here and blame me for ignoring Hamlet's affects. I do not ignore them; I just treat them differently. His emotional state—moving between melancholic moods and emotional outbreaks, serious pondering, and ironic joking—may indeed suggest, as some psychologists would claim, that hidden conflicts are also involved. Instead of guessing arbitrarily that Oedipal wishes or a general "tendency to procrastinate" are involved, I would suspect that the prince of Denmark hides a conflict between his awareness that he is the deserving heir of the throne and his reluctance to become king. He therefore fails to consider that his uncle is behaving as a usurper of the Danish crown as well as the suspected murderer of the Danish king. This conjecture is based on my assumption that Hamlet's world is that of Shakespeare, and the question of the legitimacy of rulers is so central in the latter's tragedies that his audience cannot but wonder why Hamlet is silent about it. I might, therefore, ask Hamlet for his thoughts about the legitimacy of rulers, but not as if I were a mind-reader, or as if I knew that his monologues were just a cover for something else. I do not know that they are, and I tend to believe that my counselees do not seek to deceive themselves and others. Instead of faking "understanding" of his "true" motives, I might ask him what would happen if he found proof for his uncle's suspected deed and killed him with no further remorse.

The idea of such a question was inspired by a presentation of an ex-psychoanalyst of the Milano School of family therapy, in which he described it as an application of Russell's approach to paradoxes.[11] The ex-psychoanalyst illustrated it with the case of a husband obsessed with the question of whether twenty-five years earlier his wife had had an affair. He did not *ask* the husband what would happen if he knew the answer; he just *told* him that if the answer were negative, he would be very angry with himself for wasting twenty-five years of his life torturing himself with a silly question. I do not think that Hamlet's questions are silly, and I do not know what Hamlet would think. However, I would ask him the unexpected question "What would you do after that?," and thus enlarge his horizon beyond the act that he hesitates to perform. It would confront him with the question of whether he intends to assume the kingship, but I would suggest other ideas, such as going back to Wittenberg, joining a monastery, or going east with the army of Norway, as Danes did at Shakespeare's time, to fight Sweden and Russia on Polish soil. (I could add other options, like becoming a fool in some German court or joining a group of pirates, but I prefer to stay within the range of Hamlet's imagination.) I believe that the very act of thinking about several options might help him to see the issue of revenge in different ways (it is a pity that options other than kingship did not occur to him even in act V).

There are, of course, other questions that might divert his attention from his unanswerable questions. I could ask him about his expected mood after the act and thus focus attention on his affective state and direct the conversation to his very un-Stoic self-torturing. Unlike some psychologists, I would not dwell on the history of his emotions and their unconscious archaeology. Instead, I would invite him to discuss their rationality, and explore whether one should express his emotions, control them, divert them to other objects, or let them fade away by, say, contemplating the sublime beauty of Elsinore's coast. There are many other possibilities. In practice, however, philosophical as well as other counselors act with the ideas that occur to them at the relevant moment.

This means that despite the will to let the counselee ask his questions, express his disagreements, draw his own conclusions, and make his own choices, the philosophical counselor's personality, orientation, and background have their impact on what is happening in the counseling. I shall deal with this in the next chapter.

Summary: The Structure of the Counseling Process

The counseling normally starts with introductory remarks and self-presentations by counselee and counselor. To prevent unjustified expectations the latter should explain in a few words what is philosophical in his approach.

Then the counselee is invited to explain what brings him to philosophical counseling. He should be free to choose whether to start with questions and then explain their background and what Popper calls "the problem situation" (1957), or with a description of his situation and its background and then explain the issue that brings him to counseling. At that stage, the counselor should be patient and try to understand the situation and the issues from the counselee's subjective point of view. The counselor may ask for clarification but should not press the counselee to pose questions when the latter is not ready.[12] The counselee's talking gives the counselor an opportunity to learn the idiolect of the counselee and appreciate the level of abstraction in which the latter feels at home. He should prepare himself to reformulate (for himself) the counselee's questions in his own philosophical vocabulary but be careful to formulate his questions to the counselee in terms that are intelligible to the latter.

(Choosing terms from the counselee's idiolect and using details from his narrative may render the counselor not only more comprehensible to the counselee, but also, at least apparently, more empathic and relevant. I therefore disagree with counselors who insist that counselees speak clearly from the start and try to teach them to define their terms.[13] Counselors are not teachers, and it is they who should learn to speak clearly—and transparently—so that the counselees can understand them from their point of view.)

In the next stage the counselor suggests a reformulation of the problems, as they are reflected in the narrative of the counselee, into questions or, if possible, dilemmas. That reformulation should enable him to consider the counselee's specific question in its concrete setting as an instance of a general philosophical question. For example, Hamlet's "Can I really know whether my uncle murdered my father?" can be an instance of "Can a tribunal really know whether a defendant committed the act that is attributed to him?" It can also be reformulated as a more general question: "Can one really know that an event A occurred and caused event B?" The counselor should, in any case, check with the counselee whether the suggested reformulations convey the "intended meaning" of his narrative. If they do not, if, for example, Hamlet says "Well, I do not really care whether my uncle killed my father, I am just looking for a good excuse; he is bad for Denmark and should be dead," the counselor should try different reformulations.[14]

Whatever are the final reformulations, the counselor will probably find more than one question or dilemma. He therefore must choose, with the counselee's consent, the dilemma with which to start the philosophical explorative dialogue.

The starting point of the next stage is a consideration of why the counselee has difficulties in answering the question or coping with the dilemma. While psychologists tend to look for the reason by exploring the patient's overt emotional conflicts or unconscious conflicting wishes and anxieties, the philosophical counselor thinks of non-explicit philosophical preconceptions. The incompatibility of Hamlet's various conceptions of knowledge is a possible example. One can add to them or replace them with other unexplored beliefs, such as "One's search for truth is not biased by one's suspicions or wishes," which is contradicted by Hamlet's expressed doubts. The counselor must beware of presenting the difficulty in a way, which is too abstract for the counselee, and make sure to explain it in a way that is comprehensible to him.[15] He does not have to do it in conceptual language; he may use parables or metaphors, even illustrations from comics. He does not have to share with the counselee the opinion that the counselee's conviction is "a particular instance of a general philosophical problematic position." He may leave it on the level of analogies—"What you say reminds me of what Alibaba said to the robbers when . . . does this sound reasonable to you?"

In the next stage the question is what to do with the difficulty. The counselee, assisted by the counselor, could try to solve it (in Hamlet's case, for example, they would examine which theory is the most reliable); accept it as an unsolvable difficulty (in Hamlet's case they would contrast the juridical theory with Hamlet's awareness that he is not going to get the evidence he looks for, and talk about accepting the possibility of remaining permanently in doubt); change the perspective (in Hamlet's case, asking him what would happen if he had the answer and killed the uncle). If the conversation goes in a more philosophical direction, the counselor might offer alternative conceptions of knowledge (which are beyond the counselee's present horizon yet can be acceptable to him), let the counselee explore which among them appeals to him and discuss its implications with regard to the initial problem (in the case of Hamlet, exploring, for example, theories which put the stress on uncertainty and fallibility [it is Popper adapted to a man of the Renaissance, but I could have mentioned Montaigne] and identify their implications with regards to, say, irreparable deeds, such as the death penalty).

The suggestion and discussion of alternative conceptions may encourage the counselee to think of other alternatives and create new options that should be examined.

If the process does not solve or dissolve the other questions or dilemmas, and the counselee wants to continue the dialogue, he or the counselor may choose another of the initial issues or a new issue that has come to the fore in the meantime. Hamlet, may, for example, be interested in the question "What should I do?" even if he gives up the idea of avenging an unproved act, and the counselor can introduce to him the possibility of choosing among practical rules according to a moral principle. If the idea of a moral principle is too abstract, he can ask him how he would rule Denmark if he were the king. Would he choose Plato's conception and pretend to be the philosopher-king, follow Machiavelli's advice (and continue thereby the tactics of his uncle), or explore which laws should prevail in order that Denmark cease to be a state in which "something is rotten"? (Shakespeare, Hamlet, I, 4) It is a sort of proto-Kantian question for a pre-Kantian prince.

It can be found, occasionally, that beyond the "practical" questions (including the questions about punishments or rewards in the afterlife), the counselee is bothered by existential questions, for example, "what is the meaning of life?" If Hamlet were my counselee, and I want to understand the meaning of the question for him, I might suggest that he think about the texts in which his inventor, Shakespeare, talks about the meaninglessness of life, as when Macbeth says that it is "a tale told by an idiot" (Shakespeare, 1993b, V, 5). I would also suggest that he explore the contexts where such declarations are made. I do not know what Hamlet's conclusions would be, but I would try to help him arrive at conclusions that are his own. The answer to such a question must, to my mind, be subjective: "So or so makes sense of *my* life story," "So-and-so may make *my* life meaningful," and so on.

No philosopher can pretend to know "the" philosophical answer that is valid for everybody. (That is my reason for not dwelling on the answers to Kant's third question. It is also the reason for assuming that Hamlet's answer to Kant's fourth question—"What is man?"—can be found in the Shakespearean text which concludes that the "tale. . . full of sound and fury . . ." is "signifying nothing" (ibid.). In Hamlet's words, "How weary, stale, flat, and unprofitable /Seem to me all the uses of this world! /Fie on 't, ah fie! 'Tis an unheeded garden / That grows to seed" (Shakespeare, 1993a, I, 2, lines 133–36). I hope that, unlike Richard III, he will arrive at the conclusion that a man is a being that despite the "winter of [his] discontent" is *not* necessarily "determined to prove a villain" (Shakespeare, 1993c I,1, lines 1–2).

Comparison with the "Real" Story

Of course, Hamlet did not really consult with me, and what happens in Act V of Shakespeare's play is independent of our imaginary conversation. Yet it is interesting to compare.

In Act V Horatio gets a letter telling him that Hamlet has secretly returned to Denmark and will meet him at the cemetery. When Hamlet arrives at the meeting place, he discovers that the grave being dug there is for Ophelia, and indeed the whole court, including Ophelia's brother, Laertes, comes to the funeral. In their bereavement, both Hamlet and Laertes jump into the grave. The former is trying to explain what he is doing there, but the latter, believing the king's claim that Hamlet is responsible for the death of Ophelia and their father, rejects him vengefully.

Hamlet tells Horatio that on the trip to England he became suspicious of his childhood friends, searched their pouches, and discovered there a letter from his uncle to the king of England with the request to kill Hamlet on his arrival. Hamlet replaced it with a new letter, sealed with his father's royal ring, containing a request to kill the letter's carriers. He also tells Horatio that he is determined to kill his uncle, and says, for the first time, that the murderer also deprived him of the sure opportunity to become the elected king. Horatio supports him, but when the king invites Hamlet to a non-lethal duel with Laertes—as an act of reconciliation in which the better-trained Hamlet will surely be the winner—Horatio advises Hamlet to refuse. Hamlet insists on participating, not knowing that the king conspired with Laertes to use a poisoned dagger in the last round. He also does not know that the pearl put by the king in Hamlet's goblet as a bet on the latter's winning, is envenomed. During the last round of the duel the rivals unknowingly exchange their daggers, both get wounded by the fatal instrument, while the queen mistakes Hamlet's goblet for her own, and drinks the poison. After the deaths of the queen and Laertes (who had in the meantime realized that he was deceived and forgave Hamlet), the dying Hamlet stabs the king with the same poisoned dagger and forces him to drink the rest of the poisoned wine. The king dies, while Hamlet still has time before his death to tell Horatio that he gives his vote in the election of the next king to the Norwegian prince (who has in the meantime invaded his country). Horatio declares that Hamlet should be mourned and buried as the king of Denmark.

Hamlet was liberated from his "vengeance obsession" without the assistance of philosophical counseling: He still has no proof that his uncle murdered his father, and he still wants to kill him, but now he has more urgent matters to consider and does not have to solve the old dilemmas.

He knows for sure that his uncle planned *his* death and has realized that he himself could be the king. No assumed Oedipal conflicts or "tendencies to procrastinate" seem to inhibit him anymore. In fact, becoming "a man of action" turns him into an impulsive guy, whose hastiness brings about the tragedy of errors in which he and the other main protagonists perish. He fails to realize his ideal of equilibrium between emotion and reason. Ironically, in his first responsible act as the legitimate heir of the Danish crown, he gives his vote in the election of the king of Denmark to the foreign conqueror of his country.

I do not know whether any psychologist would be content to meet the new Hamlet. His new personality is certainly not the aim of philosophical counselors. (Shakespeare and Hamlet think that Horatio rather than Hamlet realizes philosophical ideals [ibid., III, 2], but Hamlet represents the human condition with which philosophical counselors try to cope.)

Could their counseling have prevented the tragedy? Some philosophers believe that "spiritual exercises" can change one's character after several years of intensive training. However, impulsive persons have no patience for such exercises, and even the most patient counselees do not persist more than several months in counseling. In any case, I do not think that philosophers should aim at changing character. Philosophizing enables widening horizons and more critical thinking, and thereby, perhaps, better self-control and a better life within one's resources and constraints; but one's actual self-control, whether it depends on one's will or on more complex structures, does not depend on the opinions and didactic efforts of one's counselors.

Hamlet represents, perhaps, the human condition; in him, Shakespeare succeeded in portraying a personality whose complexity can fit various philosophical conceptions of that condition. I do not know whether "ordinary" counselees are less complex, but their stories are certainly less dramatic.

Lawyers and social workers sometimes need to cope with the moral dilemmas that occurred to me while dealing with Hamlet: Should they, as counselors, share their knowledge about the murder of their client's father with the client, thereby both preventing "procrastination" and precipitating another crime—or should they share with the authorities their knowledge that their enraged client is considering a slaughter? I imagine that philosophical counselors who are active in communities where blood feuds exist, or where murder is considered an acceptable way of protecting "family honor" or where political terror is encouraged, also have such dilemmas. My counselees are normally involved with less lethal problems. Yet dealing with the Kantian questions that troubled Hamlet may matter to their lives in unexpected ways. I shall illustrate this, as well as my moral dilemmas, in chapter 4.

Back to the Hypothetical: The Deceptive Hamlet

An expert in continental philosophy who read the manuscript asked me why I trust Hamlet: He might lie to me or worse, deceive himself, like one of Sartre's inauthentic persons. In response to that challenge, I invite the readers to a second imaginary conversation with Hamlet. It takes place toward the end of Act V. Hamlet has been stabbed with the poisoned dagger, but he is still alive and asks for philosophical counseling. When I arrive, he tells me what happened since our last conversation. There are two versions of what happens next: in one, I am talking with the dying Hamlet; in the other, Horatio gets an antidote for Hamlet, who survives and recovers.

At that point, I, the counselor, know much more about Hamlet than I knew in our prior meeting, and have *some reasons*, which I had not before, for suspecting Hamlet of both dishonesty with me and a self-deception. I was already acquainted with Sartre's analyses of "mauvaise foi" when we held our first conversation, but then, as always, I tried to follow my version of the "rule of charity": I do not suspect that the person with whom I am talking is lying *just* because I know that people sometimes lie. In the second conversation, I am less trustful because I have discovered in the meantime that Hamlet is not always trustworthy. For one thing, I now know that the man who presented himself as struggling with the moral problem of killing a single suspected murderer without proof of his guilt did not hesitate to falsify a letter demanding the killing of two innocent others to save his own life. I also know that the philosophizing prince, who seemed to be so thoughtful, is not even aware that he failed to consider less egoistic ways to survive. Still worse, this moralist was ready to kill, or at least wound, an innocent man in a pointless duel to come closer to his aim of killing the king. Moreover, the detached prince, who pretended to be free of political ambitions, always carried his father's ring with him, the one with the royal seal. Finally, the pacifist, who wondered about the audacity of Fontinbras of Norway to lead twenty thousand soldiers to their deaths in a remote country, recommends that mass murderer to be the next king of Denmark. Considering this information, I wonder whether there was not already at our first conversation a difference between his declared dilemmas and the issues that really bothered him, and I start to think of new interpretations of what he said about those dilemmas.

Yet I would not let my suspicions direct me in the scenario where Hamlet is dying. I would wait for Hamlet himself to ask questions, as I would in any scenario. As I am not a priest, I would not expect him to confess his sins, or to repent, or even to express remorse. In fact, I have no specific expectations at all, as I have no general knowledge about the concerns of people facing their imminent personal end. I have not had that experience, nor have I counseled people who were in such situations. And those who might be teachers, the philosophers and psychologists who talk about death anxiety and urge us to take our own personal finitude seriously, are still talking about *an abstract possibility*.

So, let me assume that the dying Hamlet, seeing his dead mother, asks me, perhaps in contrast to Shakespeare's prejudices, whether femininity has a divine pole. Maybe he asked this because he regretted his biased attitude to the queen, maybe because he wanted to reassure himself that despite his cruel games with Ophelia he was, overall, a lover worthy of his own self-acceptance. I do not know, and if I asked, I would not expect to get an answer. But I would be able to evoke his tacit last reflections by asking him which he prefers: the monotheistic morality of avoiding harming others and respecting their human dignity despite their imperfect complexity, or the proto-theosophic morality, inherited perhaps from the "unconscious" of his Nordic ancestors, according to which one's moral duty is toward oneself—one should become a whole, accepting oneself with all the lights and the shadows. And "all the rest," as Horatio would say at the end of Act V, "is silence." (It is silence, however, only for the earthly witnesses; Hamlet's ghost may go on talking in a Dantean afterlife with judges, demons, cellmates or visiting poets, or alternatively, somewhere in Valhalla, continue heroically with his monologues.)

My suspicions as well as Sartre's insights would be relevant in the second scenario, where Hamlet has recovered and expects to endure in his earthly life. I do not mean suspicions of the first order, for example, thinking that he lied to me about his true motives for wishing the king's death—his envy of the king's power or his jealousy of the uncle for being loved by his beloved mother. They are not more justified now than before, but they are not relevant to my concern. What *is* relevant is my suspicion that there might be a connection between Hamlet's prior *difficulty in deciding* whether or not to take revenge for his father's assumed murder, and his present *difficulty in deciding* whether he really wants to be the king.

Let us assume that I wonder, on a meta-level of the discourse, whether his previously hesitation was real or just pretense, while, he was convinced that he deserved to be the king, was wiser than his uncle and less corrupted. He faked hesitation but he was afraid of failing to be as resolute as kings should be. Perhaps he was thinking that it would be better if, rather than making a bad political choice, he spent the time deceiving Horatio and me with his fictitious dilemmas and confusing the rest of the world with his bizarre behavior, without speculating about the unexpectable consequences of such games. In this case we have a classic instance of "mauvaise foi" [bad faith], where the avoidance of deciding is a decision—it is the decision not to decide, and the avoider is deceiving himself by thinking that he did not decide, and therefore he is not responsible for the consequences. However, I still need an occasion to test my hypothesis, or rather to induce Hamlet to explore such a possibility, as the issue is the latter's ability to cope better with his difficulties.

Hamlet would give me an excellent occasion if he would start the dialogue with his usual litanies about the cruelty of fate and the declared philosophy of life of many Shakespearean protagonists, that life is just "a tale told by an idiot." In such a case I might ask him which of three famous philosophies of life sounds to him adequate: the mythological (or Augustinian) view that all is in the hands of fate (or providence) and does not depend on our intentions and decisions; Kierkegaard's opinion that we cannot control the hazards of life, but crises are occasions for self-transformation (or self-transcendence); Sartre's claim that we are choosing freely our deeds and faults, but in order to avoid responsibility we deceive ourselves that our behavior and our lot is the result of external causes and internal uncontrollable forces. I know enough about Hamlet to know that he does not conceive of himself as a protagonist in a Greek tragedy, who cannot avoid his predestined fate. Nor does he conceive of himself as Psyche in Hades, searching, as the Jungians say, for her "true self" as well as the limits of intellectual reason. He is also not an early and still confused Kierkegaard. The prince, I assume, has read Shakespeare's plays, and he shares his opinions. He knows that the protagonists of those plays, the tragic as well as the comic, are responsible for what happens to them, and eventually realize it. I would give Hamlet room for choice but guess that he would identify Sartre's view as the most adequate. After all, both of us know that it is not Shakespeare who speaks about the idiot's tale, but the self-deceiving Macbeth, and we do not mistake the rhetoric of protagonists for their (or their author's) actual convictions.

If Hamlet admitted that Sartre is more or less right, we could start investigating which decisions he tries to avoid, his reasons and aims for this avoidance, his tacit assumptions and expectations, and we could explore whether there are better alternatives than those that occurred to him in the past. I leave the continuation to the imagination of the readers and hope that they will not imagine me teaching Hamlet to use Sartre's terminology.

It is, of course, possible that Hamlet would like the non-Shakespearean ideas of Kierkegaard and would prefer learning more about them to investigating his present difficulties. It is also possible that he would choose to deceive me or himself in new ways. I do not elaborate such scenarios here because I am only trying to illustrate when Sartre's approach might be relevant.

Notes

1. Several of those approaches are described and discussed in Amir (2008). Many others were presented in conferences about practical philosophy and philosophical counseling.

2. In chapter 5 I discuss some of those approaches.

3. Spinoza says at the end of Ethics: "If the way which, as I have shown, leads hither seem very difficult, it can nevertheless be found. It must indeed be difficult since it is so seldom discovered. . . . But all noble things are as difficult as they are rare" (Spinoza, 1954).

4. Shocks might, indeed, initiate occasionally desirable changes, just as wars, economic crises and personal catastrophes sometimes do, and there are stories about gods who do not hesitate to inflict them for the sake of improvement. Yet, philosophically speaking, that is not a good enough reason for causing them.

5. There is, of course, no philosophical or methodological justification for putting such judgments in brackets when the adequacy of psychological or philosophical counseling is the issue. Logical or moral flaws in general approaches or their specific applications should be pointed out in professional meetings or in public presentations.

6. Unfortunately, there are psychotherapists (and perhaps also philosophical counselors) who reject, as misplaced "judgmentalism," complaints about their morally questionable behavior toward clients, trainees, and other concerned persons.

7. The process of understanding or correctly interpreting the counselee is certainly not complete at any stage.

8. Personal communications with psychologists at a psychiatric hospital in Israel.

9. He has other questions, e.g., about women and their loyalty, and about theater, but they are not among the issues that brought him to philosophical counseling.

10. Which he does, in fact, in Act V, but from a different perspective.

11. Oral communication in the early nineties. Unfortunately, I do not remember the lecturer's name.

12. As it happens sometimes in "demonstrations of counseling" at international conferences and other public shows.

13. *Clara et distincta* is a Cartesian ideal, created in a period when rationalist philosophers believed that one can construct a philosophical system *moro geometrico*. Since then, philosophers have learned a thing or two about the language and logic of mathematical systems, which thinkers of the seventeenth and eighteenth centuries could not even guess, but of which twenty-first-century philosophers should be aware. Moreover, philosophers, have also learned that it is impossible to realize in philosophy the ideal of clarity and distinctiveness. Philosophy is an endless process in which terms are, indeed, being explicated, but at the same time new distinctions, meanings and uses are creeping in. I do not see any reason to deprive the nonphilosophical counselee of the privilege of participating in such a process: gradual clarification of initial conceptions, new distinctions, and options to explore.

14. He also ought to consider whether he should continue the counseling as Hamlet's accomplice. The principle of loyalty to clients, at least from a philosophical perspective, does not automatically overrule other moral principles.

15. "Too abstract" should be distinguished from "far-fetched": when a psychologist does refer to a patient's assumed tacit thoughts—e.g., attributes to him a "regression to an infantile way of thinking," such as "mere wishes can cause real injury to a real object,"—it is the psychologist's theory-dependent a priori interpretation of behavior that is beyond the subjective meaning of the patient (who is not conscious of his alleged belief that mere wishes cause real events and does not think that his guilt feelings, if any, are due to such a belief) that psychologist's interpretation is far-fetched. The abstract thinking of the philosophical counselor, which, in an extreme case, is "Hamlet knows that 'if p then q' and assumes that 'if p than r'; he only knows that q and infers erroneously that p and r," is, perhaps incomprehensible to Hamlet, but it does not attribute to him something that is beyond the same message expressed in plain English.

CHAPTER THREE

The Philosophical Counselor

The Impact of the Philosophical Counselor

Presupposing that *Idiōtēs* Are Not Idiots

Philosophical counseling is a philosophical dialogue between counselor and counselee. 'Counseling' (or, as some say: 'consulting'), should, however, be used as a temporary title, until a more adequate one is found for a philosophical conversation that has nothing to do with advice giving and only little to do with guidance.[1] It is not a counsel-giving activity of a person, already "initiated" to the sect of the "wise," explaining to a "novice" or to a "layman" [which is one of the meanings of ἰδιώτης—*idiōtēs*—in ancient Greek] what is wise to think or do under given conditions. It may be a conversation between a professional philosopher and a colleague who shares with him his personal doubts or problems. It may be a conversation with a relatively ignorant shoemaker; in any case, the philosophical "counselor" considers the "counselee," even if the latter is not a "professional" philosopher, as a partner to a philosophical conversation.

In philosophical conversation, the speakers challenge each other's positions. They are not necessarily claiming that the position of the other is wrong; they may argue only that it is not *necessarily* right, or that it is not *exclusively* right, since one can see the issue in different ways, rely on different assumptions, different plans, from different perspectives, and so on. In a professional debate, philosophers might, regrettably, be very rude, and try, in the polemic hit, to expose their rivals as almost morons ("idiots" in the modern, derogative, sense of the word). There are, moreover, teaching philosophers who might, not without a dash of sadism, belittle their students and make fun of their questions or ridicule their use of terms. But even if they are not ideal persons, they do not, as philosophers, presuppose that their rivals or students are not partners to a philosophical discussion. Whatever is the explanation for their aggressive conduct, they certainly do not assume that the rival or student cannot find valid philosophical reasons to challenge, in his turn, their own positions. The philosophical counselee can also disagree, philosophically or otherwise, with his counselor; but in the specific situation of counseling, where one person shares his concerns with another, while the latter seeks to justify the former's trust, the counselor should not allow himself to take such "liberties."

The Counselor's Role and the Asymmetric Relationship

Philosophical counseling is an asymmetrical relationship between partners, even when the counselee is a colleague and the problem that bothers him is his difficulty coping with a theoretical question in his specific field of expertise. The asymmetry is not necessarily due to the counselor's better knowledge, although he is frequently better acquainted than the counselee with philosophical theories and ways of thinking. It is due to his role: to examine why the counselee is, so to speak "stuck," and help him cope better. Horatio, with whom Hamlet shared some of his concerns (Shakespeare, 1993a), did not take that role. In the Shakespearian world, only "fools" and some "untamed" women or innkeepers could challenge the opinions of persons of higher ranks; friends of princes normally limited themselves to saying "Aye, Sir" or something similar. When Horatio finally dares to express a different opinion, Hamlet does not even listen, and goes to the fatal duel (ibid., V, 2).

The counseling role that Horatio could have played can be fulfilled in a variety of ways; the approach of the counselor, his philosophical background, his moral views and so forth determine the kinds of questions he asks. They influence the conversation even if the questions are just a trigger to the counselee's independent reflections and explorations. Perhaps most important, they indicate directions; different questions could have led the counselee to another place. This gives the counselor a substantial responsibility. He should be aware of this responsibility even if he does his best to encourage the counselee, from the boldest to the most timid, to express objections to what he, as counselor, is saying, to consider alternative options and to decide for himself. The counselor should be aware of it although he does not control, nor can he predict the counselee's later development. I therefore disagree with philosophical counselors who believe that the counselor can stay neutral. They come in two main groups:

The first group claims to follow the method of Socratic midwifery (*maieutics*) in which the counselor is supposed to detect by his interrogation the counselee's latent beliefs, and help him, by logical methods, identify and "abort" the false ones and "give birth" to the true ones.

Counselors of this group like to rely on Socrates's alleged self-presentation as the wisest man in Athens, the only man in town who "knows that he does not know anything." Socrates did not speak English, and we do not know precisely what he could mean by the word 'knowledge' had he spoken English. It seems, however that if he meant what his disciple and presenter, Plato, named *epistēmē* [ἐπιστήμη], that is, perfect knowledge, beyond doubts and errors, of absolute truths, then he, like any human, indeed did not know anything. In particular, he could not know whether at least two of his (or Plato's) basic convictions were true: the metaphysical conviction that there is a correspondence between well-examined and non-falsified beliefs, on the one hand, and a system of logical-semantical relationships in the "World of Ideas" on the other hand, and the psycho-epistemological conviction that true beliefs (or adequate concepts) are innate, "forgotten" but "retrievable" by adequate questioning. In the light of these convictions one can see that Socrates's self-presentation as "knowing that he does not know anything" was ironic, as were many other things that he (or Plato) said. The last thing Socrates (or Plato) believed was that the maieutic teacher is transparent, that his own beliefs and values did not intervene in the dialogue. Indeed, Socrates would not have asked the sophist Protagoras, who was allegedly teaching virtue (or excellence, *arete* [ἀρετή]), whether virtue can really be taught, or whether virtue's "parts" are the same (like "the parts of gold") or different ("like the parts of a face)" (Plato, 1997, *Protagoras*), had he not been already convinced that virtue in all its different aspects is a matter of knowledge but the kind of knowledge which is to be logically "recalled" rather than learned from sensual experience or others' opinions (Plato, 1997, *Meno*). Socrates is certainly not a transparent interrogator in Plato's dialogues, and modern maieutic teachers and temporary philosophical counselors still must prove the philosophical neutrality of their questioning. (I personally believe that the new "masters" are somewhat ironic, while their quickly trained disciples are simply unaware of their unexamined philosophical convictions. I refer to this issue in chapter 5.)

The second group is inspired by phenomenological and existentialist ideas, as some philosophical counselors and existentialist psychologists interpret them. Phenomenologists believe in the importance of exploring phenomena "as they appear to consciousness."[2] I shall not dwell on the question whether and how prior presuppositions (or linguistic habits) of the phenomenologist might interfere in his exploration of his own mind; but philosophical counselors have to do with what "appears" in the "consciousness" *of other persons*, that is, what the counselees *say* (without any phenomenological pedantry) about the supposed "phenomena that are appearing" to them. So, counselors cannot just listen; they must ask clarification questions which might orient the counselees to directions that perhaps interest the counselors but not necessarily the counselee. The same applies to counselors that are influenced by existential psychologists. The latter (whether they are inspired by Kierkegaard, Heidegger, or Sartre)[3] are interested in overcoming what they conceive as existential anxieties in ways that seem to them authentic. I do not think that such an option is wrong, but philosophical counselors should be aware that their interpretations are oriented by specific beliefs and values—and talk frankly about their personal "bias" with the counselees.

In any case, whatever are the methodological convictions of the counselors, what the counselees say in the dialogues might confront them with dilemmas regarding their own moral responsibilities.

The Counselor's Questions

My Strategy of Dealing with Dilemmas

Although I am certainly not the only philosophical counselor to try to help counselees cope with their dilemmas, I do not know how many of them share my approach. It is based on my meta-philosophical interest in the differences, from epistemological and logical perspectives, between various philosophical schools in coping with difficult philosophical questions.

There are various strategies philosophers may use to try to solve the dilemma "whether A or not-A." The following description is very simplified and schematic. Some search for new ways to argue that one of the options is correct while the other is wrong. Others suggest that option A may be reasonable from one perspective while the option not-A is reasonable from another. Still others argue that the two options do not exhaust the possibilities, and that there is a third option. Thus, Plato's dialectic is often based on the proof that the two initial options (All/always A and No/never A) are wrong but the option "in the middle" (some/sometimes/in some respects A and some/sometimes/in some respects not-A) is correct (In the case of the example from Plato: "Virtue is a matter of knowledge, and teaching which helps one to get rid of false beliefs about either virtue or knowledge is relevant to one's becoming virtuous, but the knowledge which guides the virtuous man is innate and not taught by others"). Hegel's dialectics is supposed to represent a developmental process. At first A is the right option, but then its opposite develops, and the process results in the emergence of B, in which A and not-A are accepted as partial aspects; B, in its turn, is the acceptable option until it is contradicted by its opposite, but later emerges C, in which B and Not-B are partial aspects, and so on. In terms borrowed from Fichte: from "thesis" to an "antithesis," and their opposition is "cancelled out by their lifting" [in German '*aufgehoben*'] to partial aspects of a "synthesis." According to Hegel, "dialectical processes" will go on until they reach a final, all-comprehensive solution, where "all the [philosophical] oppositions" are both dissolved and united. I do not share Hegel's convictions with regards to necessary developments or final solutions, but I try quite often to help my counselees realizing that if they look at the things from another perspective A and not-A can be both accepted as partial aspects of B. Some philosophers, in contrast to both Platonic and Hegelian dialecticians, claim, as does Kant, for example, that some dilemmas are unsolvable because human reason cannot prove any of the options, and the "dialectic" from A to not-A, and back to A and so forth, is just the result of "Reason's" hopeless attempts to apply human "understanding" beyond the scope of its intellectual tools. Some, and among them Freud as well as Kant, say that sometimes the dilemma (or conflict) is unsolvable, and one should learn to live with the ambivalence or ambiguity that follows from the duality of human nature. Some, unsatisfied with such a position suggest, as did, Nietzsche, Husserl, and Heidegger, changing the standpoint and asking other questions from the new perspective. Some philosophers apply Kant's first-mentioned strategy, the one regarding circular "dialectics," but go further. They dissolve the dilemma by calling into question the adequacy or meaningfulness of dilemmas that "are beyond the scope of our intellectual tools." Instead of "criticizing" our "intellectual tools," however, they criticize what they consider fallacies with regards to language. Russell, for example, dissolves paradoxes, which are, like the liar paradox, tricky kinds of dilemmas (if one assumes that A is true then it follows that not-A is true, and vice versa), by the claim that they are involved with "category mistakes," that is, mixing different levels of discourse. Ayer and Wittgenstein and his followers dissolve philosophical dilemmas by claiming that both options are meaningless and that the question they are supposed to answer is a pseudo-question. They challenge one or more of the presuppositions of those who insist on solving the seemingly unsolved dilemma (as I have demonstrated in chapter 1 with regards to the question "Why there is something rather than nothing?"). Some, like Wisdom, propose a "curing" analysis, apparently parallel to psychoanalysis, for those who are "obsessed" with unsolvable philosophical difficulties (see chapter 5). Psychoanalysis, in its turn, was inspired by Locke, who claimed that philosophy, or at least metaphysics, with all its dilemmas, is based on "unnatural associations of ideas." I suggest regarding these various approaches as an arsenal of strategies that the philosophical counselor can use, with no commitment to the specific convictions of their original designers, when he is helping other persons with other convictions to deal with their dilemmas. The arsenal contains, of course, other strategies, and the orientation of the philosophical counselor is often not-meta-philosophical. Yet, whatever is the chosen strategy, the practitioner should understand its rationale; learning just "techniques," without understanding their logic and limitations, is wrong both in philosophical counseling and in psychotherapy.

My Choice of Strategies

With this arsenal of strategies at the back of my mind, my approach to the dilemma of the counselee depends on both my personal position with regards to the dilemma, and my appreciation of the counselee's perspective and situation. Thus, if we go back to the case of Hamlet, I do not believe in ghosts or demons, and the dilemma, whether the appearance is of a ghost saying the truth or a demon tempting him to sin, does not bother me, but they exist in Hamlet's cultural world (he is not the only one in the play that saw the ghost), and I cannot help him dissolving the dilemma by suggesting that he is just imagining things. This is, however, not the main thing to be considered: I can use his language of ghosts and demons and invite him to think about his moral conflict (revenge as a son's duty versus murder as a cardinal sin) without sharing his beliefs in unnatural beings. The problem is that once he stops hesitating, or as some psychologists might put it, "procrastinating," and chooses to become a "man of action," Hamlet might kill his uncle. My choice of a strategy depends here on my own dilemma: is my role as a philosophical counselor to help him overcome his conflict and thus enable him to act according to the decision that seems rational to him—in other words, to be his neutral coach—or is my role also to try to deter him from killing? My "actual" strategy in the case imagined in the previous chapter was to show him that his dilemmas are unsolvable and that he should learn to live with his doubts (and let the uncle live). It was influenced not only by my moral conviction that human fallibility is a sufficient reason to avoid as much as possible irreparable acts such as death penalties, but also on my state of knowledge when the imagined conversation took place: the end of Act IV, when I (and Hamlet) did not know that the uncle was planning to kill Hamlet.

If he had come to counseling in the middle of Act V, when he was already a different person, and I had new information, I would have had other considerations, used other strategies, asked different questions.

Hamlet's case is extreme, concerned with questions of life and death, not only of the counselee but also of other persons. As such, it hints at the relevance of the counselor's moral considerations, and I will return to this in my discussion of the ethics of the philosophical counselor. My present purpose, however, is to stress that the philosophical counselor has to take a variety of considerations into account and make a variety of decisions. It is, therefore, logical to assume that other philosophical counselors, even those who share my general conception of counseling, my strategic approach, and my pro-epistemological "bias," might, in any given case, choose other strategies and pose other questions. I too might have made other considerations if I had met that counselee on another occasion.

Philosophical counselors with different "biases" may work in other ways. They may work with dilemmas without being theoretically interested in the various approaches to them; they may use entirely different philosophical strategies. They may have other aims and attitudes. In any case, their background and personal decisions have an impact on the conversation with the counselee, and they too, if they work philosophically, are aware of their responsibility.

I am therefore not convinced that training people to do "philosophical counseling" according to some formula of philosophizing strategy—such as asking "Socratic questions," encouraging "self-reflection," going through "philosophical exercises," dealing with "spiritual issues," detecting unjustified "practical syllogisms" or dealing logically with dilemmas—is sufficient preparation. The practitioner should have a much wider philosophical knowledge, a better ability to understand other persons' points of view and a much deeper awareness of the responsibility of interfering in the lives of others. I deal with this in my discussion of training philosophical counselors.

The Counselor's Ethics

Not a Matter of a "Professional Code"

Several experts in "professional ethics" propose the formulation of an ethical code for philosophical counseling. They claim that every decent profession has such a code, and if philosophical counseling aims to become a recognized profession, it should have its own list of ethical rules. There are, however, several arguments against such proposals:

Firstly, practitioners of other professions did not, presumably, take courses in moral philosophy and, lacking a sufficient moral awareness, might need codes to guide or restrain them. Philosophers, on the other hand, who are trained to do their moral deliberations by themselves, can do without written codes.[4] Moreover, from a philosophical point of view it is immoral to let a written code rather than one's own autonomous deliberations decide what is the proper behavior.

Secondly, codes represent the views of their writers, and other people may have other views. An agreement to accept such a code might sometimes be necessary, but only when enforcement is involved: that is, when there is a professional tribunal that has the authority to judge violators and impose sanctions. However, the actual degree of disagreement among philosophical counselors, even among counselors of the same orientation, does not enable the constitution of such a tribunal.

Thirdly, ethical codes cannot cover the variety of moral questions that a professional might encounter in practice. Behavior according to the code might therefore cover up more serious malpractice. Thus, ethical codes of psychotherapists prohibit sexual intimacy between counselors and counselees. But they do not protect the counselee against the malpractice of a therapist who, say, undermines, with inappropriate ways of communication, his patient's self-confidence. Nor do they protect the counselee against the negligent treatment of a patient with post-traumatic syndrome, which might sometimes have much graver outcomes than certain kinds of misplaced intimate relations. Moreover, other considerations, such as solidarity with other members of the profession and loyalty to the employing institution (which are often part of the demands of professional codes) might deter practitioners from testifying against colleagues or institutions whose practices are ethically or professionally inappropriate.

Fourthly, professional ethical codes usually pay too much attention to the interests of clients and colleagues (and employing institutions), and do not take sufficiently into consideration the harm that the professional activity might indirectly cause to others. Thus, a psychotherapist or lawyer, who should indeed inform the police if they know that their client is planning murder, might support his non-murderous plans, although it might mean depriving his wife of her rights or neglecting his children. I believe that a philosophical counselor should at least consider whether he should challenge the counselee's presuppositions which justify such plans. For that reason, philosophical counselors should have their personal principles, be ready to make judgments and *initiate informal discussions with colleagues concerned about their moral dilemmas and hesitations*, irrespectively of the question whether they will eventually agree on a professional ethical code and create an enforcing tribunal.

The Counselors' Morality

Some ethical experts try to distinguish between the "philosophical counselor's commitment to truth" and the "psychotherapist's commitment to the patient's well-being." I believe that such a distinction is wrong. Both are, or should be, committed to the aim of helping their client to cope better with his problems, and both are, or should be, committed to the ideal of truth. On the one hand, both may try to foster the client's happiness, or else, doubting whether happiness, well-being, or welfare should be regarded as an aim rather than a possible by-product, and try to foster other aims. On the other hand, both philosophical counselors and psychotherapists recognize that there might be a difference between what they and their client consider as true. Both can distinguish between a difference that is due to perspective and background and a difference that is due to a failure to distinguish between reality and fantasy. Both distinguish between the subjective perspective of the client and their own perspective, although I suspect that psychotherapists tend more often than philosophers to identify their own perspective with that of their specific sub-discipline and mistake the latter, with its conceptual schemes and criteria, with "the objective." I suspect that the belief that only philosophical counselors care about truth is related to the importance that many psychotherapists attach to what is "psychologically true" for the patient. But those psychologists' endeavor to change what is initially "psychologically true" for the patient into something else which they believe is better for him and is something that *should* be "psychologically true" for that patient when the treatment is completed. Moreover, not only the aim, but also the methods by which those psychotherapists try to induce such a change do not depend on what is "psychologically true" to the patient. Those methods are based on theories, experiments or accumulated clinical experience, supposed to be approved by the discipline's criteria for efficacy, efficiency, and sometimes also ethical propriety, all of which are most often not transparent to the patient, nor are they part of his "psychological truths." Philosophical counselors also start from what is "psychologically true' for the counselee and aim to arrive with him at something better. However, the better option, from their point of view, should be not only acceptable to him as his "psychological truth" but also chosen by him as his philosophical preference. Philosophical counselors try to achieve this using philosophical dialogue, which might be influenced by theories and methods with which the counselee is perhaps not yet acquainted, *yet he is invited to participate in the conversation as someone who is able to philosophize*.

Hence, the first ethical rule that should, to my mind, direct the philosophical counselor is a sort of a Kantian imperative that is more basic than the concerns for well-being or truth. It can be formulated in two ways: "The philosophical counselor should respect the counselee as a rational being who can be his partner in a philosophical dialogue" is one of them. The other is:

"The philosophical counselor should never treat his counselee in ways that might impair his capacity to be a partner in a philosophical dialogue."[5]

That capacity might be impaired not only by the medical use of drugs, electric shock, and other physical modalities, but also by "psychological" means which attenuate a person's capacity to think clearly. These include inappropriate and confusing ways of communication (I recommend acquaintance with what psychologists call "double binding, "gaslighting," "brainwashing," etc.), and techniques for raising his level of excitement, emotionality, and enthusiasm or, alternatively, fear and anxiety, sorrow or pain (and trying to persuade the client under such conditions) and methods with hypnotic effects that might relax not only his tension but also his critical faculties.[6]

Moreover, the counselee's participation as a partner might be neutralized as irrelevant or obstructive by treatments that are supposed to cause changes on the unconscious levels of a person's mind. Such treatments are sometimes beneficial, and their application does not necessarily imply disrespect for human beings, but it certainly does not respect their capacity to be philosophical partners. Disrespect for the other as a philosophical partner is, however, not confined to treatments that are based on bio-psychic processes beneath the patient's threshold of consciousness. Treatments that are based on claims of knowledge about spiritual matters that are beyond the limit of the counselee's understanding also fail to respect the latter as a philosophical partner. In ancient times some philosophers aspired to get out of the "cave," as described in Plato's parable; others hoped for a mystic union with the Neo-Platonic "One." Some religions, inspired by such ideas, are still fostering their sufis, kabbalists, and saints, while other traditions are still adding gurus and shamans and the like. However, the spiritual claims to actual knowledge (as distinct from faith), which were always debatable among respective theologians, are not acceptable nowadays by philosophers even as a matter of debate.

Hence the second basic rule: whatever distinction the philosophical counselor makes between knowledge and belief, he should not mislead the counselee into thinking that he knows something when he is aware that it is something he just believes or assumes. He should not ask counselees to rely on his supposed knowledge of things that are beyond the counselees' capacity to explore and understand. He may, of course, be better acquainted than the counselee with some ideas, theories, or controversies, but that does not entitle him to present them as truths that are inaccessible to the counselee nor does it give him the authority to tell the counselee what he ought to think, feel, experience, or do.

The counselor's understanding that his own philosophical convictions are not absolute truths, and his awareness of their possible impact on his questioning and interpreting, justifies a third basic rule: the counselor should be honest with the counselee. He should present his relevant convictions plainly. If the counselee comes from a culture different from that of the counselor, for example, if the latter does not share the religious worldview of the counselee, he must ask the latter's permission to challenge, when it fits, the counselee's relevant culturally dependent presuppositions. However, such a challenge should be based on an acquaintance with the counselee's culture and the existence within it of alternatives to the counselee's presuppositions. For example, if the counselee presupposes that the blood-feud is a religious obligation, the counselor may mention other interpretations, from within the same religion, which claim that blood-feud is a sinful custom. It follows that a counselor working with a counselee of another culture should inform himself about that culture. He can sometimes get the relevant information from the counselee.[7]

I do not dwell here on ethical rules that are very important but seem to me obvious, such as discretion, avoidance of abuse, exploitation, and taking advantage of the counselee's weakness for any purpose. Yet there is room for three additional rules.

The fourth rule demands the counselor to be honest and admit, on the appropriate occasions, his incapacity to help the counselee. Some psychological difficulties are not resolvable by conversations of any kind, while other treatments—behavioristic training, medication or other medical (and some say also spiritual) ways—may cure or at least temporarily alleviate suffering. Philosophical counselors, psychoanalysts or religious guides who oppose such treatments as a matter of principle might cruelly and irresponsibly cause additional suffering by deterring their "client" from them. The philosophical counselor should, instead, let other experts help and offer his moral support. A person who is diagnosed as, say, schizophrenic who needs medication and sometimes hospitalization can, however, still benefit, during remissions, from conversations that foster his human dignity and abilities despite his condition.

There are, on the other hand, difficulties with which the counselor is not ready to deal for his own, moral reasons. Perhaps he believes that helping the counselee would enable the latter to realize immoral plans; perhaps he is reluctant to deal with, say, a counselee with racist opinions. The counselor should be sincere and refuse to engage with the potential counselee. There are, of course, counselors who believe that they can convert the immoral counselee to a better person; some believe they can prevent their own antipathy from influencing their counseling. But, with all due respect to their courage and determination, they need directing feedback from others. I personally think that philosophical counselors as well as psychotherapists should have, like judges, the right, and sometimes the duty, to avoid cases in which their own values and views as well as interests might lead to malpractice.

The fifth rule says that the philosophical counselor should include in his consideration not only the well-being of the counselee, but also those whom the counselee effects. While professional ethical codes demand that the practitioner try to prevent specific harms that the treatment or the client might cause to a third party, the morally guided professional takes into consideration harms that those codes ignore. The philosophical counselor, who is acquainted with moral theories, should be directed by the same moral principles that direct him at times to prefer the general good to the interests of his family and friends, and his loyalty to the counselees should be similarly—and sincerely—limited.

The sixth rule is that the counselor's loyalty to the counselee obliges him to warn the latter of dangers of which he is unaware. Psychotherapists sometimes speak of "poisonous" people and warn each other from "manipulative" patients or colleagues, yet many of them do not share with the patient their opinion that his parent or spouse is "double binding" or "gaslighting" him, and a insists that he "examine himself" and "take responsibility" for the problems (which is a wrong interpretation of the Stoic recommendation). There is, however, a Biblical rule: "Do not [sic] put a stumbling block in front of the blind" (Leviticus, 19, 14) that might be completed by "and remove, or warn of, blocks put by others." This is morally more basic than all the later rules of rabbis, popes, imams, ayatollahs,, or professional ethics codes, which sometimes prefer communal peace to the well-being of the victim. It should also prevent the hypocrisy of psychotherapists and guide philosophical counselors to consider whether collegial solidarity should be always respected.

(In chapters 5 and 6, where I refer critically to some phenomena in philosophical counseling and psychotherapy, I deal with the possibility of harmful applications of specific approaches, not with harmful practitioners.)

Training Philosophical Counselors

Philosophical counseling is a new profession. The philosophers who practice it had to find their own way of using their acquaintance with philosophical theories and approaches and help counselees, most of whom are non-philosophers. They work in a great variety of ways, and have few things in common, one of which is the fact that they were not trained to be philosophical counselors. I believe that most of them started to practice because they believed, each in his own way, in the relevance of philosophy to life, and were convinced that their philosophical background gives them the permission and the ability to apply it in counseling. Some started in one way and turned later to another; they seem to have learned something from their pioneering experience.

The issue of training came to the fore when, on the one hand, jobless graduate students in philosophy, with no prior interest in making philosophy "practical," heard about, and were drawn to the new activity, and, on the other hand, some partisans of the new cause tried to spread the message and encourage the practice of philosophical ways among educators, psychotherapists, social workers, nurses, and others. Some of the pioneers brought the message to countries where the ways of dealing with philosophical themes as well as problems of life were not inspired by the Greco-Roman heritage of philosophical dialogue and debate, nor influenced by Western conceptions of psychotherapy, whose founders were inspired by the Western philosophical tradition. The message arrived also in countries where maintenance of the Western tradition was obstructed by political or religious factors (former European communist countries, for example, and some Middle East states). The different backgrounds gave birth to different conceptions of philosophical counseling and ways of training.

The training programs started with workshops, seminars, and personal tutoring by the pioneers. Training programs are still the main avenue, but nowadays one can also find programs and courses in academic institutes, often as one of many options for counseling, in departments of education or psychotherapy, rather than in those of philosophy. As far as I know, there is no conventional syllabus or general agreement about prerequisites, requirements or aims of such courses.

According to my approach, philosophical counselors should have a philosophical background. They should not only be acquainted with the field, but also aware of the variety of possible approaches to philosophical questions. They should also have experience in philosophical debates, in which implications are discussed and presuppositions are called into question. Students of philosophy acquire such a background during their postgraduate studies, but it can be acquired in other frameworks as well, when various worldviews are confronted and systematically and critically discussed. (I insist on "systematically," as I share Locke's opinion that disputes in parliaments and chats in cafés, pubs, or tea parties, do not create such a background.) I stress "a variety of worldviews" as I do not believe that the difficulties of counselees are due to their failure to think rationally, and do not believe that elementary courses in formal logic or informal reasoning provide sufficient tools for helping counselees to deal better with their problems.

The required background is, however, not sufficient. Although advanced students (or their professors) may be aware of the practical relevance of theoretical debates and recognize actual cases in which philosophical dilemmas are concretely illustrated, they are not trained to look for philosophical questions, confusions, dilemmas, and the like, in the nonphilosophical discourse of counselees.

They are also not trained to respect the subjective viewpoints of "laymen" or listen politely and patiently to what they say. They do not always know to restrain their polemic Socratic genes, reduce the aloofness of their Stoic ancestors, slow down inherited Hegelian tendencies to dialectical processing or calm down urges to Nietzschean provocations, Derridean deconstructions or knockdowns of rivals in philosophical-analytic style. In this respect, they can learn a thing or two from psychotherapists yet forget what the latter claim to know about "human motivation" in general. They must learn to tune themselves to the individual "problem situation" (Popper, 1957) of the specific counselee. They must also learn to adapt their language and their tendency to generality and abstraction to the level on which the counselee can feel that he is a participant in a dialogue that is intelligible and relevant to him.

I believe that a philosophical counselor should not impose on the counselee his own philosophical positions, but work in ways that are in harmony with his personal convictions and style of thinking. Accordingly, I do not favor dictation from above regarding procedures, targets and aims. That does not mean that philosophical counselors should learn to do counseling without any method. The counselor should identify and challenge those latent philosophical beliefs, principles and values, which obstruct the counselee's attempts to cope with his difficulties, and help him realize that there are alternative approaches. He should do this by a philosophical dialogue in which the counselee is a partner, not a patient or client. But the counselor should apply the dialogical method it in his own way, adapted according to his understanding of the specific counselee's problem and situation.

Although the philosophical counselor cannot be sure that the counseling dialogue will be helpful, *he should believe that philosophizing may help*. In other words, he should believe that, in principle, philosophy matters. I therefore start working with my trainees by asking whether their studying philosophy and philosophizing changed anything in their personal life. Their first reaction, usually, is to cite a theory about the assumed benefits of philosophy or the philosophically proper way of life, and I have to direct them to specific occasions in which philosophizing influenced (or could have influenced) their ways of coping with a specific difficulty. I do this by bringing up examples from history novels, the theatre, films as well as my own and my counselee's experience. For some of them it is the first realization that philosophy really changed something in their life. Once they understand and describe such an experience, we explore together (I prefer to do this in the company of other trainees) how and why their experience occurred. The next question, designed to highlight the existence of personal differences, is whether they think that what worked for them would work for others in similar situations. The discussion that follows is the introduction to a series of conversations about self- understanding and understanding other persons.

In the next stage, the participants learn about the tacit philosophical beliefs and questions that underly peoples' thinking and coping. They are taught to detect them in philosophical and nonphilosophical discourses and to realize that different persons might detect different philosophical presuppositions. The importance of exploring, whether the relevant person presupposes them, is stressed.

In the following stage, we discuss which presuppositions it is relevant to challenge in the attempt to help the counselee, and which beliefs should not be touched, as the harm this might cause is greater than the expected benefit. We explore, in non-imposing ways, the alternatives that can be offered to the counselee, and examine non-harmful ways to challenge him, leaving room for the counselee's discoveries and deliberations.

The issue of handling a philosophical conversation in which the counselee, who is most often a "layman," is a respected partner is the subject matter of a further training. The option of using metaphors, allegories, and other non-conceptual ways of expressing ideas is discussed, and the trainees are invited to try "talking philosophy in simpler terms" in imaginary conversations with figures known to them from politics, football, TV shows, movies, literature, and so on. They also learn to listen to feedback from other trainees, discuss prejudices with respect to "lay" people, and failed attempts to discuss issues philosophically with parents, spouses, and others. The moral issues that may be raised in such conversations are discussed in special seminars.

When the trainees come from psychoanalysis, psychotherapy, social work and the like, I start the teaching by explaining what is, in principle, philosophical in their work and what distinguishes it from the nonphilosophical aspects. We also discuss which of their patient's philosophical beliefs and questions might be relevant even though the practitioners are not used to seeing them as such. (Some prospective counselors are "born philosophers," but I do not expect much success if the trainees are "resistant to philosophy"—if they are too "practically oriented," or think dogmatically, or prefer to apply ready-made formulas to thinking their way through, or convinced that being philosopher is being considered the wisest person in Athens.)

I also expect little success when the trainee—psychotherapist, religious guru, or antirationalist thinker—is convinced that being a philosopher means avoiding "deep unconscious truths" and preferring "shallow rationalistic" discussions to "higher sources of wisdom" (to which they allegedly have access). Being a philosopher does not mean assuming that preferences, choices and decisions, on the theoretical or the practical level, must always be arrived at by explicitly rational methods. It does mean (among other things) being ready to explore critically, *when relevant*, any claim to knowledge—however "high" or "deep" are its alleged sources—and any preference, choice, and decision, whether arrived at by rational or nonrational methods.

Notes

1. Cambridge Dictionary defines 'counseling' as "the job or process of listening to someone and giving that person advice about their problems" and says that its synonym is "guidance." In psychotherapy it acquired a more limited meaning: "professional guidance in resolving personal conflicts and emotional problems," a rather vague description of a variety of psychotherapeutic approaches by professionals whose formal education did not then entitle them to enter the guild of "psychotherapists." 'Philosophical counseling' (or 'consultancy') is supposed to be the translation of the name Gerd Achenbach gave in the eighties to his activity, '*philosophische Beratung*.' But '*Beratung*' in German is also 'discussion' or 'consultation among colleagues, politicians etc.' And, in fact, Achenbach, who sought to convey by that title his opinion that personal conflicts and emotional problems are basically philosophical and not medical issues, also insisted that he is offering his "guests" a discussion rather than giving them advice or guidance.

2. As one reader, an expert in Husserl's phenomenology, has commented, this is a rather "thin" presentation of the approach, lacking as it does the "transcendental reduction" or the "transcendental ego" and, I would add, Husserl's analytic techniques or theoretical aims. However, phenomenologist counselors or psychologists are not operating on the level of Husserl's investigations; rather, they are trying to understand the lived experiences of the other on a mundane level, sometimes with "reductions" from specific social and biographical contexts to more abstract and general levels.

3. As I noted in the last section of chapter 1, the interpretations and presuppositions that justify the practical ways of applying their theories are sometimes incompatible with the theoretical positions of the respective philosopher. Here, the difference between the "theoretical" and the "practical" consists in more than operating on different levels and asking different questions.

4. Some of my academic colleagues disagree with me. I must admit that sometimes I myself doubt the readiness of certain philosophers to examine the moral aspects of their behavior (or the moral implications of their theories). Yet I assume that they can do it more thoroughly than people who rely only on their moral intuitions. If they can but do not care to—"toothless" ethical codes will not change their attitude

5. I could have added more details about Kant's "categorical imperative" and the equivalence, according to Kant, between its different formulations: first, respecting

the human dignity of every person, second, never treating a person as just a means rather than also as "an end in himself," and third, the claim that the criterion for the morality of a personal practical rule of behavior is its ability to be a general law in a kingdom of rational beings: if everybody always follows it, it does "not destroy the conditions of its possibility to continue to be a general law" (Kant, 2002a). My simple paraphrasing does not respect the nuances of Kant's distinctions between a person conceived as a "phenomenon" and the same person perceived as a "noumenon," or between a real state of empirical humans and the hypothetical kingdom of rational citizens, where each is an end in himself.

However, philosophical counselors speak with concrete, real others, whom they perceive only from their outside perspectives. From their contingent viewpoints, they sometimes find it difficult to accept what those others are saying as rational, honest, or meaningful. I therefore recognize the importance of Levinas's moral approach, according to which one's moral responsibility to the other person does not depend on the other's assumed personality, capacities, or intentions. The "rule of charity" in human communication, as formulated by Quine or Davidson and its reformulation as a "rule of humanity" by Grandy and Dennett (see p.l.e., 2022 for telegraphic hints), demands that we try, as much as possible, to interpret what the other says as rational and honest according to the interpreter's criteria. In contrast, my rule demands that we try to create an atmosphere which enables the other, the counselee, to remain (or become more) rational, honest, and comprehensible by our shared criteria. Like Kant, I am talking about "conditions of possibility." However, I am not concerned with possibilities from the perspective of the transcendental I, but in the intersubjective realm of a philosophical conversation (even when Gadamer's ideal of a "fusion of horizons" [1989] is not achieved).

6. That does not mean that the use of such techniques and methods is always wrong. For example, using music to create a certain atmosphere or to encourage people to dance usually has nothing to do with disrespect for rational beings, who enjoy other things in life besides philosophizing. Nor does it mean that psychological or medical treatments which use them are ethically wrong. In cases in which a person is psychologically suffering and rational discussions are ineffective or impossible (as in the case of phobias, some addictions, psychotic crises or deep depression) it might be immoral to insist that only philosophical dialogues or at least "talking therapy" are "ethically adequate for rational beings."

7. I assume that a counselee who is considering revenge but seeks philosophical counseling is already aware that there might be morally better alternatives. There are, however, counselees who meet a philosophical counselor for the first time having already committed a crime, for example, prisoners for whom philosophical counseling is part of the rehabilitation program. Jose Barriento, who is conducting such a program in Spain, claims that it is oriented by Christian values, and this brings us to another important point. The counselor may be oriented by his religious or cultural values, but the prisoner may not share them, and it is my belief that the counselor should talk to the prisoner in the terms of the latter's culture, not his own. There

are of course qualifications. If the counselee's culture unequivocally endorses blood feuds, the moral rule that prohibits the encouragement of counselees to harm other people overrules, to my mind, any rule that demands respect for the counselee's culture. The respect for the other's culture follows from the respect for the other as a person, not from respect for the other culture per se. I am not acquainted with philosophers who favor blood feuds. But if I were dealing with such a person, my moral duty to act against him would overrule any ethical rule that demands collegial solidarity.

CHAPTER FOUR

Some Concrete Examples

The examples are drawn from counseling dialogues.[1] They do not describe processes in their entirety. Concrete persons are not protagonists personalizing a central problem in a well-structured Shakespearean play. They come to counseling with a whole pack of issues that bother them. The examples illustrate the relevance of philosophy to some of their problems, and the impact of their philosophical "treatment." They do not illustrate complete personal stories, and do not offer typical solutions to types of problems. They are examples of specific dialogues with specific persons about some of their specific problems. I divided them into types of questions for the purpose of presentation.

"Why Did It Happen to My Child?"

Questions of the type "Why did it happen to my child?" are often asked by parents whose children suffer from severe physical or mental handicaps, whether from birth or because of an accident or other events in later life. The apparent similarity among those parents—the feelings of sorrow, the burdens of caring, the worries, does not mean, however, that it should always be interpreted in the same way or that there is one formula for dealing with it.

In this respect, philosophical responses are different from religious ones, which tend to explain suffering as a punishment, a test, or the arbitrary will of Divine beings, and recommend, with or without special acts of repentance and atonement, continued faith in the supernatural powers and acceptance of their rule (and the authority of its earthly representatives). An alternative religious explanation, for example that of some kabbalists, sound to me even more detached from the concrete case—and from philosophy: it links a person's earthly misfortune with disorders allegedly caused in heavenly spheres by another person. Philosophical counseling is also different from formulas sometimes used by rehabilitation therapists or social workers, who do not pretend to know the answer to such questions, but "know" that readaptation after catastrophic events should start with mourning rituals, in which one separates oneself from the "lost object"[2] even if that "object" is just the subjective parental pre-catastrophic hopes, while the real "object," daughter or son, is still there, with all the daily ordeals.[3]

I acted as a volunteer in two different frameworks: organized groups of parents of schizophrenic persons, and spontaneous individual conversations with close relatives of recently paralyzed persons, most of them while the injured were still in a rehabilitation center. There were very great differences in the socioeconomic and educational levels of those counselees, and there were cultural and religious divergences. For some, being the parent of an innocent victim of an accident was a matter of shame and social rejection; for others, coping with a confused and confusing child was a reason for pride; some believed that "all is in the hands of Heaven" or Allah, and others believed that that Heavenly "bug" can be fixed by rituals, prayers, magic, or good deeds. Some carried the yoke without religious consolation, while others found relief in intellectual or artistic activity. None, I should say, looked for a Stoic equanimity or existential authenticity: some elitist philosophical ideals were not designed for caretakers of other living souls.[4]

Lina, a middle-aged woman, was "obsessed" with the question of why (precisely) her daughter, despite her "happy childhood and good up-bringing," was afflicted with schizophrenia. She was restlessly seeking scientific explanations. Many philosophers, from Bacon through Hobbes to the Positivists, and from anti-positivist Nietzsche through Heidegger to Foucault, say that people seek scientific knowledge to obtain power or control (Bacon, 2004, part 1, aphorism III; Hobbes, 1981; Comte, 1961; Nietzsche, 1966; Foucault, 1978). Others, for example, Sartre, suggest that it is a way of getting rid of one's responsibility, or a way of fleeing from guilt and shame (Sartre, 1993); Nietzsche would add, with Dewey's consent, that it is a flight of the weak from uncertainty (Nietzsche, 1954; Dewey, 1929), while Kierkegaard or Heidegger would say that it is a flight from anxiety (Kierkegaard, 2014; Heidegger, 2013). (Psychotherapists offer parallel hypotheses, fitted into their theories and terminologies.) Any of these hypotheses could fit Lina. However, I did not focus on the motives for Lina's quest, but on the ability to get an answer for her question. Science is currently and will probably always be unable to fully explain individual concrete events, and it is not going to tell Lina *precisely* why her daughter has schizophrenia. So, I chose to talk with Lina about knowledge, challenged her presuppositions, talked with her about the limitations of science, and explored with her whether alternative claims to knowledge, religious or mystical, would satisfy her. Unexpectedly, this not only induced Lina to abandon her "scientific project," it freed her to dedicate time and energy to projects that interested her before the appearance of the illness' symptoms. This in turn enabled her to accept the incomprehensibility and ambivalence in her daughter's situation, and treat her, in consequence, more patiently.

Accepting the partiality and limitedness of our knowledge may empower us. Spinoza also connected knowledge and empowerment. He thought that understanding that whatever happens, happens necessarily, might help the wise to avoid weakening, "passive" emotions, like regrets and hopes that lead to disappointments. In contrast to Spinoza, I do not rely on what the perfect knower should, theoretically, know while thinking of the world *sub species aeternitatis*. We live *sub species temporalis* and should learn to be tolerant of uncertainty and ambiguity. I am not talking about Kant's recognition of the limits of knowledge, which, from his perspective, means that our metaphysical ignorance leaves room for moral freedom and the hope for just rewards in the afterlife. I am referring, from a Popperian point of view, to what is relevant to parents of disabled persons: awareness of human fallibility, understanding that past parental mistakes are not necessarily the cause for present misfortunes and, despite the present need for reorientation, parental hopes should not be given up, as the reliability of medical diagnoses and prognoses is limited.

Despite my "bias" to epistemology, I do not think that philosophical discussions of knowledge are always in place. Sara, another parent of a schizophrenic daughter, was satisfied with the answer given to her by a Hasidic Cabalist missionary, which, she said, "gave meaning to the suffering." I did not challenge that belief, although the kabbalistic claim to know and justify the ways in which The-Holy-Blessed-Be-He runs the upper and lower worlds (or the missionary methods of persuading despairing people to convert to that version of Judaism) is questionable. Her new faith did not obstruct her coping and was not involved with fanatic aggressiveness against others. I could not offer her, in her state of mind, a more comforting meaning.

I learned what such kabbalistic "meaning" meant from Abe, and in his case, I found it proper to question and challenge it. Abe was the depressed son of a drug-addicted father, a famous violinist in his country of origin, who was degraded to the status of a poor street musician in the new country. When Abe was still a child, the father used to send him to beg for money. to cover the cost of the father's drug-enabled flight from his dire reality. Social workers, who collected children like Abe from the streets and sent them to boarding schools, changed his life. As an educated adult he helped his less fortunate siblings and formed his own family. Yet he was very unhappy. As I met him soon after his conversion to an Ultra-Orthodox Judaism, I asked him whether the conversion affected his mood. The question changed his gloomy face into a shining one, and he said that he now knows the meaning of his suffering: "it is an atonement for sins." When he told me that the sins were not his I falsely assumed that he meant his father's misdeeds, and challenged him with the Biblical announcement: "The one who sins is the one who will die. The child will not share the guilt of the parent, nor will the parent share the guilt of the child" (Ezekiel, 18, 20), and we discussed matters of responsibility and justice. The fact that I let him teach me his conception changed his mood and trust, yet he did not reveal to me Cabalist secrets, and I prepared myself for the next conversation by reading. I discovered that according to some kabbalists one might suffer for sins committed centuries ago, and it is not a punishment but rather a privilege to be elected to suffer for the "correction" of "a damage" in the upper worlds caused by an unatoned sin of one of the Just who died before full repentance. The man seemed to me strong enough to survive a challenge of the new belief that gave him meaning but left him as unhappy as before. There was, however, no need to do it: I had already acquired his trust and in our next meeting he asked me if "bad blood" can pass from father to son. His basic question then, was not only "Why did it happen to my father?" but also "Will it happen to me too?" which bothers more than one kin of persons with physical, mental, or moral defects, and that sends us to issues of knowledge, free will and hope.

Discussion of such issues had no room in the case of Meir, married to a sick wife, father of a paralyzed daughter and a drug-addicted son. Meir's despair led him to drinking. He neglected his vegetable store and in consequence lost his source of income, which led him to still heavier drinking. I first met him, in the middle of the Gulf war, when Saddam Hussein was shelling Israel with Scud missiles. He was distrustful, and answered every question with "I don't care," including the question whether he sought shelter when his area was the target of the Scuds. As his answering sounded automatic and mechanical, I looked for a question that could move him yet take him out of the context of his personal troubles. I knew that he was born in Iraq, so I talked to him about that country with the intention of reminding him of his childhood and asked him whether he cared about the bombardments in Iraq. He was surprised and surprised me with the answer: "Of course, they are good people!" I told him that he lied to me when he said that he did not care about anything, for he cares about people, even those in the "enemy's camp," while most people in Israel do not.

In the next conversation he told me that "all the people" in his neighborhood were asking him to pray for them, "for God listens to good persons." Meir did not ask why his daughter was injured or why his son was addicted. His question, which my unintended provocation enabled to emerge, was "Can a person who is unable to help his family be a worthy man?" We discussed, accordingly, the issues of helplessness and human worth, exploring the latent beliefs and values that prevented him from looking for better solutions than drinking.

It should be clear by now that I do not share Spinoza's *Amor Dei intellectualis* toward a world that from my experiential perspective and that of my counselees is not always lovable. I also do not share Spinoza's rather Stoic opinion about the emotions. To my mind, both regrets and hopes (which might, indeed, be disappointed) are "active" attitudes that may deepen our moral sensitivity and add meaningfulness to our lives. I therefore do not accept even the mild version of Spinozism of my atheist and non-determinist colleague, who bases her counseling on the understanding that we cannot change the past. That is certainly true, but we can change its present interpretation, and that might make a real difference in the counselee's life. It did in Abe's and Meir's cases, and it did in the cases of relatives of schizophrenic persons. Their change of perspective enabled them to see in a new light the confusing events and their past reactions. It also enabled at least some of them to renew their sources of energy by doing things other than caring for their disabled loved ones.

Limited resources, or at least the feeling of their scarcity, bothers many parents who need to decide how to allocate them between their children. The difficulties do not involve only emotional conflicts and the clashing interests of the parents, but also, as we know since God preferred Abel to Cain, and Jacob favored Joseph over his brothers, involve the possibility of problematic relations between the children. The relations may be even more difficult when one of the children is handicapped, and it is certainly not solved by recommending what Gilligan identifies as the feminine morality of caring, which is motivated by compassion rather than by criteria for fairness and justice (Gilligan, 1982).[5] The daughter of Sherley, who was also the mother of a schizophrenic man, accused her angrily of unfairness, and stopped talking to her.

Sherley, still wondering why "it" happened to her son, was upset by her daughter's detachment. The morality of caring did not help her, as the morality of allocation of a limited caring capacity among those who need it is a question of justice rather than compassion. I did not talk with Sherley about her motives, and I do not know who her favorite child was. I also do not think that my philosophical mission is to change emotions. A justified allocation, like the decision of who among wanderers in the desert should receive the last can of water, is not made by changing emotions or ceasing to feel them, but by making considerations that disregard them. (It not only sounds like a Kantian conviction. It is.) Shirley and I discussed the criteria for a just allocation, which enabled Sherley to be more assertive, feeling compassion for her angry daughter, yet not being remorseful for dedicating herself mostly to her son—and to the artistic hobby that satisfied her and gave her energy to go on. It also enabled her eventually to renew contact with her daughter.

"What Would I Have Lost If I Had Let Him Get What He Wanted?"

When such questions are asked, my first association is of a businessman recalculating a past transaction and regretting his refusal to make a minor concession that would have given him a chance for a great profit. The second is of a politician making the same kind of calculations. The third is of a grandfather, urging his stubborn grandchild to let his cousins play with his favorite toy while he is playing with other gadgets. The fourth is of a mother in a traditional patriarchal family, where matrimony is a matter of matchmaking rather than the couple's mutual choice, trying to convince her daughter, a reluctant newlywed, to comply with her husband's sexual wishes. This leads me to an incident told to me by one of my colleagues, whose elderly aunt told her about her last meeting with a moribund friend with whom she had had a love affair in her youth, and her refusal to respond to his plea to sleep with him "for the last time." The aunt finished the story with the "What would I have lost if . . ." question. I do not know whether it was supposed to express regret and moral remorse, pity, bragging for having had an affair with the (now famous) dying man, or pride for still being an object of desire. My colleague, with her Kantian convictions, mentioned it humorously in a conversation about the morally justifiable limits of conjugal compromises.

I am not sure that the aunt or Kant are good guides in such a case. Their life experiences seem to lack some aspects that are relevant to making moral judgments in the domain of sexual relations (with regards to Kant, see Greengard, 2015). I doubt whether Socrates, who according to Plato's *Protagoras*, believed that ethical questions can be discussed in terms of loss and profit (Plato, 1997, 746–90), and, like the aunt, refused in Plato's *Symposium* to have sex with his lover (457–505), would be a better guide for interpersonal relations. His calculations regarded the benefits to his own soul, and he justified his chastity by the claim that the lover really loved another, apparently a poet named Agathon. He probably also meant that the young lover should realize that he really loved ἡ τοῦ ἀγαθοῦ ἰδέα [the Idea of Agathon], that is, the Good in itself, discussed in the Plato's *Republic* (1997, 971–1223), rather than a degraded substitute in carnal pleasures. Such a recommendation is perhaps relevant to the Christian monks, who thanks to their "spiritual exercises" became, according to Hadot (1974) "true philosophers," but not to my counselees. Socrates, being the husband of the unfairly ill-reputed Xantippe and the father of her children, proves that heterosexually he was less ascetic; but with all his concern for love of others and love for Ideas, he does not seem to have any concern about being a loving (or a beloved) spouse or parent. Many counselees are, in contrast, concerned with their conjugal, parental, filial, and other interpersonal relations, and Socrates and Kant are not the only philosophers who, to my mind, seem to have little to offer them. That is, of course, a matter of debate: My above-mentioned colleague claims that the altruism that according to her analyses follows from Kant's anti-egoistic morality could justify her aunt's regret.

I prefer to challenge my "aunt-like" counselees by mentioning that according to Nietzsche, pity or compassion, though it may be a way of caring for one's own soul, is a form of contempt for the other, a gift-giving of a "superior" to an "inferior," without the needed imaginative knowledge of the perspective of the other (Nietzsche's multifaceted attitude to compassion and pity is discussed in Frazer, 2006). I challenge them because I think that a moral attitude should consider the other's perspective: some persons are not interested in gifts, sexual or not, which are given because the other is "altruist," even if the latter is ready, in his "altruism," to "lose something" by "letting them get what they want." The giver's soul may gain some benefits, but the other sometimes wants love, not favors.

Yet the question "What do I lose if . . ." or, better said for our purposes, "What should one *not* lose in making concessions to others?" has a central place in interpersonal conflicts and in counseling dialogues. Some of my counselees were concerned about losing control or freedom, and some felt exploited, cheated, or betrayed. Some cared about their career or so-called self-realization, and some complained about sexual frustration or other demands with which they were not eager to comply. Although each case demanded references to specific questions and presuppositions, in all of them philosophical questions with regards to selfhood—identity, subjectivity, autonomy, respect, dignity, vitality, and the like—were discussed, and many presuppositions with regards to obligations to others were challenged.

It was also important to distinguish between the Kantian moral indignation of being treated by the other only as a means rather than also an end in itself (Kant, 2002a), and the discontent, influenced by Hegelian "subject-object" dialectic and its influence on some existentialists, postmodernists, and feminists with being "turned into an object": this is a conceptually confused discontent. For example, an engineer may be a perfectly moral person, but if he wants to prevent, say, elevator accidents, he must sometimes relate to the passengers as the aggregate weight of physical objects, while the SS troops, in their efforts to humiliate their victims or obtain their cooperation by cheating them, treated them as conscious subjects. The rapist or sadist who enjoys the victim's suffering, the boss who sexually harasses his secretary, as well as the masochistic and the altruistic woman who lend their bodies for the other's pleasure, may be confused about the other's or their own body, but they are not turning other persons or themselves into things. Such philosophical distinctions matter to the counselees, and sometimes make real differences.

Sheila, a victim of abuse, was empowered by the understanding that her abuser could not, did not, and did not wish to "objectify" her. Noa became capable of saying no when she realized that her body was, subjectively, herself, and not an object that she could "altruistically" lend to her husband. Benny, who was sexually abused in his childhood by the religious leader of his community, and punished by his denying parents for his complaints, became less eager to please people who were taking advantage of him when he learned to conceive of himself as an active person—cooperating as well as resisting—rather than a passive thing.

Yet I should concede that despite such insights, the counselees' fear of losing other things that the relationship, however problematic, provides might prevent significant practical changes.

"What Is the Meaning of All That?"

Some of the counselees who ask such a question may be dissatisfied with their present situation—with their job, family, personal losses, health, responsibilities—yet seem to know what they would have done had their situation been otherwise. Others may feel that their life is meaningless and would be meaningless under any conditions. Some put the focus on their personal life, which is narrated by them as a series of failed attempts to realize plans, hopeless struggles to overcome difficulties or being just a boring, purposeless story. Some counselees who are disoriented for a variety of reasons—immigration, for example, or the loss of religious faith, or suffering a major injury—may be interested in general questions, such as the source of injustice or the purposelessness of the universe. Asking such a question does not, mean, however, that that is necessarily the philosophical question that is relevant to a helpful conversation.

The dialogue with Billy, a young architect, started with his dilemma over whether to abandon his job, family, and country and join a Buddhist monastery. Buddhism seemed to him more appropriate than "the Western worldview," as it enabled peace of mind. He talked about boredom and meaninglessness and said that he wished he were like a ball, with minimal contact points with others. I tried to understand why contact with others bothered him, but he remained vague. He drew a comparison between the study of architecture, which gives room to imagination and creativity, and working as architect, with all the compromises that one must make with the bosses and the "mediocre clients." He also mentioned his children as a burden.

The ball that he repeatedly mentioned had only its geometrical essence, and I wondered why he wanted to resemble such an abstract entity. Therefore, I asked him about the concrete features of the ball: was it light or heavy, transparent, or opaque, light or dark, and so on. I was inspired by the example of John Austin, who in his struggle against the metaphysical pretension of conceiving of the essential meaning of general and abstract terms like 'being' or 'reality,' gave examples of the variety of uses of the words 'is' or 'real' in in different concrete daily linguistic acts (Austin, 1962). The astonished Billy tried to concretize the idealized ball and finally described a very light, elastic, pink plastic balloon, (while I, under the impact of his talking about buildings, had in mind a huge, heavy, and gray cement ball, placed in front of a New York–style skyscraper). I asked him what one could do with such a balloon, and he answered: Play on the beach. Before leaving he said, "That question was like a koan, thank you!"[6] I do not know which of Billy's beliefs I challenged, as after that "enlightenment" he stopped coming. One of my guesses is that it was the illusion that playing with abstract ideas can help one get rid of concrete responsibilities. If I am correct, Billy's basic question was "Which worldview can help me live without the yoke of responsibility?" rather than "with minimal contact."

The conversations with Jerry also started with his discontent with his job and a sensation of meaninglessness. Although he was still in his twenties, he was talking about earning and investing money for his retirement, when he would be free to do what he wanted: continue reading his recently bought encyclopedia for teenagers, but without the fatigue he felt after a grueling day of work. A change of job would necessitate academic studies, which he did not want.

He never liked studying, and preferred sports. As a child he excelled in capoeira, at high school he was on the volleyball team, and from his theoretical studies there he remembered only some boring courses in anatomy, which his mother recommended because it was relevant to sport. The encyclopedia, which he was reading in alphabetical order, was therefore a revelation for him. I suggested that he look for further information about entries that interested him, which was the first step in his future searches.

Jerry's first concern was, in his words, his "personal identity," which seemed to be threatened by any social pressure to do what he did not want to do, or by insulting responses to his own demands (like a soldier's reaction—"go fuck yourself, son of a bitch"—to his order when he was the one on duty). My first efforts were, therefore, to challenge the confused cluster of ideas that he called "personal identity," and to find some Archimedean fulcrum of internal strength. My guess, that he was stronger than he was then ready to admit, was based on the fact that during his military service, where he at first felt reduced to the most monotonous drudgery, he made a huge effort to be moved to another unit: he studied by himself from a textbook in a foreign language (which he read word by word with a dictionary), and succeeded in understanding all the preparatory material that he had neglected in high school. He was admitted, against the expectations of his commanders, to a course in computers that was designed for soldiers with much better academic records, and when he finished it successfully, was given a responsible role, thanks to which he got the needed qualifications for the job he would later hold in civilian life. His considering himself as rational, and his reactions to what he was finding in the encyclopedia also suggested that he was less "dumb" than his original self-description, so I talked with him (in his terms) about the differences between "personal identity" (whatever it is), "self-presentation" and "self-image," and tried to help him improve the latter in light of a reinterpretation of his past, including his daring capoeira somersaults and his role on the volleyball team. He conceded but started to talk about the "lack of meaning" he was experiencing. I mentioned some philosophers and authors who could be accessible to him. He read about Camus, and we discussed his conception of the happy Sisyphus. I also recommended some novels and movies, but he was not attuned to any form of art besides singing Middle Eastern songs in karaoke bars. When he surprised me with the news that he had listened to some sections of Bizet's *Carmen* on the radio and enjoyed them, I told him about the opera, suggested that he read the plot before listening to it, and try to think of which protagonist he could identify with. Thus, the romantic novella of Prosper Mérimée, adapted, simplified, and abridged by the author of *Carmen*'s libretto, and further "digested" for the readers by Wikipedia, was probably his introduction to the world of literary fiction. I also mentioned Viktor Frankl, and he read avidly not only Frankl's book (Frankl, 2006), but also articles about Kierkegaard, Heidegger, Sartre and some existentialist fiction writers that he found on the internet, about whom he talked more intelligently than some of my sophisticated philosophy students. The impact was enormous. Jerry started to talk about the differences between the "I" that chooses, and the "not-I." He spoke about his personal dispositions, wishes, and feelings, said that his "awareness of his existence" gave meaning to his life, and said that he was proud to have arrived at that awareness. I believe that in the face of the confusing contrast between his past, which, in his words, "just happened to him," and his ability to be daring and make "somersaults" to unknown areas, between his shyness and his curiosity, between him, a potential philosopher, and the people around him, "who take things for granted and do not ask questions," his basic questions were "Who am I?" and "What am I worth?" I do not know what the next development will be, but Jerry is already in another mental place. Although I now suspect that when our conversations started, he was not as philosophically "virgin" as he presented himself, I still think that his story demonstrates how philosophy can matter (and how a counselee can change the prejudices of the counselor).

Sonia had fantasies. She was bored with her life as the wife of a successful businessman and had dreams about owning a bar where intellectual lectures and artistic performances would entertain bohemian and celebrated guests. At the beginning, her husband was ready to finance the project, but she hesitated to waste the family's money for risky plans, and he gradually lost interest. I do not believe that she sought counseling as encouragement (she already had a coach and a business advisor); it seemed that she had moral doubts. In her youth she was an athlete and a sports trainer with little interest in intellectual or artistic matters and did not impress me as having the capacity or the needed social connections to establish and run the imagined bar. Our conversations made it gradually clearer that she did not really want to go on with her project, but from her present perspective of a luxurious life, she could not imagine finding a meaning, a sense of independence and a feeling of "self-realization" in a less "brilliant" role. I started to challenge some presuppositions that probably limited her horizon. The process was, however, interrupted suddenly: a girl accused her son of sexual abuse while both were drowsy in his room after a drinking party with other teenagers. Sonia was convinced that nothing happened, but the girl returned home late, and her angry brother convinced her to make a false accusation. Sonia intended to dedicate all her energy to saving "the clean record" of her son.

Some of her tacit beliefs were shuttered: she still had other risks and responsibilities besides the fate of the family's money, and she found herself in an unexpected role, beyond her previous horizon, which gave a new meaning to her life. It was not the result of philosophical conversations, but I hope that our dialogues contributed something to her faith in her ability to fulfill a "non-brilliant" job, helping her son to prove his innocence (or, better, improve his capacity to have a justified clean record).

In some cases, my efforts were totally in vain. Thus, Adel, a retired librarian, divorced, in her late seventies, stayed convinced that nothing was meaningful in her entire life, and nothing could bring her to feel a little bit happier, not even her daughter and family, about whom she "did not really care." Adel stopped coming after several meetings, and I cannot say whether this was because of my failure to call up some of her joyful memories and so discover sources of energy, or her inability to explore possibilities that could change her apathetic stance.

The New Questions of Professional Philosophers

Several of my teachers and colleagues in various departments of philosophy were sometimes, like other humans, frozen in their difficulties, which ranged from illness, depression, bereavement, and family conflicts to identity issues and political despair and could not deal satisfactorily with them. Some had professional worries. They were "stuck" in their research, or reluctant to elaborate or publish their ideas. Others, frustrated, preferred to seek a more meaningful way of life in nonacademic activities. Whatever were their initial philosophical interests and questions, the hazards of life led them to ask new questions. Not necessarily "the" questions that according to some theories "true" philosophers should ask, but philosophical questions that were meaningful in their specific situations. Some certainties that they had previously taken for granted were called into question. Some of their long-held presuppositions were challenged by friends and colleagues, spiritual gurus, or psychotherapists.

A few, each a wisdom-lover in his own way, loved even more to be considered the wisest in town. They were clever enough to convince others of their intellectual superiority, and unhappily succeeded in deceiving themselves as well, without understanding whence their sense of meaninglessness. They were, like everyone else, unaware of the impact of the horizon-limiting philosophical presuppositions that prevented them from thinking of the theoretical and practical advantages of intellectual modesty. Some of them could probably be helped by philosophical counseling that challenged their urge to be, without Socratic irony, the wisest in town. Conventional therapists challenge the urge to be the wisest; gurus believe that only God, Prophets, Nature, or Being deserve the title; philosophical counselors know (or should know) better: that there was never an agreement on the criteria for such an epithet (or its relevance to human knowledge, truth, faith, love, morality, a sense of fulfillment or well-being).

Notes

1. All the names are changed.
2. It is supposed to be an expansion of Freud's theory about the stages of mourning. But in Freud's *Mourning and Melancholy*, in which he adds his ideas about Oedipal guilt to Locke's explanation of "madness" as a difficulty in separating the memories of a dead person from present experiences (Locke, 1975), the "lost object" is a dead parent (Freud, 1957). Freud wished to free the patient from irrelevant guilt feeling toward the dead, not kill the memories of parental hopes with regards to living children.
3. Some therapists organize such rituals (with the expected scenes of denial, anger, collective weeping and apparent reconciliation with reality), even when the disastrous events occurred many years ago, the parents in the support groups come from different backgrounds, have tried different ways to sooth or ignore the sorrow, and passed through very different reorientation processes. I do not know what happens after such a ritual, as I was not ready to work with the social worker who organized it and achieved, as she later told me proudly, a wonderful success: the whole group was crying bitterly.
4. I am, however acquainted with some children of sort-of-Stoic parents, and their experience of being neglected by those parents, whose Stoicism was, perhaps, a kind of withdrawal from the difficulties of parenting. The credit for such an interpretation should be given to Vladimir Jankélévitch (as I understood it as a young foreign student attending his lecture in the Sorbonne).
5. Gilligan reacted to empirical studies according to which few people, male or female, arrive at the sixth level of morality on the Kohlberg developmental scale (Kohlberg, 1976), where what is moral is determined by a moral principle, and many more males than females arrive at the fifth level, where what is moral is determined by rules based on mutual agreements. Gilligan made two claims: a factual one, that boys and girls acquire their moral notions in different kinds of games (rule-governed competitive games versus sharing-and-caring games as in playing with dolls); and a moral one, that the "woman voice," expressing compassion, and not just the "man voice" talking of fairness and justice, should be heard. I do not know whether Saint Paul (morality of love) or Hume (morality of sympathy) played with dolls while the philosophers of the "social contract" played football, and Kant (obedience to the moral law) grew up without playing. Philosophically, it does not matter. The

question is which approach offers better solutions to moral problems. "The Jewish Rabbis" (who, according to Saint Paul, prefer obedience to the written Law to Love) speak of both Law and Compassion (although they are as unfair as their colleagues in the other monotheist religions, and do not listen to women's voices at all). The Muslim wise say that Allah's mercy is limitless, but they too are aware that human love, sympathy, compassion, and the capacity to care are not. Scarcity creates problems of morally justified distribution. Therefore, the leaders of all these religions, males like most past philosophers, tried to define principles for it. Moral approaches that concentrate on moral motivation and ignore such dilemmas will not solve them even when all children grow up on gender-neutral computer games.

6. A koan is an apparently senseless question that the Zen teacher asks with the aim of provoking the student and inducing him to call some of his beliefs into question.

CHAPTER FIVE

~

Who Does Not Need Academic Philosophy?

The Idea of an Alternative Philosophy

Some of the advocates for practical philosophy claim that academic, or at least modern academic, philosophy is not really philosophy. As the title of one article says, "There are nowadays professors of philosophy, but not philosophers" (Hadot, 2005). It is not really philosophy because its teachers do not generally aim at changing the students' life, and when they occasionally do, they locate the students' personal choice of a practical way of life "at the end of the process of [abstract and theoretical] philosophical activity, like a kind of accessory or appendix," rather than starting with it (Hadot, 2002, 3). According to some other campaigners the problem is not the teaching but the subject matter. They claim that theoretical and abstract philosophy is irrelevant to the issues that engage people in their real life. Some complain that it is irrelevant to the mundane problems that a person must cope with; others believe that it cannot reach the emotional, unconscious, or otherwise irrational level of their problems. The most salient in that group are convinced that it does not help solving the "existential" or "spiritual" dilemmas, enigmas, confusions, quests for meaning or feelings of lack, which are, perhaps, always in the back of one's mind but come to the fore in times of crisis. Few, finally, maintain that relevant philosophy should not deal with problems of any kind; instead, it should enable new kinds of problem-dissolving experiences.

Spiritual and Other Exercises

Some of those campaigners suggest relying on an alternative kind of philosophy. Some of them follow Hadot, who proposes that we turn back to ancient

Greco-Roman philosophy with its character-forming "spiritual exercises" which encourage students to live philosophically (Hadot, 1995).[1] One of them, who considers himself as a follower of Erasmus, was probably inspired by Hadot as well (but is apparently less acquainted than Hadot with either Greco-Roman or modern philosophy[2] and closer than him to medicine). He seems, however, to sometimes prefer physical exercises, like philosophizing during peaceful promenades in gardens and woods, allegedly following thereby the Aristotelian "peripatetic" tradition.[3] In contrast, another one, who had formerly seen herself as the most loyal disciple of Gerd Achenbach, started to practice spiritual exercises toward the end of her life. What inspired her was not Hadot's erudite analyses of ancient Greco-Roman texts and his idea of character formation, but rather the ideas of the sixth-century hermit Johannes Climacus and his experience of living in the Egyptian Sinai desert, aspiring to climb, by performing such exercises, the "Jacob's ladder" of ascent toward unity with God (Schuster, 2010).[4] She believed that such exercises could help those who are terminally ill and those who have lost their dear ones. One of them would agree with Hadot that philosophers must change the way of life of their students (or counselees). However, he does not believe in the efficacy of logical dialogues, which focus, to his mind, on a critique of the student's or counselee's confused concepts and the incoherence of his thinking. As such, they do not help the latter change his perspective and reorient himself in new situations. Instead of spiritual or physical exercises, he suggests a "poietic" approach, using poetry both for reinterpreting the client's self-presentation and changing his perspective. It does this by turning the view from the small and trivial to the great and important (Barrientos-Rastrojo, 2006).[5] He too is interested in helping people in times of crisis, but his approach, unlike the former fascination with the Greek-Orthodox spiritual conception of proper dying, is closer to a Catholic conception of proper living. He has developed special plans and training programs for working with prisoners. Some are less interested in a "philosophical life" and more in the Greco-Roman philosophical ideal of the "good life." The pioneer of modern philosophical counseling, who was initially interested in the clients' search for meaning (Achenbach, 1987), seems nowadays to hesitate between a Heideggerian "*Gelassenheit*" or "letting-be"[6] (rather than wishing to control and change external things), Stoic "equanimity" and an ascetic disdain for "capitalistic" values and competitive state of mind, all of which are supposed to enable the serenity and peace of mind that modern people allegedly lack (Achenbach, 2010). Another one is interested theoretically in the ideals of "good life," but doubts that it is humanly possible to attain them (Amir, 2018). Instead, she proposes exercises (though not to counselees) that are supposed to enhance our capacity to regard with humor our "risible" human condition, where there is always a tragicomic gap between our aspirations and attainments (Amir, 2019).[7] Júlian Marías, motivated by other reasons, would agree with her that complete happiness is unattainable in this world (Marías, 2005). His approach to persons (Marías, 1997) inspired another practical philosopher to establish in his practice of applied philosophy the "project" program, whose aim is to help people find their possible happiness by approaching the person in his "radical reality" as a "multi-vectorial" being living in specific circumstances. He describes his method as a combination of the Christian approach to love and hope and the wish to understand the counselee from a multi-vectorial perspective. The aim is to help the counselee, using narrative methods, discover her personal vocation as a project to the future, and encourage him to live for that project (Humberto Dias, 2015). Discovering "personal vocations" is not specifically Catholic, but it is a religious notion, which presupposes the predestination of individual souls to specific missions (by some God or other). Although the very religious Pascal, to whom I referred in Appendix A, did not presuppose any *human* ability, however "non-geometric," to discover predestined personal *tasks*, he would agree that academic philosophical dialogues are not very helpful in such domains.[8]

Maieutic and Parrhesia

Some philosophical counselors claim that academic philosophy is irrelevant to practical philosophy because the role of the teacher, facilitator, monitor or counselor is that of the maieutic helper [Greek: μαιευτικός—obstetric] who, by using Socratic questioning, assists people to give expression to their latent opinions, and like an experienced midwife helps them abort the false or otherwise invalid ones and give birth to true or authentic ones. Some practitioners apply it to liberate counselees from false beliefs about themselves. Those beliefs are supposed to be the cause of their psychological problems, and obstruction to their reaching excellence (Grimes, 1998). Others apply it to make the counselees aware of some truths about themselves. Their intention is to "provoke consciousness," which means, according to one of their speakers, "not being concerned with social codes, but with reason," according to the paradigm of parrhesia.[9]

Parrhesia [Greek: παρρησία], which means literary "free speech" in the sense of frank and fearless questions or statements. It was practiced by the ancient Cynics and Epicureans. It seems to me, however, that the more direct inspiration is the approach of Michel Foucault, who interprets parrhesia as:

> a kind of verbal activity where the speaker has a specific relation to truth through frankness, a certain relationship to his own life through danger, a certain type of relation to himself or other people through criticism (self-criticism or criticism of other people), and a specific relation to moral law through freedom and duty. (Foucault, 2001, 19)

The cover copy of Foucault's book Fearless Speech distinguishes between the *history of ideas* and the *history of thoughts*, and says that while the former is concerned with the "analysis of a notion . . . in the setting of other ideas . . . " the latter is "the analysis of the way an unproblematic field of experience becomes a problem, raises discussions and debates, incites new reactions, and induces crisis in the previously silent behaviors, practices, institutions" and also of "the way people become anxious, for example, about madness, about crime, about themselves, about truth."

According to some philosophical counselors of the Paris Institute for Critical Thinking, academic philosophy is irrelevant to the work of the "midwife" or the "problematizer." By adopting an attitude of Socratic irony and Cynic disdain for theories, they are attempting to replace dialogues that deal with ideas with activity of parrhesia, which is intended to require students or counselees to rethink behaviors and practices, especially ways of communicating and attitudes that they otherwise take for granted. They perform, in accordance with Foucault, "a verbal activity in which the speaker expresses his personal relationship to truth" (ibid., 20), and although the practitioners do not thereby literarily risk their lives, they "recognizes truth-telling as a duty to improve or help other people (as well as themselves)" (ibid.).

People who come to their public workshops or presentations, whether as students or curious colleagues, are often confused and sometimes upset, while the "counselor" is rather cool and "uses his freedom and chooses frankness instead of persuasion, truth instead of falsehood or silence" (ibid.). "The counselees" or interviewees probably expect the interviewer to solve a problem they *already* recognize as a problem and offer an answer to the question they raise, in a dialogue where they are also free to present perspectives, explore and clarify them, pose questions and object to the suggestions, as is the case in philosophical dialogues from the "academic" philosophical point of view. As it turns out, they get something entirely different: The interviewer is busy, for once, "problematizing" something they do and say, something they have never considered problematic, at least not until the interview with him.[10]

As Foucault describes it, parrhesia is not necessarily a philosophical activity. As the Biblical reproving *navi* [Hebrew: נביא, who, contrary to the standard translation, is not necessarily a prophet] did it in the name of God rather than reason, so does the modern journalist appeal to alleged facts, the "engaged" play-writer creates imaginative scenarios, and the political activist uses whatever is available. The members of this group conduct the interview through questioning in which they try to lead the interviewee to clarify and make precise his use of philosophically relevant words and, perhaps more importantly, to become aware of his philosophical "pathologies." Since dealing with "pathologies" sounds more like an idea for alternative psychology than alternative philosophy, I will discuss the group's procedure and claims, in the second part of the chapter. It will be an appropriate bridge from the present chapter to the next, where I deal with another domain whose practitioners often declare that academic philosophy is irrelevant to psychotherapy.

Contemplation

The word 'contemplation,' which sometimes describes a kind of a pensive mood, meant, for most modern Western philosophers, a very systematic intellectual effort to deal with general and abstract philosophical questions. The importers of Eastern ideas and practices to the West borrowed the latter term, as well as the close term, 'meditation,' to design a group of entirely different mental "meditative" exercises, which are based indeed on a philosophical worldview about the "true" irrelevance of some human problems. Though some of those exercises, even when they are detached from their cultural context, are very beneficial for the dissolution of problems, at least temporarily, they are, to my mind, mental technics, rather than philosophical activities. 'Contemplation,' which has recently been borrowed for new activities, at least has some "post-discursive" Western past: Platonic synoptic intuition of the world of Ideas, Neo-Platonic spiritual "vision" of, or mystic union with, the One. Ironically, the Greek term for such "visual" contemplation is 'θεωρία' [theoria], while philosophical practitioners who use the term insist on the non-theoretical nature of their version. Some of them satisfy themselves with an activity in which the participants read an aphorism, a citation or a short tale chosen by the facilitator, presented out of any context, and share their subjective impressions and reflections. Thus, the opinions of the author of the text or its erudite interpreters are not considered (and the impact of the practitioner's philosophical positions on the choice of texts is not discussed). Others offer something more complicated.

Some of the latter look for an alternative philosophy in the meditative tradition of Buddhist cultures and its problems-dissolving worldview. At least one of them is ready to borrow the Greco-Roman ideal of purposeless and egoless contemplation, reject its ideal of character formation by dialogues and exercises, since they are, to his mind, as logical and problem oriented as modern academic philosophy. He finds proximity between, on the one hand, the Western existentialist disinterested attention to Being, the mystical religious experiences of Hasidic rabbis, and the longing for the spiritual and the sublime of nineteenth-century romantics, and on the other hand, Eastern philosophical approaches, states of minds and exercises inspired by Taoist or Buddhist monastic traditions. In some of the exercises, paragraphs, phrases, or even single words, selected from philosophical texts that speak in favor of the facilitator's contemplative attitude, are read loudly by the facilitator and the participants. The latter, who are instructed to avoid "judgmental" thinking, are invited to explore together the experience of that reading, its interior resonances, and the issues that they bring to the fore. The group calls such "contemplative" or "meditative" exercises deep philosophy. They claim that philosophizing in this way involves on the one hand, the whole person and not only his intellect, and, on the other hand, places "really important issues" rather than "petty problems," in the forefront. Thus, it is a deeper search for wisdom than any academic discussion of theoretical problems. Its practical effects are, according to them, deeper than the attempts of some philosophers to help people solve philosophically their practical problems, whether "mundane" or "spiritual" (Lahav, 2021).[11] While the author of the just-mentioned text seems to believe that such problem-dissolving philosophizing can free us from both our problems and our problem-oriented approach, some other exponents of such "deep philosophizing" maintain that it may provide us with true self- and world-knowledge (for example, Borisov, 2020). They believe that such experiencing is free of any preexisting concepts, structures, or questions, and therefore enables the participant immediate contact with both the contemplated object and him as the contemplating subject. They maintain that that is also the aim of phenomenological investigations.[12] Such approaches call for an exploration of the difference between philosophical counseling and religious experience, which is beyond the scope of the present book.

The Quest for Subjective Meaning

Subjective meaning is another aspect that theoretical philosophy, modern as well as ancient, seems to lack. It is not necessarily the personal commitment of the philosopher to live "philosophically" according to an "objectively true" philosophy—as if the philosopher were the wise person who knows what truly makes a person "virtuous" or what is really "the good life." Nor is it the commitment to one's own declared philosophy. Despite the claim of some cynical logical positivists that "one should no more expect a philosopher dealing with ethics to be moral than one should expect the geometrician to be a triangle," philosophers have always been criticized for failing to live their lives according to the practical implications of *their* declared theoretical positions (see Gruengard, 2018). It is also not a matter of one's students' commitment. Modern professors of philosophy would not admit (despite their possible wishes) that they expect *their students* to be practically committed, irrespective of their personal preferences, to living according to the subjective preferences *of their professors* (and that is, by the way, my answer to Hadot and followers). Personal commitment is different from "subjective meaning."

Theoretical academic philosophy aims at positions that are, in some sense, objectively valid (among equally valid alternative positions). It seems, however, to lack the ability to answer the subjective *question* of a *specific individual*: "what is the meaning of [*my*] life," or as some interpret it: "what is meaningful in [*my*] life?" (cf. Kasher, 2002). Some are inspired by Søren Kierkegaard (1980), (see, for example, Yaguri, 2018, and Von Morstein,1994, 1999).[13] The logo-therapists follow Victor Frankl (2006). Their approach should be distinguished from the reliance of existentialist counselors on the Heidegger's ideal of authenticity, (Heidegger, 2010) or Sartre's ideal of "being-for-self" (Sartre, 1993) or Camus's rebel's position (Camus, 1992). Those influential philosophers indeed maintained that academic philosophers failed to ask the "right philosophical questions." [14] They failed to relate to the person as a concrete being-in-the-world who has to give his own meaning to his life, make personal choices and take responsibility for them rather than "flee" to the "general" in order to avoid the burden or anxiety of finitude, selfhood or freedom, and seek refuge in abstract theories, social conventions or the opinions and expectations of others. Yet they did not necessarily believe that the *answers* to philosophical questions are subjective. They thought, for example. that their own answers to questions such as "what is authentic?" or "when is a person responsible?" have an objective validity[15] Practical philosophers who insist on "subjective meaning" insist, in contrast, that *the individual answer* is—and should be—*subjective*. Their position follows from the nature of the personal question and not necessarily from the conviction that academic and theoretical philosophy is never relevant to life issues.

Theoretical Philosophy Matters Nevertheless

Although my counseling does not concentrate on questions about the value or meaning of life, I share the opinion of the last-mentioned group, regarding the importance of *subjective meaning* and *personal choices* and *the personal relevance of theoretical philosophy*. However, I only partially agree with some of the other counselors mentioned above. Some of the "alternative philosophies" (of which I gave some examples rather than a comprehensive survey[16]) are perhaps alternative, but they are not philosophical. Some are philosophical, but only on the first, nonreflective, level. They are no more philosophical than citations of wise sayings.

I therefore start with some comments on the "contemplative" alternative. I sometimes see on social networks a few lines from a text written by a famous philosopher or guru, taken out of any context. They are cited neither as an answer to a possible question nor as a question-raising statement. Thus, according to a message sent to "friends" on Facebook by one of the "contemplative" counselors, Hobbes wrote in favor of peace. The sender did not raise any questions; he also did not mention that Hobbes was writing about peace in the context of his justification of autocratic absolute rule (Hobbes, 2010). "Well," I thought to myself while reading it, "the sender favors peace and peace is, of course, desirable; yet some partisans of dictatorship used their declared love for peace as an excuse for their aggressive policies. Why," I asked myself, "is the sender not citing one of them instead of Hobbes? Is it because Hobbes could be taken as a *philosophical authority*?" The sender, interested in the "spiritual," has a PhD in philosophy, so he surely knows that Hobbes was not only a metaphysical *materialist* but was also morally concerned with the mundane and "*materialist*" values, which that sender disrespects. I would guess that he also knows that among such issues were not only earthly and egoistic pleasures but the right of the ruled to rebel against a life-threatening souverain even when a rational and voluntary social contract is the source of the latter's authority. "If so, why does he not mention that the peace-lover Hobbes was *not* for peace at any price?" Those were my allegedly irrelevant academic private reflections. I continued, however, to ask myself what the receiver of the message, who perhaps knows nothing about Hobbes, is supposed to do with it, especially when he is asked, as that sender usually asks in his workshops, to be "nonjudgmental": become a pacifist? add it to the statistics of pro-peace citations? join Hobbes's lines to the slogans he has learned from others? Feel the "inner resonance" of Hobbes's cited words? With the word 'Leviathan' (the title of Hobbes's famous work) echoing in my "judgmental" mind and remembering that some peace-loving philosophers believe that distinctions should nevertheless be made between "just and unjust" wars (Nardin, 2015), I thought that such an alternative way of using philosophy or philosophers was adding, at best, some partial and therefore biased information to the participant's first level philosophy. I do not consider such additions philosophical on any higher level, as philosophical counseling should be. They may, on the other hand, persuade a naïve peace-loving participant to adopt uncritically the practitioner's philosophical (or religious) position regarding other matters.

Postponing judgment, or putting one's doubts "in parentheses," may have an important role in philosophical as well as psychological and other explorations; but when persuasive teachers, preachers and psychoanalysts demand a "nonjudgmental" attitude from their students or "clients," they misplace and misuse that tool. The culture of academic philosophical debates is, perhaps, not free of dogmatic biases; yet by fostering a "judgmental," i.e., critical, attitude and awareness of alternatives, it is the best guarantee against *tacit* persuasion.

The "peripatetic" alternative which, at least in my limited experience as a workshop participant, consists in encouraging participants to ask philosophical questions whenever they occur to them, perhaps as the group pauses under some trees, and spontaneously suggest answers to the questions of others during the next pause under other trees, may sound more philosophical. It is not: the group in question was heterogeneous, with no common background, the questions came out of the blue, the answers were intuitive, there were no dialogues. Such a social recreation, which may be useful as an introductory exercise for schoolchildren to let them experience cases of philosophical *wondering*, is very different and less philosophical than the legendary walking dialogues, based on *shared* rote-learned texts, of students at Aristotle's *Lyceum*. It is also less philosophical than the interpretative debates, held while standing or sitting, between the students in a traditional Jewish *yeshiva* or a Muslim *madrassa*. In those frameworks there are at least connections of relevance and logic between what is asked and what is answered. It is also a far cry from the legendary instructive promenades with a Zen teacher. Philosophical wondering is great, and the encouragement to get out of the closed circles of the obvious, dogmatic, dictated or indoctrinated is important, but it should be relevant to somebody's concern—at least in counseling.

The users of maieutic methods may be helpful, but they still must defend the claim that they or their model, Socrates, do not orient their dialogues according to prior "academic" theories.

Performers of parrhesia in the "critical thinking" or other styles are also far from doing it like academically tabulae rasae; although they do not necessarily share the same background philosophical knowledge or convictions. I do not relate to those whose philosophical education is largely concentrated in a few workshops, and like their counterparts in other counseling (and psychotherapeutic) orientations, they try (mostly in vain) to imitate the exemplified "techniques."

Parrhesia Has Other Additional Dangers

The Talmudic Sages used the word *perhessia*, which is derived from parrhesia, when discussing the propriety of free speech or other acts performed *in public*. This suggests that the Epicurean provocative activity (with which those sages were indirectly acquainted) took place primarily in front of an audience. By playing the jester, Socrates, who used to have dialogues in the agora, was able to fool a sophist in front of everyone, and to get the man to admit that, logically, his dog's mother was also his mother (see below). Socrates's teaching ethics would not always be approved by the old sages, but I'm not concerned with teaching here. I want to examine the propriety of *counseling* in the agora of seminars, conferences, workshops, and videos available on websites and social media.

The following dangers are not specific to the public *expositions* of the "critical thinking" counseling method. Some members of this group sometimes demonstrate that the advantages of doing it in public may be important despite some perils, and take upon themselves to promote free speech, at least among students and teachers, in countries where tradition or political authorities discourage it. However, I am not referring to such risks.

Experience has taught me that the completion of any counseling project, irrespective of the method, will usually require more time than the duration of the public performances. Yet the counselor, while demonstrating publicly how his method works, might also wish to demonstrate how successful it is. Therefore, he may take disingenuous shortcuts, jump from one topic to the next, and force his volunteer "counselee" to admit what she does not believe, while he himself jumps to conclusions. Although it is done for educational purposes, it still counts as a show, and the "counselee" is only playing the part; she can either obey the "counselor" and show how his remarks are helpful or, on the contrary, see it as a duel, and show that she, the counselee is cleverer. Thus, the show might be superficial, and distort both the weak and the strong sides of the presented approach.

If the counselor claims to be able to identify a counselee's errors or pathologies, the performance in the agora may be even more deceptive: the "counselee" may regret accepting the role, and what appears to be her recognition of the image he claims to "reflect back" at her, is actually a ploy to stop him before he "discovers," that is, exposes in public, all her "defects."

The counselor's indiscretion is not the only risk in such a situation. Although sophists who claim to teach what they do not know sometimes deserve public ridicule, and some students do not care to be "teased" for the sake of wisdom or just for fun, counselees should never be embarrassed in front of others. Counselors may use their dialogue to persuade their *audience* instead of helping their client; they may use the client as a means rather than an end. Counselees should not be treated in this way, even if they volunteered to play the counselee's role.

Some other of the proposed alternatives to "academic philosophy" are philosophical, but only on a secondary level. Some of them are inspired by philosophers who found that the rationalist tradition in philosophy failed to address, not to say solve, questions that only religion could answer. These counselors *do* call the initial convictions of their counselees into question. They assume that those convictions are responsible for the counselees' practical difficulties or unhappy states of mind, and instead propose beliefs, values or ways of life that are better according to their religious convictions (which they have, perhaps, adapted from the inspiring philosopher). They consider the counselee's "multi-vectoral" *personality* and living context, but they do not seem to consider that his multifaceted *rationality* may also be relevant. They try to reach him in a variety of "alternatives" to logical dialogues, ways that are important when one deals with people who are not attuned to abstract thinking, but it seems to me that they fail to offer him their preferred option as just *one of various* possible alternatives to his initial positions. They do not invite him to examine their proposed position and do not leave him a space for exploration, and thus deprive him of a higher degree of freedom of choice.

I would address the same reproach to any religiously based guide who claims that there is only one practical and moral interpretation of his religious heritage or that only his own religious heritage is an option, or that the option must be religious. I assume that the philosopher that inspired those counselors examined various options, and the nonreligious option, and *opted knowingly* and philosophically for his personal way. However, that was *his* personal decision, and I, as a nonreligious person, respect it as much as I respect the philosophical but individual choices of some thinkers, with whom I share a religious background, to convert to another religion. I am not sure, however, that the counselors who were inspired by the religious philosopher have passed through a similar process. Even if they did, it does not entitle them, as philosophers, to do the job of a Catholic missionary, just as an Orthodox Jewish counselor who has adopted Maimonides's interpretation of Judaism, is not entitled, as a philosophical counselor, to re-educate the counselees in a Maimonidean spirit, as if he were their rabbi. The philosophical counselor should, of course, take into consideration the religious background of the counselee's culture and the counselee's attitude toward it, and try to understand it; he should adapt his language and metaphors to the latter's conceptual and metaphorical world. Yet if his background and position are different, he should be honest about it, and remember that his role is not to correct the counselee's religious "errors" or convert him to a "better" religious faith.

And that is why I do not accept, with all due respect to Hadot's expertise in the Greco-Roman philosophical tradition, his onslaught on "modern professors of philosophy" for their alleged failing to be "philosophers." Modern academic institutions in Western countries may be responsible for their teachers' tendency to prefer publication and personal promotion to education, or their students' tendency to prefer notes and diplomas to knowledge and wisdom. Their *liberal* pretense of guaranteeing the freedom of thought of students and protecting them from the persuasive methods that were applied in monastic education and its parallels in other religious schools is *not* a failure to enable their professors to be philosophers. Institutional liberalism is, unfortunately, not always successful: many teachers still wish to "form" the mind as well as the character of their students, and political and other groups still want to determine the direction of the "formation." However, to the extent that modern schools succeed, they realize ideals of tolerance developed by philosophers who were aware that philosophical opinions and ideals, principles and values, conceptions of virtue or the good life are a matter of debate and not of "formation." Psychologists, as I shall argue in chapter 6 and Appendix C, sometimes do intend to "form." That is why I personally opted for philosophical counseling.

Stoic equanimity, Heideggerian "letting-be," ascetic or non-competitive ways of life as well as authenticity, self-realization, becoming a subject, self-awareness (or other ideals) is also a matter of philosophical debate. Their realization, if possible, is always at the cost not only of material interests, but also of other spiritual or otherwise "philosophically decent" ideals: I assume that philosophers who hold any of them made their decision knowingly, after having considered some of the alternatives. As philosophical counselors they should enable the counselees to make their own searches and their own decisions. For that purpose, counselors do not have to turn the counseling session into an academic course about philosophical ideals. But they need theoretical understanding and academic experience to facilitate philosophically the *personal search of the counselee*.

However, some of the "*disciples*," following mechanically a philosophical "master" who has deliberately chosen his way, operate without sufficient academic philosophical background, and seem to take the method as a technique for treating, say, "logically" all kinds of issues, among them cases which Aristotle would have considered as ἀκρασία [*akrasia*, in Greek: "lack of command," in modern philosophical parlance: "weakness of the will"], such as smoking and similar addictions. When I skeptically asked one of these "disciples," a follower of the "masters" of the Paris Institute for Critical Thinking, whether it helps, he answered: "Well, if it does not, I tell the counselee that there is nothing to do: she simply *does not want to be rational.*" He did not seem to understand that the counselee, who came to him *because* she knew that her behavior was *against her best judgment,* did not need him to become aware of her irrationality. (I do not know whether the "masters" deal with addictions in their counseling, but I am convinced that the attitude that they would "problematize" in such a case would be something that the counselee had not already suspected.[17])

Philosophical Practices Where Academic *Opinions* Do Not Seem to Matter

There are several branches of so-called philosophical practices in which the philosophical *opinions* of the "academic experts" are avoided *on purpose.* These practices, of which I describe here just a sample, share the common purpose of educating nonphilosophers to think, reason and communicate better—more clearly, coherently, logically; yet one can divide them into two different groups: those whose purpose is pedagogic and those whose purpose is so-called therapeutic, assisting people in their attempts to cope with the life issues that concern them personally.

Pedagogic Practices

Let Us Discuss

Philosophy for children and the "café-philo" meetings are clearly in the first group[18]. Participants are invited to discuss philosophical issues, but the purpose is not to solve philosophical problems or become acquainted with the attempts of philosophers to deal with them. Rather, it is to enhance the participants' awareness of issues that are matters of philosophical wonder as well as debate, and encourage them to think about them logically, express their own opinions, listen to those of others, respond to objections, acquire tolerance of disagreement and criticism, and encourage openness to different perspectives. Whether the teacher or facilitator chooses to mention the relevant opinions of some philosophers under their own names or whether he avoids that, the participants are not supposed to treat them as authoritative. What matters is the *philosophical exercising* of the participants and not the philosophical *truth, depth, or importance of their conclusions.* In such contexts, the opinions of the "experts" are indeed irrelevant, although the teacher or facilitator should know a thing or two not only about logic, but also about the fallacies, the dangers of sophistry and demagogy, the pressures of dominant groups and the persuasive power of his own authority. He should be acquainted with a variety of philosophical opinions as well as with pedagogical debates among experienced teachers.

Socratic Dialogues

The practice of the so-called Socratic dialogues (see Nelson, 1970; Heckman, 2018; VanRossem, 20) stands between the activities of the first group and the practices of the second. Unlike the discussions with children and the guest of café-philo meetings, the Socratic dialogues are highly structured conversations. They were originally conceived by Leonard Nelson, a philosopher of mathematics, with the hope of fostering clear and logical thinking in schools and among the general public (and thus enhance democratic tendencies in post–World War I Germany).[19] They were later developed into tools for other purposes as well, such as dealing with conflicts, mediating between employers and employees, improving communication and cooperation, and enabling more agreement between rivals; in short, they became a tentative way of political and social healing, and are also applied in the new profession of "business [philosophical] consultancy" (Horikoshi and Kono, 2020).

Unlike the ancient dialogues, in which Socrates, pretending to know nothing yet claiming to be the wisest person in town, posed questions to refute the answers of his rivals and thereby expose the falsity of their claim to knowledge, the facilitator of the modern dialogues encourages the participants to express their opinions in a friendly and accepting setting. He is not trying to refute answers, and as he is not the only one to ask questions; he is not inviting the other participants to critically examine the answers to their questions and expose their logical flaws.

Unlike the ancient teacher, who discarded answers that related to particular cases, circumstances or categories and encouraged the participants to relate to the common trait "in itself" and say what it is "in general" (or, in modern terms, to find "the" essential definition of a general concept), the modern facilitator proposes a theme, and starts the conversation by asking the participants to describe in which *concrete situation* the proposed theme was *experienced personally* by any of them as relevant or problematic. In the next step the group votes among the answers and the personal case of the participant which got the most votes will be the base for the discussion which will follow. The facilitator explains the procedural rules, and in the next step the other participants pose questions to better understand the situation and perspective of the protagonist in the chosen case. Without entering the details of the procedure I will sum it up by saying that he and the others are invited to define the issue before and after listening to the others' perspectives, and attempts are made to find what is common to the different views.

While the original Socratic question should be answered by yes or no (I am using for illustration the already cited questions from (Plato, 1997, *Protagoras*): "Can one teach another person how to be a virtuous man?"), the modern initial question is open ("If you have been in a situation where the theme of, say, teaching somebody how to be a virtuous man was relevant—what did you experience?") The logic underlying Plato's description of Socrates's dialogues is that two contrary answers to a question, positive and negative, cannot both be true. The modern assumption is that considering the different backgrounds and perspectives of the participants—both may be plausible, and more important, meaningful. The Platonic dialectic, which presupposes that both negative and positive answers can sometimes be refuted and that when that happens, one should start a new series of questions ("Is there something common to all the human virtues?") with the aim of eventually reaching an answer that negates the prior alternative and proposing a third possibility ("One cannot teach another person to be virtuous yet being virtuous is a matter of knowledge"). When such a conclusion is also not satisfactory, new sets of questions follow until the prior "aporias"—undecidable dilemmas—are solved by "the" satisfactory answer ("There is knowledge that is not learned from others but rather "remembered" with the helpful questioning of the Socratic "midwife," and such knowledge is needed to be a virtuous man in all respects).[20] The modern Socratic dialogue does not presuppose that the answer is a matter of innate, "intellectually intuited in the eternal sphere of Ideas," or otherwise objective knowledge; it rather aims, despite personal differences, at a better *intersubjective* agreement, or else an exchange of perspectives.

Instead of dealing with logic and dialectics, the modern Socratic dialogues allow for "meta-dialogical" interruptions, where questions of procedure as well as participants' complaints and emotions about breaking their rules are discussed.

What is common to the ancient and modern Socratic dialogues is the irrelevance of the positions of other philosophers. Such positions may sometimes be the source of the discussed theme (e.g., a philosopher's claim that he can teach his student how to become virtuous), but the conversation does not aim at learning from him or understanding him better, and his reasons as well as other opinions are irrelevant to the process. Socrates did not need them, for he believed that true knowledge is not learned from others. The participants in the modern Socratic dialogue do not need to be acquainted with the opinions of philosophers because the participants are exploring their views within their group and examining their relevance to their lived experiences.

Although it might seem that the only thing the facilitator needs is good training in the method, I believe that to conduct it wisely, he also needs to be acquainted with various philosophical approaches and debates.

"Therapeutic" Practices

The second group, which concentrates on philosophical counseling, aims to heal individuals from their internal disagreements, from mental stress, helplessness, inability to decide or perform, emotional difficulties, bad habits and addiction as well as intellectual confusions. It does not accept the psychotherapeutic dogma that physical or mental diseases or otherwise chronic "disorders" or "weaknesses" are necessarily responsible for such states, and opposes the tendency in modern Western societies to seek help in psychiatric drugs and psychotherapy (so-called *clinical treatment* in the psychoanalytic, psychodynamic or behavioristic styles).[21] In this respect the second group resembles other groups of philosophical counselors. It differs from the others, however, in its conviction that *flawed reasoning* is the principal cause for such states, and in its claim to be able to help people get over them by fostering their ability or readiness to think more clearly and logically. It is, therefore, apparently not interested in their opinions, aims, values, principles, or attitudes *in themselves*; it deals only with their logical relations and coherence. The opinions of other philosophers about things in which it is not interested are therefore irrelevant.[22]

Eita Veening is, to my limited knowledge, the mildest in that group. He acknowledges his debt to Karl Popper's approach to rationality in everyday life, an approach that Popper started to develop, in opposition to Freud's and Adler's ways, when he was a doctoral student of cognitive psychology (Popper 1928, Alt, 1982): a tentative problem-solving according to the "logic of the situation" (Popper, 1957, 1967, 1982). Veening's counseling is not reducible to finding contradictions, fallacies or just failures to think in clear and distinct terms. His orientation is goal-directed: assisting the counselee to deal with his problem situation by rational actions. He invites him to describe what bothers him (monologue), helps him (through dialogues) to define the problem and examine rationally alternative feasible changes that can solve or alleviate it; choose, in light of the conclusion and in accordance with his principles and values among alternative aims and select the best available means to get the chosen aim, encourages him to realize the tentative plan, correct wrong assumptions, and cope with unexpected obstacles.

When the process gets stuck, he explores with him (in a metalogue) why it is stuck. The reasons can be emotional or cognitive, moral, or ideological; in any case he tries to help him define the interfering factors and choose rationally whether and how to go on with the project (Veening, 1987, 1994). I assume that Veening does not cite opinions of philosophers in the metalogue, yet guess that his way of guiding the exploration, which, as he insists, should be philosophical rather than psychological, is based on the ideas of more than one "theoretical" philosopher.

Elliot Cohen, in contrast,[23] believes that he must help the counselee deal with his flawed thinking rather than the problematic situation. As the title of his book *Caution: Faulty Thinking Can Be Harmful to Your Happiness* (Cohen, 1994) suggests, he cares more about the counselee's state of mind than his problem-solving capacities. His work reminds me of that of the cognitive psychotherapist Albert Ellis, whose theory of "musturbatory thinking" is based on the idea that people get stuck in psychological difficulties when they think in the modality of "must" when "can" or "will" would be more appropriate. A simplified example would be the frustrated client who thinks "I did not pass the exam, yet I *must* pass it" instead of "I did not pass the exam although I *want* to pass it; maybe I *cannot* pass it." The purpose, of course, is not to correct the patient's use of modal verbs but to lead him to a *realistic acceptance* of the unattainability of his aim. I guess that Ellis was inspired by Hume's "ought-is" fallacy, while the "musturbation" makes a comic allusion to the "compulsive-obsessive" insistence of the patient on getting his unrealistic aim (see Ellis, 1994). I have some philosophical reservations with regards to the logical element in that example: I do not know whether Ellis's patient is really unable to pass the exam, or whether he really believes that he must pass it. I am quite sure, however, that he is *not* committing a logical fallacy like the fallacy of inferring from one modality to another. Cohen, in contrast, does not pretend to teach the counselee what is realistic or what is wrong in trying to realize unrealistic aims. He assumes, instead, that the beliefs that are responsible for the patient's mood may prevent him from improving his means to get them. He believes that his unhappy patient, who is complaining about a sheer psychological *fact*—his *mood*—as the *result* of a sheer *event* ("I failed the exam and therefore I [feel that] am a failure"), is unknowingly deducting a conclusion of a "practical syllogism": The major latent premise is a rule (which contains a "rating"): "If I failed my exam, then I myself am a failure." The counselee's feeling ("I am a failure") is in fact a belief inferred from this rule and the factual report, the minor premise, "I failed my exam" (Cohen, 1988). Cohen assumes that the rule was inferred from other premises, and ultimately from the very general premise "I ought to be perfect in everything I do" (ibid.), which means that Cohen agrees with Ellis that the conclusion contains a tacit "must." Cohen thinks that not only the "must" premise ("I ought to pass every exam"), rather than the facts, is responsible for the counselee's state of mind: the "*rating*" premise ("failing means being a failure") or the *moral* premise ("a failing person is a worthless person") are its accomplices. Yet Cohen's use of logic is not meant to correct logical errors more than Ellis speaking of a cognitive failure is meant to improve cognitive functioning. Both want to draw the counselee's attention to what they consider as his "irrational premises" (ibid.). Their strategy is philosophically valid, even if psychologically it is not sure whether the counselee's belief that he is a failure is a matter of a logical deduction or, as a psychoanalyst would say, associative thinking.[24] I suspect, however, that both Ellis and Cohen are aware that the counselee's belief reflects a predominant opinion of some of the counselee's "meaningful others" or a worldview that is prevalent in his culture. In other words, both Ellis and Cohen are challenging some *philosophical presuppositions* of the counselee *and his environment*.[25]

Cohen seems to me more aware than Ellis that that the cure is not commonsensical "sanity" but alternative philosophical positions; he therefore proposes to the counselee, as "antidote" to such venomous premises, alternative philosophical positions, such as that of Kant or Mill, Nietzsche, or Heidegger, toward failure, self-evaluation, ambitions of perfection etc. (ibid.). Hence, he is not thinking that academic philosophy is irrelevant. Yet he will enable his counselee to be even more philosophical if he invites him to examine whether his troublemaking premises are also irrational and venomous from *his* perspective, explore several alternatives and choose among them, instead of choosing for him the one that, according to Cohen's opinion, is appropriate in his case (ibid.). I believe that such an exploration might reveal the counselee's *philosophical dilemmas*—for example, compliance with a dominant popular philosophy or having other criteria for human worth; the importance of parental approval or the importance of one's personal aims or abilities. Such an approach would be more compatible with Davidson's "rule of charity," Dennett's "rule of humanity," and my first moral rule (see chapter 3, the section about the morality of the counselor, including the notes). Philosophers may have thought they could solve such dilemmas for everyone, but that can still be debated, and the counselee has to deal with it independently.

Other kinds of *logic-centered therapy* or counseling may have different orientations. However, most of them assume that the counselee's difficulties with the specific problem or kind of problems that trouble him are *not due* to his specific beliefs or attitudes but to his failure to think in clear terms, check the coherence or logical implications of those terms, and to inconsistencies and incompleteness in his technical, moral, or other considerations. They therefore assume that the *opinions* of any other person are irrelevant. Here, again, I wish to distinguish between the opinions of others, which are perhaps not mentioned *in the dialogue*, and the philosophical theories and perspectives with which the counselor should be acquainted. Moreover, there are many occasions for *flaws in the counselor's questions, inferences, and recommendations with regards to reasoning*. To minimize them practitioners have to be acquainted with various approaches to reasoning, various issues that are dealt by the philosophies of science and language, modal logic and other sources from which they can learn that the logic learned in the first year of college *is perhaps insufficient* for reasonable inferences from what people say or do to what they know, believe or want. They must know more than what one can learn in a first-year course of reasoning, where one gets acquainted with lists of fallacies to be avoided. Debates among philosophers as well as linguistic analyses on higher levels show that what should count as a fallacy according to past logicians may nevertheless be non-fallacious in some theoretical or practical contexts (and vice versa). They must know much more than logic in order to make inferences from the declared intentions of their counselees to their actual deeds or defaults, the actual results of their behavior, or their responsibility for those results.

They should also remind themselves that *persons* are neither propositions nor theories, and that they can be helped by acquaintance with philosophical discussions about the possible differences between them. The dilemmas which I suggested as replacements for the judgment of "irrationality" in Ellis's and Cohen's analyses are meant to remind the "logical" counselor that the counselee must make "existential" decisions—decisions about his values, criteria, aims and ways of life—whereas propositions and theories are not bothered by such "trivialities."

"Curing Thinking Pathologies"

In this part of the chapter, I am concentrating on some claims and illustrations of one of the "masters" of the Paris Institute for Critical Thinking, but my aim is to examine the assumption that the concepts of *philosophical* pathology or health are needed by philosophical counselors or, more generally—are philosophically justifiable notions.

Criticism Based on Misunderstanding

Common sense, and rationality are declared by practical philosophers from the Paris Institute for Critical Thinking to be the cornerstones of counseling.

The counselor should focus on clear communication and coherence, while discussing academic theory is unnecessary. Other philosophers took these statements seriously and pointed out some logical fallacies and faulty dialogical procedures in the practice of one of a central member of that group.[26]

The counseling interviews of members of that group start always by inviting the counselee to ask a question. Some of those accusations would have been justified *if* the following of the interview had been meant to deal with that question as counselors normally do: explore what is the problem that the counselee wants to solve, why he needs help and cannot find himself a satisfactory answer. In such a case the interview would proceed with explorations of the aim of asking that question, the counselee's beliefs, values, principles and their relations to his wishes and emotions, aims and intentions, actions and reactions, and the counselor's indications of inconsistency, incoherence, arbitrariness, biases etc. in the counselee's thinking. The critics correctly assume that in such a process the counselor himself might commit errors of inconsistency, incoherence, or arbitrariness. But this is *not* the aim of the interviews with practitioners of that group. Although the purpose of their practice is rarely mentioned in conferences and workshops, it can be learned from explanations in courses recorded in videos or from written description of the approach and its rationale (for example Brenifier 2019, 2020; see video April 2018): In those presentations the person playing the "critical thinker" is not attempting to help the "counselee" with the problem *as the latter perceives and expresses it* in his initial question (the only question he is permitted to ask!).[27] As Foucault taught, that "counselor" aims to "problematize" an experience and "induce crisis" into a domain that was previously silent (Foucault, 2001, 19). While the counselee believes that his question expresses a philosophical problem which will be discussed in the interview, the counselor intends to help him to understand *that it is not his real problem*, but just one *manifestation* (if that counselor were a psychologist, he would call it a *symptom*) of another problem, of which the counselee is unaware of: "his pathological philosophical attitude."[28]

Increasing Self-Awareness to Attitudes

Hegel's theory about knowing persons seems to provide the theoretical basis for this approach: the counselor, from his "objective" outside perspective, can see things in the counselee's behavior, which the latter, from his "subjective" inside perspective, cannot see. A person's self-knowledge should be an integration of both perspectives. Therefore, in order to help the counselee become more aware of his attitudes and behaviors, the counselor should reflect back to the counselee his "objective" image. (Brenifier, 2020, 30–37).

Personal characteristics, according to Hegel, can be altered and rectified if a person is alive. This means that knowledge of living persons is only ad hoc. Accordingly, the critical thinking counselor focuses on the counselee's *current* philosophical attitudes. He believes that those attitudes, or what Foucault would call [ways of] *thinking*, should be addressed and corrected before philosophical discussion of the counselee's *ideas* can begin. I do not know precisely what those philosophical counselors do when they discuss their counselees' *ideas* with them,[29] but it seems that they assume that the "pathological philosophical attitudes" are responsible for the counselees' difficulties in coping with mundane as well as philosophical problems.

The approach is therefore purposeful and deliberate: What seems to the critics as out-of-context questions, flawed inferences, ad hominem and other apparent or real fallacies, as well as the dialogical rules, which, over and above limiting the counselee to one initial question, prohibit qualified answers, complaints or objections to the counselors' questions (Brenifier, 2017), are *devices* for "throwing the counselee into the void," that is confusing him in order to trigger "unruly" behavioral and verbal reactions. The intention is to obtain information about his personality—his attitudes and motives. The counselor *le met en abîme* [places him between opposing mirrors], that is, he reflects the counselee's images back to the counselee as they are seen from the counselor's point of view; while doing so, he emphasizes the repeated expressions of "pathological" attitudes the counselee has unknowingly displayed. Thus, the counselor confronts the counselee with the knowledge he has attained about him. The counselor's task then becomes to integrate the counselee's answers and other reactions (or, to my mind, the counselor's interpretation of them) with the counselee's initial question (or rather, the counselor's interpretation of that question) and more importantly, with what he identifies as the counselee's reasons for asking that question, into a coherent narrative. If all goes well, the counselee will eventually acknowledge the narrative as a reflection of what he said. (See the video Brenifier, 2010.) The acknowledgment is supposed to indicate that the counselee realizes that it is the truth about him. The counselee's denial, on the other hand, might indicate that the process must continue, sometimes despite the counselee's expressed desire to quit (De Haas, 2012). Alternatively, it might mean that the counselee is one of the many individuals who "do not want to be asked" and do not wish to "learn the truth" or "be reasonable."

Since the process reminds me of the psychoanalytic interpretation of the patient's behavior in what is called "transference," I allow myself to add that some psychologists would refer to the refusal as a form of "defensive resistance."[30] Unlike some of the latter, Brenifier admits in his books that his conjectures may be false, and that his questions are not always to the point. Yet he believes that the process eventually leads to the emergence of the "dysfunctions." So, despite the recognition of the possibility of error, the counselor, like the psychoanalyst, is basically right. I personally belong to a philosophical tradition that abhors methods whose reliably is beyond doubt.

For obvious reasons, the critically thinking counselor does not share the secrets of the method with the counselee or the audience in his public presentations. The lack of transparency is problematic. Such a lack is quite frequent in some kinds of psychological experiments and treatments. Yet, if the philosophically minded, critically thinking counselor were a psychologist, he would have been aware that at least some of the psychologists obey ethical codes which say *when* nontransparency in research is *permissible*, and when "debriefing"—revealing the truth to the subjects of the investigation—is *obligatory*, and whether the tacit "therapeutic contract" between the therapist and the patient allows, if ever, the use of secret devices. As a philosopher he is probably aware that many philosophers believe that in philosophical dialogues such a lack is improper; partners in such dialogues expect attacks on their allegedly mistaken assumptions and fallacious reasoning, not cunning detections of their alleged *dysfunctions*.

Psychologists who try to understand why a real dialogue between Freud and Jung became impossible, tend to explain it psychologically: Freudians tend to speak of father-son entanglements, Jungians of differences in their alleged cultural unconscious. There were indeed many reasons, psychological, ideological, and moral for their mutual grudge. But what made impossible any *dialogue* between them about their *philosophical* differences was the pretentions of each of them to know which *dysfunctions* causes the rival to hold his allegedly wrong *ideas* (see Gruengard, 1998, 2006). I personally do not believe that psychological expertise includes the ability to judge the correctness of philosophical ideas or attitudes, and, even if it were applicable to such issues, I would insist that philosophical counselors, whatever their psychological assumptions about the counselees, should not put themselves in the position of psychological experts.

One should distinguish between the *philosophical propriety* of the procedure and the efficacy and the methodological adequacy of the *psychological* tactics of the counselor. Not all philosophical counselors are acquainted with the complexity of the issue of causal explanations, whether of seeming problems that are allegedly caused by the counselee's "dysfunctions" and whether of the counselor's actions which are supposed to trigger "dysfunctional" behaviors. The critically thinking counselor should know a thing or two about the reliability inductive conclusions in general, and the validity of conclusions derived from a single case study. They should listen to what research psychologists have to say about the differences between the reliability of discoveries in conversations in front of an audience and their reliability in conversations in the privacy of the clinic, or about the reliability, in both cases, of the opinion of a single explorer, whose personal style might affect the behavior of the explored subject, and whose personal biases might affect his conclusions. I shall return to those issues, which are also relevant to the practice of psychoanalysis, in the following.

The Method in the Madness

Brenifier and those who endorse his view of philosophical practice claim that their "Socratic questions" as well as their criticisms of the counselees are based on reason, logic, and commonsense, and that academic philosophy is irrelevant to their work. As I am dealing in the present book with the relevance of academic philosophy to philosophical practice, I must try to refute that claim. I am going to use my prior knowledge of academic philosophy, Brenifier's texts, and his counseling and teaching expositions "in the *agora*" to identify some of his possible academic sources of inspiration. I am referring only to Brenifier, as others in the group may get their ideas from other academic sources. (Some of them also use the method differently, being less "Epicurean" and more "user friendly.")[31] I admit that I aim at two birds—identifying academic sources and pointing to some risks in the approach—but I hope that nobody gets harmed.

The critically thinking counselor's questions appear arbitrary to the critics, since they presume that he derives his assumptions *deductively* or *inductively* from what the counselee says. By inferring the counselee's character from his words, the counselor *appears* to be committing an adverse ad hominem. However, in Peirce's terms, that counselor infers *abductively*; that is, he makes *conjectures* and *hypotheses* which seem *reasonable* to him, based on what has been said or done by the counselee (Brenifier, 2000, 39), and then seeks to confirm them (ibid., 40). The critics, who, over and above finding flaws in Brenifier's "*esprit de géométrie*," accuse him of lack of refinement must nevertheless admit that he does it with "*esprit de finesse*."[32]

The woman who answered Brenifier's question with 'I'm not sure,' 'perhaps,' or 'not precisely' in the dialogue discussed in De Haas (2012) had previously asked Brenifier a question. For simplicity, let us assume she asked whether gray clouds always signify an imminent rain. The counselor abducts that she seeks security. However, he does not share with her his conjecture, but tries to collect more information about her by his explorations, which are presented as questions that will help her to improve her conceptual clarity.

The explorations lead him eventually to ask whether she believes clouds are always black or always white. According to the rules, commenting on the question or making assertions about clouds sometimes being *gray* is not allowed. The constrained counselee says she is uncertain, which, to my mind, means that she is *certainly* not ready to say either that clouds are always white or that they are always black. I am quite certain that she is *fully certain* that the counselor misinterpreted her initial question, which presupposes that clouds are at least sometimes gray.

Making fun of the counselee's *use* of the qualifiers 'not really' and 'perhaps,' or asking the counselee whether she is *greedy* because he "wants more certainty than she may obtain" (De Haas, 2012), is a strategic device which may remind one of John Dewey, John Austin, Ludwig Wittgenstein, and John Wisdom, who were all interested in the issue of certainty. Dewey (1929) uses the expression "quest for certainty," and I believe Brenifier borrowed it from that author. Brenifier, moreover, admits having read Wittgenstein and incorporated some of his ideas in his work. He does not mention the two others, but Austin, the author of *How to Do Things with Words* (Austin, 1975), has perhaps inspired him to do *funny* things with words, and Wisdom, who compares some philosophical stances to psychological pathologies (Wisdom, 1952), perhaps gave him the idea of curing philosophical "dysfunctions." But is Brenifier following them?

The following example demonstrate the variety of their different approaches to the topic of certainty: *In an informal conversation with colleagues*, I recall that Socrates sometimes played the jester, and although I do not remember exactly in which of Plato's dialogues I found it, I *say* that *I am certain* that he once caused a man to admit the validity of the following nonsense: "It is true that whatever belongs to someone I own belongs to me as well, and it is true that I have a dog and the dog has a mother, so, I must admit, I am a son of a bitch." Dewey (1929) would say my certainty is sufficient for the practical purpose of the collegial dialogue, but if fanatic fans of Socrates or Plato are listening and threatening to sue me for libel, I should be more careful about the wording and provide more specific references before *claiming* my certainty. Austin (1962) would say that the warning might be too late, because *saying* 'I am certain,' just like *saying* 'I know,' is an illocutionary speech act which might be interpreted as a *promise*, a *commitment* to prove my claim. And indeed, some fanatic fans of Socrates (or Plato) hear about my claim and sue me for libel. Wittgenstein would now advise me to insist that 'certain' is used differently in the "language game" of collegial joking than it is in that of legal discussions. I choose another strategy. Once in court, prepared with the exact citation from the right Platonic dialogue, I concede that in Socrates's Athens saying of someone that he is a son of a female dog perhaps did not mean precisely what the expression 'son of a bitch' means in present colloquial English, but, as some classical experts would certainly validate, it was not a compliment either. I argue that Socrates knew this and purposefully induced the poor man, a sophist, to conclude that, logically, he was the son of his dog's mother, to embarrass him. The plaintiff's attorney responds that classical experts may, perhaps, validate my claims about general linguistic facts, but not my pretension to know Socrates's personal intentions. If, after I have introduced *all the conceivably possible evidence* for Socrates having been teasing when he induced that sophist to admit that his dog's mother was his mother, the plaintiff's attorney insists the evidence does not prove that Socrates *intended* to be teasing, *and a philosopher supports this claim*, Wisdom would intervene. He would probably say that the attorney is sane, as lawyers obviously know precisely what they want (to win their case), but that the supporting *philosopher*, who aims at philosophical truth about the possibility of knowing what is happening in "other minds" in general, needs an analytic treatment. Although both the attorney and the philosopher *have no idea what additional evidence* might prove *to them* that Socrates *really* intended to be insulting, only the philosopher is "sick," as the attorney is not really seeking more certainty, while the *philosopher's* quest for more certainty is an *unsatisfiable obsession*. Austin and Wittgenstein would not use psychiatric terminology but would agree that *philosophers* (unless they are analytic philosophers of language of the right kind) need philosophical therapeutic analysis.[33] Dewey would add that the "quest for certainty," which is motivated by the "fear of peril," is reasonable when one knows what is certain *enough* for his *relevant practical purposes*. If the judge is wise enough to understand that the issue is not my claim to knowing the mind of another person but the *interpretation* of what a protagonist says in a fictive dialogue in a literary work, he will accept my evidence as sufficient for the justification of the claim that Socrates's behavior *may be interpreted* as teasing. If this is the case, I can calmly claim my certainty. However, Dewey himself would not claim certainty about judges being always wise, and therefore he would concede to Austin that my claim might be risky. He would not say that peril is a sufficient reason for not making it, as sometimes the political right to express one's convictions even if it irritates some fanatics justifies taking risks. Yet he would be epistemologically cautious and avoid generalizations. He would say that we sometimes wish that some general statements, in life, in science, in philosophy or in religion were true, and that general practical rules were always valid, as this would give us a sense of security. But, to his mind, that security would be just an illusion; the quest for certainty *on such levels* is futile and therefore irrational. Wittgenstein would object to that generalization; to his mind, it is true that we cannot be sure that all judges are wise, and that we cannot be certain that everybody always believes that 2+2=4; but while it is a mistake to think of a general definition of 'wisdom' that is certainly valid for all the possible uses of the word, '2+2=4' is certainly and always true in the language game of mathematics.[34]

I am quite certain that Brenifier shares Dewey's pragmatist convictions, and moreover, believes that the quest for precision and the fear of ambiguity and risk may be "dysfunctional." However, I am also certain that Brenifier understands that the counselee's *saying* that she is uncertain in the context of her dealing with his purposefully confusing question *does not mean* that she is still seeking evidence and is not ready to commit herself if she is in doubt with regards to the color of clouds. In fact, he is not interested in her cognitive state of mind; he is concerned with her *use of expressions* like 'I am not certain.' Wittgenstein (1958) was also interested in the *use* of words, but Brenifier, unlike Wittgenstein, does not seek to expose or deconstruct the counselee's *conceptual confusions*, which might be the result, as Wittgenstein would explain, of "the bewitchment of language."[35] He rather explores what is behind the "funny" use of words, when one says, "I am not certain" while it is not clear which additional information could induce him to say "O.K., now, I am certain that . . ." I was tempted to conclude that Brenifier goes in the way of Wisdom, who suggests curing the "stubborn skeptic" by an analysis "similar to psychoanalysis" (Wisdom, 1952, 124).[36] However, I am sure that Brenifier is aware of something else. I dare to say that I have no doubt that he, like me, identifies the "game" his counselee is "playing" when she says, "I am not certain" while *being certain* that she *does not want* to answer the counselor's question by 'black' or 'white.' This is not a matter of identifying a "language game" with rules that one follows but understanding a "game" of *breaking the rules*, when the "intended meaning" of the speaker is different from the apparent meaning according to the ordinary use of the expression in the relevant "language game." In simple words, the polite counselee *says* she is not certain *instead* of *saying* something else. I have no doubt that Brenifier understands that there is a "subtext" and that it is different from the "text." I am not certain that the *counselee*, who is clearly aware that something is wrong with the questions, *suspects* that they are designed to incite reactions which allegedly betray her "dysfunctions." I hope the readers remember the conjecture: She seeks security. The confusing dialogue does not give her what she seeks, and both the polite "I am not certain" and the probably impolite subtext express her frustration.

I suppose that the confusing dialogue could cause the counselee to seek security even if Brenifier's conjecture is wrong, and she was not seeking it when she asked her initial question. Similarly, I suppose it is possible that the patient might wish to "kill" the psychoanalyst even if he is not "transferring" to him from a former "object" his alleged childhood Oedipal wishes. As some researchers have suggested, "crazy communicating" might create confusion and anxiety and under conditions of strong dependency, might even cause schizophrenia (Bateson et al., 1956); The causes of schizophrenia are beyond the scope of this book, but I suggest that "crazy communication" might invoke both a need for security and aggressive wishes even under less stressful conditions. Some psychiatrists have no doubt that psychoanalytic communication is somewhat "crazy" (Laing, 1982); However, I still believe that one of the motivations for fostering philosophical counseling as well as alternative, non-psychoanalytic, ways of psychotherapy is the wish to enable assistance to people by "sane" talks.

Although some of the counseling strategies described in Brenifier (2019) are reminiscent of psychological tricks, they also remind me of the fool's, or Hamlet's, teasing questions, designed to reveal hidden or forbidden truths. However, the *agora* is not a place for revealing personal truths which the counselee is hiding if those truths do not threat the well-being of others, and, in fact, what seems to really matter to Brenifier in the discussed case, is not the counselee's real or alleged secret problem but rather the education of the *audience*. To accomplish such an aim, one can employ Socrates's strategy, which is never a naive asking, and is sometimes a deliberate enticement to admit the truth of an absurd statement by means of a "logical" dialogue (as he did the case of the "son of the dog"), to teach the audience something about, say, fallacious reasoning. So, I look for additional sauces of inspiration in the libraries of academic philosophy.

Brenifier, a teacher and an almost declared Epicurean, probably wants to teach the audience not only about a misplaced quest for certainty but also about the failure to be satisfied with one's lot, which is, from an Epicurean perspective, greed. In order to connect the counselee's alleged "quest for certainty" with her alleged "greed," Brenifier not only provokes the counselee to use *phrases* such as 'I am not certain,' he also reacts to them with the question 'why are you so greedy?' According to the recordings of some of his workshops, Brenifier speak with his *students* about the discussed quest as greed which, he explains, is "wishing to have more than one can get." *I personally* would distinguish between accepting one's lot as *fate* has designed it and accepting a situation that was designed by the manipulations of a jester. But the pedagogic project can be realized if the *audience* is prepared, and it is not me, but Brenifier who prepares his audience.

Even though Socrates was sometimes joking, he is respected as a serious philosopher for his struggle against unjustified claims of knowledge or virtue. Brenifier, on the other hand, tries to bring to light the "ridiculous childishness" of the counselee's dissatisfaction with her "uncertainty" and other alleged faults. We learned from Shakespeare that sometimes there is a method to madness. In this case, we should look for it in the theoretical assumptions that underly the maddening method.

The Theoretical Assumptions

Peirce believed that abductions are based on evidence, but more recent philosophers of knowledge and science claim that such conjectures are based on presupposed theories. In Brenifier's case, I believe they are right. In the dialogue described in De Haas (2012). Brenifier equates the "unreasonable quest" with "greed," a term that typically denotes a character defect, one of the seven deadly sins. The counselee is repeatedly asked if she is greedy, and she repeatedly denies the charge; she gets increasingly impatient, and finally declares, "I am generous!" Brenifier points out that wanting to know "for sure" is greedy, as 'being greedy' means wanting more than one can receive. He speaks *as if there is no difference* between the *desire to obtain more certainty* and the *desire to have more than one needs of a scarce object by depriving other persons of their fair share*. If I had not read Nietzsche (and some other past philosophers who are fashionable nowadays), I would have assumed that only gods, godlike kings, high priests, and the like, whose exclusivity is threatened by the human quest for knowledge and certainty, would deem that human desire a deadly transgression. Philosophers today who have given up the ancient dream of perfect knowledge tend to see the desire for it as nothing more than, paraphrasing the burning Jan Hus, an "unholy simplicity" (which American pragmatists, more empathically, tolerate as "fear of peril"). However, Nietzsche tried to teach us that the search for knowledge and certainty might be a quest for superiority and power. (Nietzsche, 1968, among his other texts). Marx, as rival and accomplice of Nietzsche, believed that the ideology of the ruling classes, though mainly self-deceptive, was also motivated by a desire to keep the other classes ignorant (Marx, 2012); Heidegger linked greed to the "technological" way of thinking, and regarded the belief in the possibility of complete and certain knowledge an insult to the Being of beings and their ever-emerging truth (Heidegger, 2013); following Hegel and Heidegger, Sartre saw in the attempt to view oneself or others as objects of knowledge a Master-Slave dialectic (Sartre, 1993); Foucault combined some of these ideas in his "problematizations" of the treatment of crime or insanity in the "age of reason" (Foucault, 2001).

In my tentative list, however, Nietzsche's ideas appeared first because of Brenifier's association of greed with feelings of frustration, anger, and impotence (Brenifier, 2020, 30). Additionally, Brenifier links greed to anxiety, a desire to control, and a desire to hide one's weaknesses (ibid.). This suggests that he is interested, like Nietzsche, in "unconscious" emotions and motives. (Brenifier 2019, 2020). Brenifier has indeed a working theory about human nature and the pathologies of counselees. It is not, as Wisdom said, the "obsession" of his "stubborn" philosophical opponent, nor is it Dewey's assumption of insecurity, but rather a Nietzschean assumption that most people have a "slave mentality" and are motivated by their "will to power" to override others rather than overcome themselves (e.g., Nietzsche, 1994). Brenifier sometimes accuses the incompliant counselee with the wish to control the conversation.

In a second thought, it is possible that despite all these influences, Brenifier is not a new Zarathustra; he is just an Epicurean who, besides practicing fearless "free speech" in public and denying the importance of academic knowledge, insists on the importance of *being happy with one's lot* (See Appendix B).[37] But all those influences are in vogue, and the *audience* does not need more than vague notions of them in order to be prepared. For such an audience the "pathology" is manifested not only in the diverse behaviors and unintentionally revealed thoughts of some counselees, but in the ways of life of almost all of us. Brenifier claims to treat in private consultations, both as a teacher and a philosophical counselor, many other "philosophical dysfunctions" that result from the "human existential condition" (Brenifier, 2019, 135). Yet, assuming that we, or at least "people in general," are sometimes "slavish," "intolerant of peril," "greedy" etc., the "greedy quest for certainty" is the "pathology" that is the easiest to expose and confirm when "consulting in the agora."[38] The assumption that we all "resentfully" enjoy exposing others' weaknesses could also play a part . . .

These are, at least, *my* conclusions, and I tend to think that the fault is in the counseling in the *agora*. Brenifier is targeted because of his publicity, ability, and skill. I criticize him for his *apparent* disdain for acquaintance with "academic" philosophy, and for the risk that such an approach might have when the "game" is not in the agora, and the protagonists are not just *playing the role* of counselees in a demonstration or a workshop but are persons in distress who ask for assistance. In such a case one should, to my mind, be more cautious and proceed less quickly to conclusions than was done in the conversation described in the "Dialogue with Kim" (Brenifier, 2019, 239–

58). I believe that in his private conversations Brenifier, or other competent counselors of that school, are as cautious as other experienced counselors. But I am not sure that inexperienced followers, whether in philosophical counseling or in psychotherapy, who might apply the learned approach mechanically will do so prudently.

Pathology and Health: Philosophical? Psychological?

Brenifier often uses the "quest for certainty" as an example of a "philosophical pathology," so I shall use that alleged quest as a case study in my response to the idea that there are attitudes that are "philosophically pathological." I must admit, however, that I am not sure that Brenifier himself, despite using the words 'pathologies' or 'disfunctions,' means much more than *obstacles* which a *teacher* might come across when *teaching philosophy*, or when counseling philosophically. I am also not sure whether, when he speaks of the "second stage" (Brenifier, 2019), which occurs after the counselee has overcome the obstacles, he means counseling rather than *tutoring*. He seems to aim at educating persons who want to become *theoretical philosophers* (not necessarily *academic philosophers*), to be able to consolidate a coherent and clear view on one or another philosophical *topic*. He seems to believe that many academic philosophers and most practical philosophers still need such tutoring. Yet I allow myself to use his apparently "diagnostic" approach as an occasion for criticizing the idea of "philosophical pathologies."

Like many contemporary Western philosophers, I do not believe that absolute certainty in philosophy, science or life is an attainable aim; yet I think that the quest for it is neither pathological nor an attitude. It may take the form of a specific activity or exist as a vague aim, conceived as a practical rule, or treated as an abstract ideal, and it is sometimes based on an unwarranted belief in its possibility.

Is the case of Wisdom's "philosophical patient," the skeptic who insists, despite having all the possible evidence that is accessible to *him*, that he can never be sure what *another* person really feels, analogous to the case of the psychologist's patient who checks again and again whether the gas is turned off? Certainly not, for the psychologist knows that sometimes such behavior is reasonable (there might be somebody in the house who is repeatedly putting the gas on), and he needs more information (and other "symptoms") before he can diagnose his patient (with the very limited certainty of psychiatric diagnostic criteria) as compulsive-obsessive. In contrast, Wisdom *shares with the skeptic the conviction* that he cannot know for sure what another person feels simply *because he is not that person*. But he also theorizes about the proper *use of phrases* like 'being certain that' in the "language game" of *gossip* [as it is supposed to be "played" by analytic behaviorists], while the "stubborn skeptic" is not interested in "language games" or analytic philosophy. To my modest mind, it is not a sufficient reason for referring the latter to an analytic treatment. In the case of a "quest for certainty," in Brenifier's example (if we ignore the educational aims in the public performances) the philosophical counselor might both mis-identify the speech act of the counselee (who says politely 'I am not certain' but means something else) and make a hasty "diagnosis" of a "pathology" (which might, moreover, be irrelevant to the counselee's problem).

Some philosophers speak of attitudes—to life, to themselves or to other persons—which might seem more seriously "pathological" than an allegedly unjustified quest for precision, or the assumed "will to power" of the counselee who refuses to comply with the counselor's rules, or even the wish (against which Epictetus warns the wise) to change what is *really* beyond one's control: Sartre's "mauvaise foi," for example, or Heidegger's "inauthenticity," or Nietzsche's "resentment," "slave morality" and "ascetism," to name a few. I do not know which sickness is more serious, but there is at least one difference between the ancient Stoic and these modern philosophers: the former advises the wise to *check in every case* whether what he wants to change is within his control, whereas the latter have complex *models* of personalities or behaviors, which they present as philosophically condemnable. However, they do not explain what the readers need to check in order to know whether the models fit *them* personally, or, in fact, fit *anyone*. Those models are apparently very different from, say, the economist's model of a "rational consumer": they are not conceived by an "*esprit de géométrie*" but constructed, sometimes roughly, with an "esprit de finesse." They pay attention to lived experiences and not to measurable "materialistic concerns." They are also different from Weber's "ideal types," which may model irrational personalities and behaviors in fanatic religious wars yet are meant to be instruments for explaining social reality scientifically, although "with understanding of the subjective meaning of actions for the relevant individual agents." Yet they are *constructs*, based on theoretical speculations, and not *empirical descriptions* of concrete people. Sartre (1948, 1993) did not interview waiters, Jews, or Antisemites; Nietzsche does not even seem to have read about the "ancient Rabbis," whom he repeatedly attacked, for example in *The Antichrist* (Nietzsche, 1954); Heidegger might never have spoken with any "inauthentic person" who did not "dare to cope with his death anxiety" (Heidegger, 1993). Indeed, even the great Hegel, whose idea of the "unhappy consciousness" (2018) is reflected in Melenie

Klein's influential psychoanalytic theory about the narcissistic personality, was not acquainted with the relevant "unhappy persons"—small children in general and the mythical Eternal Jew in particular—who, because they are not mature enough to understand that God and Satan are immanent in the world and in their own as well as other's souls, are supposed to suffer mood fluctuations between unjustified feelings of superiority and envy of those who are better than them. Just as there are probably millions of persons of Islamic descent for whom God and Satan are transcendent, and yet they are *not* pathologically narcissistic, there are probably many individual people who seem to the prejudiced to be of this or that type, but who, in fact, are *not.* And just as nobody knows as yet whether there are more narcissists among non-Christians than among Protestants with Hegelian convictions, nobody knows as yet in which population of "ordinary people" the tendency to "mauvaise foi," "inauthenticity" or "resentment" is more frequent than among the "elites" who are supposed to cope more "dialectically," "authentically" or "nobly" with the human condition. Some interpreters say that Kierkegaard (1992), in his analysis of the "aesthetic," "ethical" and "religious" types, *is* talking about a concrete person: he is reflecting himself in subsequent stages of his spiritual development. And Kierkegaard (2004) does speak of "sickness," even "unto death." But if it is assumed that they apply *only* to him, then even relativists like Deleuze and Guattari (1994), authors of the theory about the idiosyncrasy of philosophers' "concepts," should admit that they are no more than anecdotical curiosities.[39] They are interesting because they are general models, yet we do not know how to decide whether they apply to any person feeling "sick unto death" besides Kierkegaard.

Thus, we have a sufficient reason for not considering such types as models of *diagnosable* pathologies that are analogous to psychological dysfunctions. The necessary reasons—a *wide agreement* that they are models of *unhealthy* persons—is also missing. Hence, they should rather be interpreted as representations of the *moral* (and some say, amoral or immoral) positions of those philosophers with regards to the question of how people *should not be* or *behave* (usually, they were criticizing thereby their alleged *Zeitgeist*).[40]

Many philosophers and others have different positions. Liberal-democratic philosophers, for example, would not agree with a great part of those elitist ideals; some of them have constructed counter-models for philosophically condemnable attitudes, like the "closed society" stances in Popper (2020). But while sociologists and psychologists who share their moral and political ideals relate to such types (for example, the "authoritarian personality" [Adorno et al. 1950]) as pathological and try to study *empirically* the conditions under which they might be formed, Popper and many other thinkers preferred to give *their reasons* for condemning them. They did not suggest treating them as *pathologies*, nor spoke of *their* favorite attitudes as *healthy*. They knew that using medical or psychiatric metaphors for distinguishing "right" from "wrong" attitudes or beliefs, might lead to the persecution—with "hygienic" excuses—of people with different opinions.[41]

Philosophical counselors do not need, to my mind, concepts of "pathology" or "health" to do their job. The very reason for proposing such counseling as an approach to human problems that at least in some cases is preferable to psychotherapy is not, as some practical philosophers claim, only anti-psychiatric; it is a philosophical antagonism to the idea of psycho*pathology*. Philosophical counselors who think otherwise should check whether they are operating with philosophical or psychological methods. They should beware of falling into the "psychological" ways, which better serve persuaders who seek to *bypass* the possible barriers to the clients' rationality. Some of those "demagogical" ways are applied in certain forms of psychotherapy, the subject of the next chapter (and Appendix C).

Notes

1. Which is based on parts of the second edition (1987) of his article on spiritual exercises (Hadot, 1981) and on ideas expressed in interviews with the editor, Arnold Davidson. Hadot dealt with such spiritual exercises even earlier (Hadot, 1974), in the context of his analyses of ancient texts.

2. Hadot appreciated some modern thinkers, such as Montaigne, Nietzsche, Wittgenstein and Foucault, as true philosophers although they did not share the philosophical preoccupations, presuppositions or ideals of the Greek and Roman thinkers that he considered philosophers.

3. Demonstrated by Peter Harteloh, in a workshop given at the 12th International Conference of Practical Philosophy, Athens, August, 2013. I believe, based on a lecture he gave in the congress that preceded that conference (Harteloh, 2013), that the idea behind that exercise was to enable the participants to experience peaceful dialogical togetherness as part of a process of peacebuilding rather than character-building. As to Harteloh's general approach, see Hartelob (2010, 2018).

4. Schuster considered herself a disciple and loyal follower of Gerd Achenbach (Schuster, 1999). As Elliot Cohen says, she conceived her philosophical practice as addressing the clients' existential problems, and "calling forth the myriad voices of philosophers to help her clients bring meaning out of confusions" (Cohen, 2016). She insisted that philosophical practice and counseling should be free of any dogmatic approach. Though she shared with Hadot an interest in the nature of "philosophical life," she maintained that it should be life according to the person's own evolving philosophy (Schuster, 2003). However, she gradually came closer to

Greek Orthodox religious views, converted, and adopted the ideals of Sinai hermits. Compare that attitude to that of Kierkegaard (2004), which was originally published under the pseudonym of "Anti-Climacus."

5. He does not think, however, that the poietic way is the only method, nor that it is always applicable. He recently published a book about "experiential philosophical practice" (Barrientos-Rastrojo, 2021). His main ideas—that philosophical practice should enable "simple people" in their dire life situations, to think philosophically and change their lives, and that the philosopher is not the "knower" but the one who thinks with them—are not very different from mine, though I would not talk of an experiential philosophy but of philosophizing in terms that are relevant to the counselees and intelligible to them. As I have learned from his recent book, however, the main difference between his approach and mine is still his being the one to decide which philosophical themes the counselees should address, and which should be their source of inspiration for answering them (for instance, Stoic views), while I believe in letting or helping the counselees ask their own philosophical questions, and reflect about more than one philosophical answer. This difference is probably due to the fact that he believes that philosophical practice should be mobilized for the purpose of a social change, and he conceives the counselees—he is working mainly with prisoners—as the "simple people" without whom such a change cannot occur, while I believe that it is up to the counselee to choose his position toward social change or any other issue.

6. Which means, according to (Davis, 2013, 168) "non-willing letting-be that is otherwise than both will-ful activity and will-less passivity."

7. Amir's idea of exercising humor is nonconventional in academic circles, but she does not offer an alternative philosophy. Her interest in the humoristic position, about which she has already published three books, is part of her serious attitude to academic philosophy. She is interested, on the theoretical level, in the relevance of philosophy to life, and on that level deals with the rationale of philosophical counseling and its principles, but she does not practice philosophical counseling. Yet she is not only teaching philosophy in the academy. Her practical philosophical activity consists in teaching philosophy to nonphilosophers who are interested in integrating philosophy into their practice. (Based on personal communication).

8. I am not directly acquainted with Júlian Marías's writings and am not sure that he believed in the discovery of personal missions. If, however, the internal complexity of the protagonists and their intricate interrelations in the wonderful novels of Xavier Marías, his son, reflects the conceptions and insights of his father, then the latter is an excellent source of inspiration for a "multi-vectoral" understanding of counselees. However, the son's novels do not suggest that his father mentioned "projects" dedicated to harmony and inner peace. As far as I know, the father believed that it depended on God's grace.

9. Private correspondence with a perplexed participant in one of the groups' courses of critical practical philosophy.

10. I must admit that I never heard any member of that group cite Foucault, and I know of only one who mentioned the word 'parrhesia'; but the citations (with less dramatic commitments) fit the conception that is expressed in his writings (Brenifier, 2019).

11. I also rely on personal participation in Ran Lahav's workshop in the fifteenth international conference on practical philosophy, Mexico, 2018.

12. "Real knowledge," and in particular "real self-knowledge," is also the declared aim of some other partisans of alternative, nonacademic philosophy, who are neither phenomenologist nor Buddhist. Such approaches, which are probably based on misinterpretations of the Greco-Roman philosophical "know-thyself" ideal, seem to reflect the partisans' intuitive notions of "selfhood" and "self-knowledge" and their unawareness of the fact that the meaning and meaningfulness of both terms are a matter of debate among contemporary philosophers (and psychologists).

13. While Yaguri is interested in dialogues about the meaning of life for the counselee, Von Morstein integrates Kierkegaard's approach to anxiety into a conception that is mainly inspired by Nietzsche and Wittgenstein. At many of her workshops, however, she presented Kierkegaard's concept as a starting point and guide to her philosophical practice.

14. Schopenhauer and Nietzsche, Bergson and Wittgenstein, Foucault and Derrida, among others, can be added to the list. One can also find the accusation of failing to ask the "right questions" in Plato's early dialogues. It expresses a new, or renewed, approach to some philosophical issues. It may imply that some "wrong" philosophical questions are not important, or they are important but not philosophical, or they are important and philosophical but unanswerable or senseless pseudo-questions. In any case, the accusation is usually supported by theoretical and methodological presuppositions and defended by rather abstract arguments. It is therefore not evidence for the irrelevance of academic and theoretical philosophy.

15. The terms 'subjective' and 'objective,' as well as 'subject' and 'object' serve in philosophical texts in various meanings, and the variety of their uses in psychological texts, does not contribute to their clarity. In the present context I mean by 'subjective' a position that is not claimed to be valid for others as well, a matter of personal opinion or attitude, and not something that is "common to (thinking) subjects," or something that is "only in the (subject's) mind, not in the real world." I do not mean by it something that is specific and innate to a certain individual or even a "mission" pre-destined to that "subject" (or "soul" or "self") by the gods.

16. Among the "alternative philosophies" that I did not mention are religious worldviews which were suppressed under communist rule and are now prevalent in Russia, Romania and some other postcommunist countries as the "spiritual philosophical" alternative to "materialism" both in Western "non-spiritual" philosophical theories and Marxist-Leninist dogmas.

17. I personally think that what may induce smokers to quit are, on the one hand, rationally planned or unplanned events that break the habit of taking a cigarette (which is an indirectly rational or nonrational "unlearning"), or, on the other hand,

information that changes the balance between the immediate pleasures of smoking and the expected displeasures that it might cause in the future. Whether such changes occur because the pleasures diminish or the threat of suffering increases, it is not a change from irrationality to rationality but in the framework of the same utilitarian logic, it is a change of beliefs and attitudes, and their subjective "weights." It is, normally, much more effective than hearing from a counselor that from some philosophical point of view not quitting smoking is irrational. (I must admit, in defense of that practitioner, that I assume that, irrespective of his theoretical description of the treatment, he somehow tried both methods before arriving at his irrationality conclusion.)

18. See Lipman (2003), Lipman et al. (1980), Matthews (1984), and Brenifier (2015) for philosophy for children and Sautet (1995) for café-philo.

19. Nelson and his movement were persecuted by the Nazis and moved to Britain.

20. The examples are taken from Plato's Protagoras, which deals with the traits of a virtuous man and the possibility of teaching them, and in Meno, which deals with "remembered," i.e., latent, innate knowledge. In order to understand the logic of Plato's dialectic, or the logic of his philosophizing, one should be acquainted with more dialogues, such as Theaetetus (Plato, 1997) and Sophist (Plato, 1997). However, whatever is the Socratic or Platonic logic, Socrates, as the protagonist of the Platonic dialogues (Plato, 1997) is not always committed to logic. Provocations and treacherous exploration such as his would be discussed in the meta-dialogues of modern Socratic conversations.

21. Philosophical counselors tend to be more tolerant of Jungian, Rogerian, or cognitive psychotherapy, which seem to them closer to philosophy. I believe that they are wrong and explain that claim in chapter 6 and Appendix C.

22. It could have considered the opinions of other philosophers about logic or coherence, which could be relevant to its endeavors, but it does so, to my mind, only very selectively.

23. I am referring to the approach that is presented in Cohen (1994) as an example, and not to Cohen's view in general (a similar reservation applies to Ellis). Cohen, I have been told, does not conceive of himself as essentially different from the former; he even collaborated with him for a while. I am speaking of the difference between the approaches in the specific case of a depressed mood after a failure in an examination.

24. This apparently minor difference is the reason why cognitive therapy is very different from psychoanalysis: the latter assumes that the "wrong premises" are endogenous. their "correction" is a lengthy process, an "archaeological search," through long chains of associations, for the "original" anxiety-raising wish -thoughts in the analysand's childhood. Those allegedly "repressed" thoughts, reevoked unconsciously by associations, are the cause of the present mistaken thoughts, "neurotic" behavior and "inadequate" emotions and moods of the analysand as well as the "parapraxes" (errors, omissions, memory failures etc.) and the "conversions" (psycho-somatic illnesses) which seen to happen to him unintentionally. Reexperiencing the ancient

wish-thoughts in a different mood and with more mature understanding enables not just the correction but also the cure. In contrast, cognitive therapy assumes that the "wrong thoughts" are exogenous, uncritically learned from others (or wrongly inferred from others' opinions), and believes that the much shorter process of searching for (and discovering of) the "logical fallacy" or the "irrational premises" and their exposition is sufficient. Some psychotherapists who share those assumptions and believe that the "archaeological inquiry" is superfluous, insist nevertheless that something has to be done about the emotional aspects.

25. I personally tend to endorse many of Ellis's opinions, but it is irrelevant to my counseling. As a philosophical counselor my aim is to assist the counselee to arrive at his own conclusions. In the process I indeed call into question some of his beliefs and values because they seem to me to be the "trouble-maker," but the conclusion of his re-vision of them is his, and can be different than mine.

26. See, for instance De Haas (2012, 10). I do not refer to criticisms expressed in papers that have not yet been published, with which I am familiar through personal correspondence.

27. In the following, I assume the "counselor" is always a man and the "counselee" is always a woman merely because I need to use many pronouns and I want to minimize confusion.

28. Responding to critics of the pathological approach, he says: "Let us say that the main test [for the readiness to deal with the difficulties of philosophical consultation] lies in the acceptance of the idea of pathology taken in the philosophical sense" (Brenifier, 2020, 135).

29. According to Brenifier, curing the pathological attitudes is just the first step. In the next step the counselor, with the tool of "conceptualization" and with more respect for the accumulated wisdom of academic philosophy, assists the counselee to form his own clear and coherent cognitive and existential philosophical positions (Brenifier 2020). It appears that that step will form part of a possible theory that will be as comprehensive, in terms of topics, vectors, antitheses and syntheses, as Hegel's entire philosophy. I am not sure how long Brenifier estimates it would take for the realization of such a project (past philosophers needed a whole academic life). I cannot estimate how many counselees would survive the first step and go to the next. But in any case, I am sure that some of their triggering issues, which led them to seek his assistance in the first place, would seem less significant at the end of the process. (Philosophizing matters, but sometimes, as they say in my cultural province, "what reason does not do time does.")

30. Brenifier himself worked for a while as philosophical counselor at Moscow's institute for psychoanalysis. One of his followers, who is now studying philosophy in France, has recently announced in Facebook the publication of her study about asking questions: that is, how to bypass someone's refusal to answer. If I had not known who she is, I would have thought that the text was destined for police investigators or economic spies. Psychoanalysts seem quite able to bypass such refusal and get what they consider to be the answers without asking questions.

31. Instead of describing other approaches within the "critical thinking" group I cite a recent post (November 20, 2022) on Facebook by Isabelle Millon, one of the central members of the group (Italics mine):

> Rigor. *Ascetism*. Learning to be clear, to be concise. *Stop being on the defensive, put his ego aside*. To think is not a matter of being wrong or right, but a matter of looking for meaning. *Learn to give up*. Reconcile oneself with slowness to enjoy the process of thinking. Clean up one's head and feel better by articulating his thoughts and *put order in them*. *Therapeutic*. Joyful. "The existent which *we must analyze*, writes Heidegger, is ourselves." *Necessary confrontation in order to grow and to be free*.

Millon is conducting workshops in many countries. I am not acquainted with her practice, but by using italics, I try to draw attention to some of her sayings, which should be "unpacked" to explicate her presuppositions.

32. See Pascal's distinction between the two in Appendix A.

33. See chapter 1, Philosophical Questions.

34. See chapter 1, note 11.

35. At that time Wisdom was not well acquainted with what is taking place in psychoanalytic analyses and that his source of inspiration, Wittgenstein, also had only vague impressions. (There are some writers today who claim that he was a fan and nearly joined the psychoanalytic camp. Given everything I know about his life and his ideas, I imagine that he would not terminate even the first hour of regular psychoanalysis, not to mention the training sessions.)

36. I was recently accused with arbitrariness by some supporters of the idea of "philosophical health" for saying that since Locke, at least some analytic philosophers believe that philosophy itself is the disease. I have to be more precise: speculative philosophy and correct myself: since the ancient skeptics.

37. If he is Epicurean, he must admit that his rules are replacing Fortuna, while Diogenes is pushing others into barrels. This is practical philosophy. His predecessors, in and out barrels, seeking justice with or without candles, were most often just loud free speakers.

38. I am not inclined to examine in depth whether a particular use of words in the context of his exposition actually reveals something about the counselee's "pathology" since Brenifier admits that although the counselor's remarks may be erroneous, they may nevertheless lead the counselee to [eventually] disclose his [true] "pathology" (Brenifier, 2000).

39. I believe that Kierkegaard's theory of reason recognizing its limit in times of crisis inspired their conception of philosophy as exploration of the limits of possibility of the philosopher's "concept."

40. It is true that some of them were able to claim that the wrong "climate of opinion" prevails since Socrates's intellectualism overshadowed the pre-Socratic insights, foreign Semitic ascetics spoiled the Dionysian festivities of "pagan Christianism," and the "technological attitude" replaced the holy mass murderer of heretics with the twentieth-century death industries. I am not calling into question rhetorical talents.

41. Nietzsche used medical terminology, and the process of his rehabilitation since Walter Kaufmann's campaign in the middle of the twentieth century does not contradict the fact that his "medical" opinions, rightly or wrongly interpreted, were used or misused by the Nazis and other partisans of "sanitary" causes. See the introduction (1924) by his translator into English, H. L. Mencken (Nietzsche, 1999), who, as the apologizing publisher admits, had negative [I would say poisonous] opinions not only about ascetic ancient rabbis but also modern "plutocratic Jews."

CHAPTER SIX

The Irrelevance of Philosophy

The Scientific Perspective

Mutual Accusations of "Ψ"s and "Φ"s

In the last chapter I presented groups of philosophical counselors who claim that academic philosophy is irrelevant to philosophical practice and counseling. In the present chapter I deal with another group of practitioners who has a similar purpose—to help people who are "stuck" in their life issues—and who also share the conviction that academic philosophy is irrelevant to their activity: these are the "Ψ" [psy] practitioners, from psychiatrists and psychoanalysts to clinical psychologists, psychotherapists, counselors, educational advisors, and clinical social workers.

This is a rather heterogeneous group, with different levels of erudition and training and a great variety of worldviews and approaches; but except for some voices here and there, they all claim that their activity is based on scientific knowledge, supervised training and clinical experience, and tend to suspect others who seem to lack adequate preparation to treat people responsibly. These "Ψ" professionals, mostly with positivist background, maintain, like Comte, that beliefs in spiritual cures are residues of a primitive, religious, mentality and that a reliance on modern, positive science and technology turns even philosophy, which is supposed to be more advanced and useful than religion yet less efficacious than science, into a superfluous activity (Bourdeau, 2006). Depth psychologists who are influenced either by Comte or his anti-positivist counterpart, Hegel (2018) seem to share the assumption that the development of the individual, from birth to maturity, repeats the development of humanity, including its philosophical development. The completely "mature" individual (if there is any) is supposed to spontaneously hold the most advanced philosophical worldview. If he failed to complete his developmental process, the depth-philosophical treatment (if "terminated," that is—completed) will help him to "grow" toward it. Thus, philosophical debates are limited to highbrow practitioners of depth psychology whose members have read some philosophical texts and are aware of philosophical controversies, but as they have also studied and to some extent deciphered the "unconscious," they claim to understand life, rationality, and irrationality even better than philosophers. Some of the "Ψ" people, having more respect for non-scientific disciplines and a greater readiness to recognize their possible contribution to mental strength, concede that philosophers are able to deal with cognitive or educational issues, but insist that they do not sufficiently understand the domain of the *affects*—desires, emotions and moods—and its pathologies. (Others, Jungians among them, claim to be philosophical, but say that mainstream philosophy, like mainstream psychology, is too intellectual, unready to attend to "intuition" and the hints of the "unconscious" or relate to the "spiritual.") Some say that philosophers do not understand the biological drives or instincts. Others claim that philosophers are competent in dealing with the *conscious* aspects of the mind, but have no access to its *nonconscious* sides, do not understand the somatic aspects of the patients' problems, or know nothing about the physiology of the brain. Finally, some say that philosophers are not trained to detect the manipulative or otherwise disturbed behavior behind the patient's seemingly rational discourse. They are therefore unable to act responsibly in critical cases, when the patient is, say, in a state of panic or psychotic attack, suffers from posttraumatic symptoms, is severely depressed or is addicted to drugs or alcohol.

The camp of the philosophical counselors, the "Φ" [phi] people, is even less united: many maintain that they do not compete with psychologists because they do not "treat" patients; others, following the anti-psychiatry trend, do not recognize the legitimacy of categories such as "mentally ill" or "disturbed" persons (Raab, 2001). Some assume that many among those who are diagnosed by the "Ψ" people as "ill" are healthy and sane and need philosophical conversations rather than "treatments" (Marinoff, 1991, 2001). Some claim that the "Ψ" people are biased, and tend to detect—using flawed diagnostic tools—"clinical" symptoms when the issues are not medical but moral, spiritual or philosophical (Achenbach, 1987, Schuster, 1999). I am among those who rely on the claims of philosophers of science that the base of knowledge of the "Ψ" professions (especially of the "depth-psychologies") is not precisely scientific (Grünbaum, 1985); all of us have heard the complaints of disappointed patients or have learned from research psychologists that the efficiency of most of the clinical "techniques" or "methods" have not been put to valid objective tests. Many "Φ" people therefore tend to interpret the "Ψ" people's negative reaction to their "intrusion" as a defense of tradition rather than a concern for the scientific quality of the therapeutic intervention. Some philosophical counselors maintain that what the "Ψ" people are doing is simply irrelevant when the problem is existential; others accuse them of thinking in causal terms, or in terms of "laws" and "statistics" and fail to understand the human quest for "meaning," "faith," "virtue" or other values. While the "Ψ" people talk in terms of "sanity," "health," and "normalcy," the "Φ" people see their activity as an attempt to reduce individuals, each of whom is unique and special, to the "average" and the "conventional." Finally, there are philosophical counselors who are ready to acknowledge that some personal problems may be treated better by the appropriate "Ψ" experts but claim that the domains of the "Ψ" and the "Φ" overlap each other and the tentative dividing lines are fuzzy.

I belong to the latter group. I believe that many of the claims of the former groups, in both fields, are based on confusion or ignorance. I do not know who competes with whom, but the territory in which the "Φ" and "Ψ" are most likely to clash is the territory of what Freud called the "talking cure," which targets beliefs and attitudes in the hope of bringing about changes and generating improvements.[1] Thus, the question is whether there is a difference in the reasons and methods of "Φ" and "Ψ" in terms of "*talking*," and this depends on their implicit meta-theories and their tacit sub-theories, or presuppositions. The theories of both "Φ" and "Ψ" practitioners include beliefs with regards to *psychological facts* and *preferences* of certain *philosophical positions*. From my point of view, the practitioner is a "practical philosopher" if he tries to promote psychological changes by exploring philosophical positions *in philosophically proper ways*. In contrast, if the methods are psychological, and the user is a philosophical counselor, he should be aware that he is working as a psychologist.

He should at least be aware that he is using psychological methods, and remember that most of the professionals among the "Ψ" people are trying to distinguish between professionally *permissible* psychological methods and methods that should be avoided because they are "psychological" in a derogative sense; that is, they are attempts at "persuasion under inappropriate conditions," including subliminal conditioning, seduction, group pressure, emotional blackmail—in short, any kind of induced disability to examine messages critically.

Philosophical counselors should be able to identify and avoid "brainwashing," "double binding," "gaslighting" and other rhetorical and psychological "techniques" that fit those who have learned the arts of persuasion—such as salespeople, lawyers, propagandists, missionaries—and are supposed to characterize naturally talented seductors, such as some narcissists, psychopaths, and charismatic deceivers. Furthermore, they should be aware that that distinction is not always easy. Sometimes practitioners in one "Ψ" camp accuse colleagues in another "Ψ" camp with misuses of "psychological" methods, and some "Φ" people blame their colleagues for their use of "demagoguery," that is, "psychological" tricks.

Yet one must be aware that some psychological methods that are permissible in the "Ψ" camp aim to induce change by targeting beliefs and attitudes *that are basically philosophical* in ways that are *philosophically improper*.

Psychologically Acceptable and Philosophically Improper

Philosophical discourse is not always clear of demagogical strategies, but whatever may motivate a philosopher to try to persuade persons in nonrational ways, philosophers in general would be embarrassed to learn that people accepted their views *because* they did not have the chance to examine them critically. Psychotherapists are not different, yet many of them believe that *in the clinical context* they should create conditions under which the *patient has little or no chance to think critically* about the beliefs or attitudes that the psychotherapist wants him to accept. Sometimes the "Ψ" people are not aware that they are dealing with beliefs and attitudes; sometimes they believe that they are dealing only with unconscious residues of infantile mentality; sometimes they believe that beliefs and attitudes can be changed only under conditions that are like those under which they were acquired—non-consciously, unconsciously, experientially, emotionally, hypnotically, and so on. Often, they are not aware that some among the beliefs and attitudes they try to change are philosophical. Most often they assume that the patients are irrational, so that the beliefs and attitudes that are responsible for their problems are resistant to rational arguments. Some believe that the irrational aspects are irrationally defended by seemingly rational excuses, "rationalizations," and therefore use methods that are designed to bypass barriers placed by the patient's allegedly misused critical thinking. Whatever are the supposed reasons for the patient's assumed irrationality, many psychotherapists believe that their role is to use rationally conceived nonrational ways of persuasion to make the not-fully-rational patient more rational, or else, "functional," perhaps happier—or, as it is sometimes the case, simply less troublesome to others.

Lightly Philosophically Improper

"Conditioning"

Radical behaviorists speak only in terms of observable "responses to stimuli" that are conditioned through repetition and "associations" between them, which are "reinforced" "positively" or "negatively" by other "stimuli" (while all the rest is, methodologically, "in the [unobservable] black box"). But that way of speaking is a translation (and, scientifically, an improvement) of the old Lockean mental theory, according to which our beliefs and attitudes are a matter of associations of ideas, and the connection between the formation of what, in more popular language are called mental habits, and the accompanying experiencing of pleasure or displeasure. Materialist philosophers and psychiatrists tried to transfer the "associations" from the conscious, but only privately observable, mind to the nonconscious brain, but the brain is also a "black box" from the behaviorist perspective. Behaviorists call their theory "learning theory" because the radicals among them believe that there is no learning and there are no beliefs or attitudes other than the "associations" between what the scientist sees as perceptible "stimuli" and the observable behavioral "responses" of "organisms." Behaviorist treatment aims at the patient's "unlearning," that is, learning not to make the [learnt] associations that lead to problematic responses. It consists in training under conditions in which the frequency or intensity of the "stimuli" and the "reinforcements" (the famous carrots and sticks) for "responses" are different from those under which the "non-functional" habit was presumably acquired.

From a philosophical standpoint, there is nothing wrong with a non-radical behavioral therapist using the technique on a child suffering from a phobia like Freud's Hans. Hans was afraid of horses, the child in the example is afraid of dogs, and the goal of the behaviorist is to help the child, whom his parents fail to convince that dogs are not that dangerous, "unlearn" his automatic and unpleasant reactions to anything that reminds him of dogs. Perhaps, this is more helpful than the quasi-psychoanalytic approach Freud recommended to Hans's father, based on his belief that Hans's phobia was related to Hans's Oedipal problems (Freud, 1990). In the case of post-traumatic phobias and nightmares that are suffered by victims of battle shock, it can be even more beneficial than a discussion with a philosophical counselor about pacifism (Gruengard, 2016). At least, it is worth trying, despite the fact that the patient, at least the child in this example, has been practically "conditioned" and not rationally persuaded, to believe that dogs are not always dangerous.

Nevertheless, it is utterly inappropriate to "condition" people to hold a particular *philosophical* viewpoint. That is why most "Φ" people and other lovers of freedom (including most of the "Ψ" people) rejected Skinner's idea of a totalitarian state run by psychologists, in which people would be "scientifically conditioned" ("which is much more efficient than liberal education") to accept beliefs, values and behaviors that "safeguard civilization" (Skinner, 1948).

Fake Cognitive Biases

Psychologists claim to have discovered various inborn tendencies to cognitive biases which (on the average, when great numbers are considered) probably have some survival advantages, but might lead to errors in specific cases, where logical thinking is relevant. However, the mistake of which Ellis talks (see chapter 5), of 'is' for 'ought,' or 'will' for 'must,' is not among them. A therapeutic approach like that of the cognitivists, which tells a frustrated but nevertheless striving patient that he suffers from a cognitive bias, according to which "everything" he wants he "must" get, is therefore deceptive even when the therapist, does it, half-jokingly, in Ellis's style (Ellis, 1998). It is doubly so when the therapist himself does not really believe that the patient is committing a cognitive error. (I am not sure whether there are no philosophical counselors who commit the same deception.)

I do not know precisely when the therapist thinks that the specific aim of the patient is not worth striving for, and when he estimates that the specific patient is unable to achieve it, whether he believes that people in general should "adapt to reality" and be content with what it is not too difficult to get, or whether he estimates that the very wish of the patient to achieve such a goal is a matter of a blind adaptation to parental hopes or conventional norms. In any case, the therapist imposes his personal philosophical convictions as "cognitively unbiased." Sometimes it works despite the deception, and the patient changes his attitude and is happier. Yet the proper philosophical way is different. A philosopher would discuss with the counselee the real issue at stake: the importance of the problematic goal relative to the counselee's other goals, his criteria for choosing or comparing goals, the importance of norms or the expectations of others, and, on a different philosophical level, his attitude to "adaptive resignation" versus "striving nevertheless."

The "Sane" and "Mature" Attitude to Life (and Other Values)

Some philosophers recommend, in the name of Stoicism, Spinozism, or cognate worldviews, or in the name of a commonsensical and pragmatic adaptation, an acceptance of what they believe is reality, and an attitude that some other philosophers may perceive as undue resignation. Other philosophers praise adherence to aims or ideals even when they seem unrealistic and an attitude that some philosophers define as determination and others—as fanaticism or sheer stubbornness. The "wise" attitude has always been a matter of debate, but since some philosophical provocations in the nineteenth century, notably those of Nietzsche, the debate is also whether the recommended philosophical attitude to life's hazards should be called "wise" rather than "courageous," "noble" or "authentic."

The founders of the various schools of what was once called "depth-psychology"—psychoanalysis, analytic psychology, individual psychology, and their more or less rebellious or creative followers—had different opinions about it and were aware that it was not only a matter of debate among philosophers but also among themselves. Yet each of them included the "correct" attitude toward the difficulty of getting what one really wishes in their conceptions of the "mature and sane" personality. As the aim of their treatment is to help the patient "grow" toward "sane maturity," the patient is tacitly directed, through interpretations of his "immature" thoughts and behaviors, toward the philosophical conception of "sane maturity," or in other words, the philosophy of life, that the founder of the approach built into his conception of psychotherapy. (See Appendix C for more details.) The actual therapist, who is applying that approach as a matter of course, is not necessarily aware that he is thereby imposing on his patient a debatable philosophical conception.

The preferred attitude to life is, of course, not the only philosophical preference that is built into their respective psychopathological theories and clinical approaches. The prevalent, though debatable, assumption was that the root of psychological disturbances and difficulties in dealing with "the normal problems of life" is the failure to fully overcome crises in the evolutionary process of the species, overcoming that everyone has to repeat in his own growing process. This led to the elaboration of developmental theories which were supposed to explain much more than psychiatric syndromes, problematic character traits or unhealthy styles of life. They were also supposed to explain the development of the abilities which, according to the explicit or tacit philosophical positions of the founder or developer, the "sane and mature," that is, the ideal person, *should* have. These explanations regard cognitive capacities and emotional sensitivities, social abilities and political tendencies, moral aptitudes and religious inclinations, intellectual curiosities and artistic imagination, professional preferences, and readiness to work, fitness for conjugal life and parental responsibility, the potential for love and the readiness for personal autonomy or self-aware individuality. Others go even further and explain the courage to confront death anxiety or the audacity to pursue meaning in life. Briefly, they assume that "sane" and "mature" people are naturally inclined to hold certain moral values, while the preference of those values is a matter of debate among philosophers (and cultures). According to some philosophers, any attempt to solve moral debates with psychological theories is committed to the "naturalistic fallacy."

I just say the patient or counselee should understand that values rather than facts are at issue here, and as such are open to debate.

Fully Philosophically Improper

Freud, Jung, and Adler included in their theories their personal positions regarding many other philosophical issues that were, and still are, matters of debate. Their differences are reflected in their positions on the role and importance of sexual development, as well as their philosophical positions about science and determinism or their conceptions of the "unconscious." Their rebellious or creative followers were inspired or provoked by other philosophers, who criticized the founders in the name of science or religion, cultural and existentialist conceptions, and, more recently, in the name of groups that were allegedly ignored or misinterpreted by the founders. They implanted, on their turn, equally debatable philosophical positions in their revised approaches.[2]

The depth psychologists follow, in that respect, philosophers who elaborated developmental psychological theories of their own, from Plato and Aristotle to Hegel, Kierkegaard, Nietzsche, Heidegger, and Sartre, to name a few. Some would add to the list the philosophical ideas of the psychoanalyst Lacan, sociologist Becker, and historian Foucault. There is nothing wrong in basing one's theory on one's philosophical positions; it is in fact unavoidable,[3] What is philosophically improper is the imposition of those positions on others *without giving them the chance to reflect on them critically*, with an awareness of alternative possibilities.

There are, however, differences between the various systematic or personal approaches with regard to the place given to the patient's philosophical awareness and the legitimacy of alternative "mature" ways of thinking and behaving.[4] Therefore, in the following, I use conditional and not indicative language.

Diagnosis of Unconscious Thoughts

Depth psychologists assume that some of the alleged facts with which they deal are non- or unconscious and have theories about the functioning of the unconscious mind and its contents. Whatever is their theory, if the clinical conversation consists of interpreting what the patient says, does, and fails to do, as expressions of his unconscious thoughts, while the patient's disagreement is systematically rejected as "defensive resistance" and his alternative interpretation is discarded as "rationalization" or "a move in a power game" and so on, the conversation is not a dialogue. It resembles an asymmetrical conversation with a physician, where the latter is the knower, who detects symptoms of which the patient, the ignorant one, is unaware. The physician then interprets them as inner disturbances, which, from the point of view of the patient, do not seem to be the causes of his complaints, nor do they seem connected with them logically.

Physicians sometimes believe that the patient's psychological tendencies and philosophical views are among the conditions that increase the risk of a physical illness or decrease the chance of healing, and recommend changing them. In this case, it is up to the patient to consider alternative positions and attitudes. However, if, the depth psychologist believes that the psychological tendencies of which the patient is unaware and his *unconscious philosophical attitude are the illness itself*, that separation does not exist. If that is the case, then his method of diagnosing unconscious *philosophical positions* as symptoms of an illness, is philosophically improper. This is so not only because philosophical conceptions are not a matter of psychopathological expertise, but also because he does not respect the patient's conscious conceptions, his ability to explore his presuppositions, his reasons for looking at things from his own perspective and his ability, when challenged, to make rational judgments and personal choices.

The "Initiated" Versus the "Non Initiated"

Some depth psychologists believe that the patient transfers to the therapist repressed wishes and emotions, which were originally parts of intentional thinking whose intentional object was one of his parents. Now the patient does it unintentionally and unconsciously, under forms that may be very different than the original intentional but "repressed" thoughts. The psychologists assume that the original "repression" occurred because, for example, the child, still unable to distinguish between mere thoughts and effective actions, or between his private world and what others may perceive, believed that those thoughts were forbidden and dangerous, and caused him the pains of guilt and anxiety. The residues in the adult unconscious mind of the unsolved childish conflicts, *including the childish way of thinking*, cause the growing person's anxious ego to continue the defensive associative processes and hide the ancient thoughts by gradually replacing their parts, including their accompanying emotions, by their increasingly remote associations.

They assume that the therapist too is not completely free of his "childish residues" and does his own "counter-transferences" to his patients, but thanks to his own analysis he is aware of it and is able to use his infantile reactions to the patient as a tool for diagnostic and other purposes. The *asymmetry* between the "initiated," with all that they have learned and all the exercises through which they have gone, and the "non-initiated" is, to my mind, a sufficient reason to doubt the properness of the conversation. It is why I would not recommend anyone to engage in philosophical counseling with religious missioners of any faith. It is also why I would not recommend as counselors some famous *philosophers* who, though not members of a sect, yet pretend to know the unconscious psychological tendencies that cause their philosophical opponents to think in ways that are allegedly typical of less developed (or more degenerate) stages.

In philosophical dialogues one challenges not only the explicit positions of the other, one also calls into question assumed beliefs, values, or attitudes of which he may be unaware. However, in a proper philosophical dialogue they are assumed because there are *logical* connections between them and the declared positions. The philosophical counselor is supposed to know that they are no more than assumptions, for the same positions can be logically justified by other sets of presuppositions.

Individual philosophes may also have assumptions about the psychological motives of their interlocutors, but, unlike some famous philosophers, the philosophical culture of critical thinking distinguishes between assumptions and facts and does not mistake the logical validity of positions with the psychological "validity" of their holders.

Persuasion under "Experiential" Conditions

If a depth psychologist believes that treatment should consist of an analysis of the "transference" under "experiential" conditions (that is, conditions in which the original situation is re-enacted, causing the patient to relive the original pain and other hard feelings) in the presence of an understanding and supporting therapist, and the psychologist "sneaks in" philosophical messages, the treatment is philosophically improper. In addition to the usual asymmetry of knowledge and power between analyst and analysand, the reenactment creates an asymmetry between the empathic but relatively cool therapist and the emotionally excited and dependent patient, whose critical and explorative capacities are, at least temporally, impaired.

Some philosophical counselors evoke Socrates or Epicure, praising their alleged practice of stunning their rivals with provocative questions or accusations, as if a confusing embarrassment rather than Aristotelian wonder and curiosity were the beginning of philosophizing. Other philosophical counselors and some philosophically minded teachers of social work agree with the psychological claim that intellectual convictions cannot bring about real change. Therefore, they add other means of persuasion and call their practice "experiential philosophy." Some of them believe in working in groups and, like some group depth psychotherapists, add social pressure to their arsenal.

I am not talking here about the efficacy of philosophical conversations but about the philosophical propriety of "experiential," "social" or other sorts of apparently efficient treatments under emotional pressure. I believe that Freud, Jung, Adler, and some of their followers, at least when talking philosophically, would agree with me. The central aim of their treatment was, after all, to liberate the patients from the effect of social and emotional pressures in their developmental process.

Avoiding emotional pressure and treatment under emotional excitation does not mean that philosophers are unable to deal with emotions or that philosophical counselors should talk about concepts and leave the "affects" to psychologists. But although affects are not just beliefs and attitudes, beliefs and attitudes are essential aspects of them (see Nussbaum, 2001). One can deal philosophically with the question of whether and when they are justified, and by what criteria. One can deal with them by asking if, when, how and according to what principles one should express or control them even when they are justified. One can recognize the value of experiencing and expressing them and still ask about their importance relative to other values in concrete life situations. One can ask whether the philosophical positions of the founding-parents of a specific school of depth psychology with regards to the emotions are justified. One can deal with them by criticizing the popular culture that fosters the expression of wishes and emotions and neglects other aspects of human life, a culture that was developed under the impact of depth-psychologies (often in contrast to the philosophical and psychological convictions of the founding-parents of those disciplines and practices). And one can deal with them by criticizing the inadequate attempts of some philosophical counselors to deal with them, by ascribing to the counselees, dogmatically, the wishes and emotions that "people like them have," according to the untested *psychological* theory of some philosopher, trying thereby to apply, amateurishly, some psychological technique or imposing, religiously, their own standard instead of inviting the counselees to a critical exploration.

Spiritual Convictions

Finally, some depth psychologists assume that the developmental process, which occurs under conditions of dependence on adults, is involved with pressures to adapt to parental expectations and dominant social norms. They assume that it involves adopting an external "persona" and ignoring the "unconscious self." In another, less Jungian, version, it involves alienation from the "true self" and living a "false" one. If the therapist seeks to help the patient find his "true self," he probably does so by ignoring the philosophical criticism that the notion of a "true self" is quite problematic. It is unproblematic only if one assumes that the self is the soul to which the gods have assigned a special mission, and the individual will "realize himself" when he fulfills it. Thus, the diagnosis of psychological difficulties as the result of self-alienation is necessarily true only if one is convinced that the gods punish disobedient souls. Otherwise, it is philosophically not clear what those psychologists are talking about. If they mean that "realizing oneself" is living according to one's talents and aspirations, is that necessarily and always more valuable, or "mentally healthier" than choosing to dedicate one's life to other purposes, which are, from one's perspective and in the context of choice, morally preferable? If they mean that one should "really" make his own decisions, what is their criteria for that "really"? If they mean that one should know his "true self," how can they know that he does? If they mean that the patient's reasoning is an expression of his conventionalist "ego" and that the unconscious "self" is discernible by attending to messages hidden in dreams, free associations, or hand-writing—how can we know that in helping him interpret those "messages" they are not manipulating him, as missionaries do, to become another "false self," this time according to their expectation instead of his parents' hopes? How do they know that his "self-presentation" and "self-image" are less "true" than the "true self"? How do they know that he "has" a "self" instead of having to "create himself" by what he thinks and does?

Some philosophical counselors have similar pretensions, and are similarly unaware of the philosophical difficulties and debates with regards to the notions of self, self-knowledge and self-realization (or the individualistic ideals that stand behind them). They know that Socrates said "know thyself," but do not seem to understand what that meant in the historical context of Socrates's philosophical activity.

Philosophically Oriented Psychotherapy

There are many therapists who practice depth psychology without being aware of the philosophical aspects of the founders or their innovative interpreters.

In this respect, they are not like psychoanalysts (including the Jungian and Adlerian schools), whose theoretical studies and training are lengthy (and whose services are practically reserved for the few who have the time and money to devote to intensive long-term treatment). In the best cases, they are clinical psychologists who have been trained in psychology departments that are scientifically oriented and do not "waste time" on philosophical questions, or clinical social workers and other therapists who, with a few exceptions, lack both a scientific and philosophical background. The latter (who often work for those who cannot afford long and expensive treatment) are practically oriented. Their "philosophy lessons" often have nothing to do with a critical examination of psychological theories, which are taught superficially, often as "techniques," which should be applied dogmatically. Unknowingly, they transmit, just like the local priest does with his rituals and dogmatic advice, the philosophical positions that are embedded in the "techniques" of the philosophically inspired founder of their respective "religions." In some cases, they realize that these "techniques" may not be useful, and so they "integrate" them with other "techniques" that were formulated within the frameworks of entirely different "creeds." Some may compare it to a syncretic popular religion lacking theoretical or philosophical integration. (There are, of course, exceptions; as they are acquainted, as teachers or practitioners, with what I am saying I hope they will pardon me the generalization.)

Consequently, parallel to the growing number of unqualified psychotherapists, there is a growing number of other professionals, from psychiatrists to social workers to dance therapists, who refuse to blindly accept depth-psychology dogmas, and refuse to play the role of the uncritical priest. The alternative developmental theories that do not pretend to know how a "mature" person should think and behave are theories that don't assume that the patient has a "psychiatric problem": They include approaches that pay attention to present social contexts, rather than looking for causes in forgotten past events; approaches that attack habits of thought, prejudices, and dogmas, pay attention to other perspectives, and detect communication problems; approaches that respect the cultural background of their patients, respect their worldviews, and work with them in ways which are, essentially, philosophical. Like contemporary philosophers, they do not "educate mankind"; they invite individual persons to re-think what seems obvious to them, and encourage them to think for themselves. I believe that both they and philosophical counselors can benefit from an exchange of ideas and experiences.

Some Prejudices

Philosophy is concerned with exposing prejudices. Some philosophers have nevertheless inherited some prejudices from their predecessors, and some psychologists have also inherited them. The chapter concludes by describing some instances of this, as well as some prejudices that may have religious or mythological origins.

Prejudices of Philosophical Origin

The Fallacy of Sterile Conditions

The first one is the claim, which I personally heard from a psychiatrist and a social worker: "A philosophical counselor may sometimes help the patient, but it may be very dangerous unless he acts under the control of a "Ψ" professional." That claim is as fallacious as Socrates's warning the young man, who wants to learn from the sophist Protagoras: "Be cautious of his spiritual food, which, unlike material alimentation, goes directly into the soul. It might poison it forever" (*Protagoras*, Plato, 1997) [my paraphrasing]. I call it "the fallacy of sterile conditions." Hearing such warnings, one might think that the possible "victim"—the Athenian boy, who is passing his time among other Athenians whose opinions and behaviors Socrates despises, or the Holocaust survivor in Tel Aviv, who has survived Hitler's camps, Israeli bureaucracy, his mother-in-law, and silly TV talks—lives normally under conditions of a strict spiritual diet in a mentally sterile environment! One should believe that both "victims" would finally get fatally poisoned, the former by attempting to learn virtue from the honest but relativist Protagoras and the latter by an "uncontrolled" dialogue with a philosophical counselor . . . (Plato, in fact, aimed at creating a sterile polis, where everybody would live under conditions of a severe spiritual diet (*Republic*, Plato, 1997).

Wise People Do Not Have Difficulties to Cope with Their Problems

Another prejudice is the conviction that one gets into trouble, or rather has difficulties to cope with it, because one's thinking is defective. Locke "knew" that the melancholic mourner, whose sorrow is reevoked by everything that reminds him of the deceased despite the time that has passed since his death, is "unnaturally" associating present with past experiences that are no longer relevant (Locke, 1975); Freud "knew" that that this was indeed the case, but his "knowledge" was more comprehensive: he also "knew" that that mourner was stubbornly making the "unnatural association" because the death reevoked in him the guilt feeling that he experienced as a small child, when he believed that anything bad that might happen to his father would be caused by his wish to kill him (Freud, 1975). Both behaviorists, who are following Locke directly, and psychoanalysts or dynamic psychotherapists, who are following him indirectly via Freudian influences, pretend to know how to correct conscious, nonconscious, or unconscious thinking.

However, just as the Athenian youth and the Israeli Holocaust survivor may be harmed by other factors besides sophists and philosophical counselors—the former, for example, by Socrates's misleading questions and the latter by an insensitive psychotherapist—the melancholy of Locke's or Freud's "stuck" mourner may have other explanations. He may, for example, feel hopeless and depressed because he does not think he can cope with other problems without the support of the person he lost. Failing to see new ways of coping is not necessarily a matter of flawed reasoning. Some say it is a lack of imaginative or creative thinking, which are matters of intuition rather than reason. I believe that it is a matter of going beyond the horizon that is determined by tacit, unexplored, presuppositions.

We Know How to Educate Humanity

Platonian censorship has been practiced intentionally by some totalitarian states and by religious and other institutions, including, perhaps, psychiatric hospitals and some schools for the "Ψ" professions. It has probably been practiced unintentionally by all kinds of "agents of socialization" and "centers of power" in liberal environments, including modern academic departments of "Φ" people. Yet (if we ignore Plato) it was never a central declared philosophical position. In contrast, the prejudice that one gets "stuck" because one's way of thinking is flawed and needs correction is central in both psychotherapy and philosophy. It goes back to the ancient Greeks and the medieval developers of Aristotelian logic. As an educational ideal, however, the "amendment of the intellect" or "correction of the understanding," for practical as well as theoretical purposes, got a decisive impetus in the seventeenth century (Bacon, 2000; Spinoza, 1955; Locke, 1975). While Spinoza mainly inspired philosophers and Bacon influenced empirical scientists, Locke, as already said, was the grandfather of modern psychology. He was convinced that "unnatural associations of ideas" are responsible not only for (senseless) metaphysics, (stupid) parliamentary speeches and (silly) tea-party chats, but also madness, as in the abovementioned melancholic mourning. As a physician, and not merely a philosopher, he was among the pioneers of what would become psychiatry, on the one hand, and behaviorist psychotherapy, on the other hand. Moreover, his explanation of all those "follies" is the basis of the psychoanalytic theory of the unconscious and its "unnatural" associations. Although Freud's theory of mind is different from Locke's, the latter's idea of "correcting the understanding" is the basis of the psychoanalytic view.[5]

Locke was also among the first of modern philosophers to look for an explanation, in mundane terms, for the fact that humans, whom God had created good and reasonable, free and equal, live under unjust and unfree economic, social and political conditions. He was among the firsts to promote the ideas of a rational social contract (Locke, 1993), better education

(Locke, 2010) and tolerance (Locke, 1991) to amend that distressing reality.[6] Those facts are relevant not only to the story of liberalism (and the labor theory of economic value and therefore also political economy and socialism) but also, indirectly, to the development of psychotherapy. He inspired Rousseau, who, with his own conceptions of a social contract (Rousseau, 1997) and education (Rousseau, 1979) in turn inspired Kant.

Kant was less optimistic than Rousseau, and bequeathed to both Freud and Popper his beliefs concerning the temptations and interventions of the "animal," "instinctive," "not-unconditionally-rational" or otherwise "phenomenal" aspects of humans, but believed nevertheless that Enlightenment is the process of the "education of mankind" (Kant, 1999). That education was meant to create people who "dare to know" and think for themselves. However, in the nineteenth century, Comte and Hegel, inspired by theories of biological evolution, developed the Kantian educational idea into a theory of history, according to which it is the story of the development of the human Intellect (Comte) or Reason (Hegel), both on the personal and the sociopolitical level.[7]

Both assumed, however, that the process is not perfect; "residues" of former stages may remain and negatively interfere in the more advanced stages. Comte, the founder of the idea of a "corrective" sociology, relied on his very imperfect knowledge of "primitive" people and conferred his interest in speculative anthropology and myth-interpretation to Freud and Jung and their "corrective" psychologies. Hegel, whom Freud, under Brentano's influence, deeply despised,[8] relied on what he assumed about the childish psychology and "unhappy consciousness" of "the Jew," who "refuses to develop" and accept Christianity and "its" Hegelian idea of the immanence of God (and Satan) in the world and in the personal soul (Hegel, 2018). Unlike Comte, Hegel did not conceive of philosophy in programmatic terms, did not share the conviction that positive science was the highest authority, and did not believe that former worldviews become obsolete. He thought that former views, with their corresponding opposites, are "canceled by being elevated" as partial aspects in higher philosophical syntheses that are gradually more comprehensive and more explicitly rational. His relevance to the story I am trying to tell here is in the reactions that his influential theory (or its re-interpretations by some of his followers, among them "left Hegelians" and Marxists) stimulated. More precisely, it is in the reactions it evoked among opponents who did not share the belief in the evolution of either Intellect or Reason, and did not accept the political and moral values that were common to the Enlightenment legacy in all its versions. The heterogeneous counter-camp included conservatives, defenders of religious traditions, and believers in the intuitive wisdom of customs, folktales, dreams, myths, religious imagery, poetry, and art, as well as thinkers who claimed to rediscover and revive alternatives to what they considered the "degenerate" dominant culture in their "forgotten cultural roots." It included local patriots as well as ethnic nationalists who considered themselves the best representatives of a larger and mostly remote "race" and fought against the "alienating" influence of "foreign" elements in their neighborhood. It included opponents of "modern materialism" as well as ancient, allegedly rabbinical, teachings. It also included elitist individualists, who sought to distinguish themselves from the "masses." Some of them were pessimists and looked for consolation in artistic experience; some longed for personal religious experiences, while others were utterly anti-religious, rejected traditional religious ideals, and believed in "loving one's fate" and self-overcoming. Some were interested in theories of knowledge and expressed insightful reservations regarding the methodological claims of philosophers of science and the partisans of explicit, clear rationality. Some sought alternative ways to wisdom, appealing to the "intuitive," "unconscious," "collective subconscious," "mystical," and "magical." They looked for insights in the words of ancient Greeks or Indians, in voices heard in dreams and in interpretations of the "true meaning" of "Being" that is supposed to be found in the etymologies of words of certain language families, or secrets about "subjectivity" hidden behind syntactic rules of a local dialect.[9] On this background grew the counter-Enlightenment version of history, according to which modernity is the end of a degenerative process in which "intellectuality" and "alien" or otherwise inadequate morality and political conceptions oppresses both individuals and cultures. The pretension to "educate mankind" and "mend" ways of thinking was not abandoned, but the aim was to correct the alleged damages of the dominant traditions of the Western world.

"Depth psychotherapy" was born in departments of psychiatry, not in departments of philosophy. But the founding fathers (later joined by contributors of other genders) of the various schools within it were children of their time, and studied philosophy, at least at some stages in the process of their professional formation. Some of them also read challenging philosophical texts that were not part of the syllabus, but were, perhaps, relevant to their personal orientation or cultural identification. They were acquainted with the positivistic approach, intrigued by its attempts to understand "primitive cultures" or explain away religion, and provoked by anti-positivist writers. The conversations they held in their circles and the theories they developed testify not only to such philosophical influences, but also a readiness to take upon themselves, in the "talking cures"—and the talking in their circles about the cures—more than the treatment of psychiatric disturbances. They wanted to take on also the treatment of the Freudians called "neurotics," that is, ordinary people "stuck" in their life problems, and, more: they wanted to explain social, cultural, and political phenomena in terms of those "neuroses." They wanted to replace philosophers and take on the "education of mankind." However, both the aims of that education and its methods have been, as I have just said, subject to philosophical debate throughout history.

Mythological Origin

The depth psychologists were psychiatrists. Their academic education fostered their critical attitude toward the religious traditions of their families of origin. Psychotherapists of later generations came to psychotherapy not only from medical or scientific psychological disciplines but also from social work and other frameworks, which were, to an extent, continuation of religiously sponsored activities of charity, nursing and education of the poor, and an unacknowledged continuation of some elements of religious legacies. I want to discuss two of them:

Therapists as Erinyes

I heard some psychoanalysts and social workers declare that experiencing pain is necessary for a cure. This astonished me. The position that painful treatments may be necessary if one wants to be cured is widely acknowledged in philosophical as well as medical circles, but the claim that the *pain is the curing agent* is not. I have heard of esoteric psychotherapists who encourage patients to scream their pain or anger "out of their system," but even they do not claim that the pain is the cure. I know that some pedagogues believe that suffering forges bodies as well as characters and that painful punishment improves learning. But the forging factor is the effort, not the pain, and the painful punishment is not supposed to do the job if the victim does not understand it as a response to his behavior, or at least its consequence. Some magicians and alternative medicine people believe in homeopathic principles—curing the same by the same, although for them, the sameness holds even if it is just symbolic or in small doses, unfelt by the patient. These observations led me to wonder whether there might be traces of religion in the education of the above-mentioned therapists. Among the religious attitudes to pain are the following: painful exercises as training the soul to ascetic habits or as preparation for the soul's special mystical experiences; self-flagellation as symbolic self-identification with a suffering God or saint; suffering as an effective detergent for whitening the dark stains of transgressions, and suffering as atonement for sins (usually, as scapegoats know, the sins of others) or, according to some ancient beliefs and newer kabbalistic versions, as restoration of a disrupted cosmic order caused by wrong human actions or a failure to do the right ones. It seems to me that the last one is the most relevant. I will translate, as follows. Thebes (or the soul) is stricken by a plague (mental disturbance) and Oedipus, not Freud's but Sophocles' (the patient or trainee), who is an aggressive person, angry with the parents who abandoned him, should suffer in order to realize that Laios (apparently an anonymous rival) and Jocasta (apparently a loving stranger), were his (humiliating and abandoning) father and mother. He did something very wrong to the former, and something atrocious with the latter. He should realize what he really did and feel the pain of remorse. Moreover, he should be humiliated, abandoned, and shamed. Only if this is done will Thebes be liberated from the plague. The psychological explanation: The anger of the patient helps him to avoid pain. But he will not be cured without feeling the pain.

I asked other experts for their opinions: Some psychiatrists told me that reviving repressed pain does more harm than good. Some psychotherapists who treat victims of violence said that in the victims' first reactions, there is usually both anger and the pain of humiliation, and that in their opinion, it is healthier to be angry at the aggressor than to dwell on the pain of humiliation. Freud, who believed that his patients were just fantasizing, did not try to reevoke emotions but interpreted allegedly reevoked wishes. He seems, moreover, to have thought that aggression is not always a simulation of something else, and sometimes it is even an appropriate reaction.

Some critics of dynamic psychotherapy say that therapists sometimes wrongly interpret their patient's justified anger against them as merely "transference" of other emotions toward other persons. I decided to leave the professional quarrels to the professionals.

In my unprofessional opinion the return of *repressed myths* may be even more harmful than that of repressed unpleasant memories, and I believe, humbly, that humans, who, unlike the Erinyes, know nothing about fate and destiny but believe in causality, do not really know which of the numerous sinful transgressions caused the specific cosmic disorder, which viruses were responsible for the plague in Thebes or what are the causes of "mental disturbances." Such causal misconceptions, reiterated in some of Heidegger's and Arndt's explanations of the horrors of World War II as well as in Jung's and Roger's explanation of psychological problems as the result of a failure to be authentic, remind me of a story: An unmarried pregnant woman came to the religious guide of her community and blamed him for her state: She drank from the blessed potion that he had given her barren married sister. "My daughter," he said, "to become pregnant you also need a man." "That is no excuse," she said, "you know that there are enough men in our town."

People say that one should not laugh at pain-inflicting divinities. But one can challenge psychotherapists, who should not inflict pain even if according to their confused causal conceptions it is the cure.

Self-Inflicted Alzheimer's Disease

Some other psychoanalysts and social workers seem to believe that their students have to join their sect with very clean minds. Some of my colleagues, who had tried, in their middle age, to be retrained as psychotherapists, told me that their supervisors told them to "forget everything" that they knew. That was not just a way of saying that psychotherapy demands an approach that is different from the academic one. It was a sort of order: "I am not able to teach you if you may be reminded of anything." Those supervisors probably do not know that Plato and Descartes have already tried that approach, but were left with thousands of unexamined doxas. As psychotherapists they were supposed to know that the only practical ways to forget everything is either to get Alzheimer's disease in an advanced state or to repress all memories. One cannot, however, rely on a disease; and what has been repressed may return, as was suspected by some churches and regimes with their inquisitorial institutions against forced "*conversos*."

So why do those supervisors make such demands? The only teachers who seriously demand that a student "forget everything he knows" are those who prepare novices for initiation into their sects or monastic orders, and missionaries who try to convert pagans: They really believe that what they are going to teach is important enough to "forget everything" for its sake, and they ignore that what they offer rests on many pagan presuppositions. No supervisor's knowledge is that important, and the demand is absurd. I do not say this just because some of my colleagues who are entering training after spending years in other careers are philosophers, but because I believe that the wisdom that a "simple" shoemaker manages to accumulate in forty years of life may contribute something of value to his future work as a psychotherapist, and his questions, based on his experience, may show supervisors that they can learn a thing or two from him.

Maybe that is the secret but true reason for their impolite demand. A bad teacher is dogmatic, envious, and afraid of "resistant" students. The patients deserve to be treated by students of good teachers. A good teacher can cope with students from a variety of backgrounds, and help them (and himself) to integrate his and their knowledge and doubts to new ways of thinking, from new perspectives, with wider horizons.

Notes

1. For that reason, I believe that the title of Lou Marinoff's book *Plato, Not Prozac* (Marinoff, 1999) is misleading. It should be *Plato, not Freud.* Marinoff, like some other philosophical counselors as well as Freud and his followers, does indeed criticize the attempt to find solutions for life's problems in drugs, but his main controversy is with those who believe that the solution is psychotherapy. In some translations of his book the antidrug position reflected in the title is therefore justly attenuated to "More Plato, Less Prozac" since Marinoff is aware, as every philosophical counselor and psychotherapist should be, that in some cases "talking therapy" of any kind is insufficient for reducing suffering.

2. See detailed explanations with regard to some of them in Appendix C.

3. However, when one pretends that his theory is not just a philosophical reflection but a more or less scientific explanation of facts, one should also propose criteria for empirically identifying the alleged facts and making empirically testable hypotheses. That is problematic when many of the relevant facts are supposed to be nonconscious instincts and drives, assumed experiences of babies, unconscious thoughts, repressed memories, and implicit intentions. One should also consider alternative explanations, at least of facts that are beyond dispute, from a factual rather than merely philosophical perspective: theories about cognition, for example, or emotions, personality, sexual conduct or social behavior that were developed by researchers who do not accept a priori their depth-psychological commitments.

4. Adler favored a kind of philosophical reflection on the patient's worldview, and Jung let patients play with the double aspects of the archetypes that appear their dreams. For limitations of space, I will not dwell here on the question of why the former is not sufficiently philosophical and the latter, like all claims to understand messages of the "unconscious self", the "collective unconscious" or the "immanent God" or "Wisdom" - that are transmitted through dreams, myths or symbols - is not philosophical at all (although among the pretenders were some famous philosophers). Psychoanalysts too do not always play according to their methodological rules. Yet one should not confuse the semi-philosophical seminars or lectures that they give with their interactions with patients in clinical dialogues.

5. See Appendix C

6. Some historians remark that as a political person he supported slavery and schools for poor children where they would work and learn to serve (Farr, 2008). This is perhaps true, but Locke was certainly not the only Enlightenment partisan who failed to apply its universal principles universally. Before accusing those liberals of flawed reasoning or hypocritical self-interest, and jumping, like Foucault, to the conclusion that an Islamic revolution offers (the Iranians) a better alternative than an imperfect liberal democracy to the Shah's regime (Afari and Anderson, 2005, 203–9), we should remind ourselves that, whatever are our explicit principles, our horizons may be limited by our own unexplored values and beliefs. By challenging those presuppositions one can enable the widening of horizons.

7. See Appendix B.

8. Freud refers to various famous philosophers in his writing in order to justify his approach to "forbidden" subjects, such as the unconscious (allegedly the Kantian Ding-an-sich) and sexuality (allegedly the Platonic eros). My assumptions about his philosophical sources and positions are independent of them, and are based on several things: his correspondence with his friend during the time he was attending Brentano's lectures (Freud, 1992), the positivistic ideas of his teachers of science, his acquaintance with Brentano's thought, Freud's own ideas with regard to thinking processes, and his remarks about Nietzsche and his counter-Nietzschean theory of the origin of morality.

9. I avoid mentioning precise references because my first encounters with that world was through a mixture of erudite messages, dogmas spread in fiction, and the prejudices of nostalgic emigrants, and also because I believe that it was precisely such a pell-mell of input that enabled the growth of many counter-Enlightenment political ideologies and theories of psychological "correction." See Noll (1997) and Sternhell (2006).

Conclusion

Relevance to Academic Philosophy

I have insisted that theoretical philosophy is relevant to philosophical counseling and other forms of practical philosophy. Some promoters of practical philosophy claim that, on the contrary, the latter is relevant to the former. I would like to examine some positions that are lurking behind this claim and see which of them deserves attention.

The most obvious one is that academic philosophy is not only too abstract, too general, tedious, and boring, it also fails to deal with "the important issues." In a similar line of argument, teenagers and shopkeepers often complain that the mathematics which they must learn in school is irrelevant to their lives. Yet no philosopher would suggest that professional mathematicians stop exploring mathematical logic because teenagers and shopkeepers do not need it for their calculations. In reality, many philosophers understand that such abstract studies contribute to the creation of devices that permit teenagers and shopkeepers to forget even the little mathematics they know (and even those who consider calculations on any level less important than philosophizing, recognize the importance of such a contribution). According to the same logic, the importance of philosophizing demands that it be applied to important things, not on the trivial and casuistic. The problem, however, is that there is no agreement about the identity of "important things," and in fact one cannot know in advance which of the conclusions reached by studies that seem tedious and irrelevant might be helpful in resolving difficulties related to "important things." I remind you of counselees from chapter 4, who were "stuck" in their effort to find answers to their questions, and the help they received from philosophical "unimportant" discussions about the limits of knowledge or the meaninglessness of certain questions. Such discussions enabled them to "move on."[1]

Other positions recognize that what seems most important to, say, Hadot, is not philosophically most important to Heidegger or Wittgenstein, although they too wanted philosophers to live according to their convictions and not just talk about them.

According to one of those positions, philosophers should ignore what seems important to thinkers they consider isolated and eccentric and deal instead with issues that concern "ordinary people" in their everyday lives. But although moral and political philosophers as well as philosophers of knowledge or action may be eccentric, and live in academic ivory towers or secluded retreats, they do deal with issues that affect ordinary people. The problem is that they sometimes do so on levels that are largely inaccessible to others. Their preferred level of abstraction may be too high, and the particularity of their philosophical jargon may impede understanding (and deter even trained philosophers that do not belong to their circle). Yet there may be reasons that justify the language they use and the methods they employ. A solution might be to remember that their works can be translated, so to speak, and made more accessible. This would allow "ordinary people," with or without the mediation of teachers or counselors, to judge for themselves whether they are reasonable and relevant to their concerns. Thus, they would be enabled to make their own judgments, independent of the biased interpretations that politicians, religious guides, and others might give them.[2]

According to another position, what is important is not "academic generalities" but one's personal perspective and interpretation of philosophical questions, which is sometimes referred to as "personal meaning." Personal meaning in this sense is, of course, important, but the academic generality in question may be personally meaningful to the philosopher who made it.

Its meaningfulness to others is not an inherent characteristic of the work but depends on the individual's perceptions and judgments. I must admit that there are many philosophical texts, created under the pressure of publish or perish, whose "academic generalities" are probably not very meaningful even to their authors. But that is an institutional problem which is not specific to academic philosophy.

Finally, some practical philosophers maintain that "ordinary people" have philosophical concerns which have not been explored by academic philosophers. In this case the experience of practical philosophers is indeed relevant to academic philosophy, as is the emergence of new philosophical questions in other practical fields.

My personal experiences in counseling have taught me to think of some philosophical issues from new perspectives. I hope I have demonstrated this in my analyses of cases and in my debates with colleagues and scholars in other fields.

My experience has also made me more sensitive to deceptive or harmful misuses of philosophical texts and ideas, whether by practical philosophers or by psychologists, politicians, or gurus. This is not just a curiosity which academic philosophers may or may not choose to address I believe it is a moral and cultural problem. It should be discussed by philosophers in academic as well as practical circles.

Notes

1. I could remind you of Heidegger and his reliance on the etymology of verbs cognate to the English 'be' in other Indo-European languages and his assumptions about their common protolanguage in his speculations about the worldview of the primordial speakers of that language in his analysis of the "true meaning" of Being and Truth (Heidegger, 1959). Practically oriented philosophers of language have, however, taught me to look for the variety of uses of any given word and not for an alleged common meaning across different languages. That is one of the reasons I do not refer my students and counselees, "stuck" in their concerns, to explorations of words in other linguistic families which are sometimes translatable to the English 'be,' and tell them, as an antidote to some of Heidegger's biases, to try to discover other meanings of Being and Truth that are, perhaps, even "deeper." In my efforts to enable them to "move on," I sometimes find that it is more beneficial to refer to philosophical studies that from a Heideggerian point of view are "merely epistemological" or "just intellectual."

2. The interpretations given by the latter, however biased, demonstrate their relevance to the concerns of nonphilosophers.

Appendix A

Wisdom: Knowing When to Rationally Decide to Be Nonrational

Some academic readers might get the impression that I am interested only in the rational aspects of philosophy, and moreover, that I prefer the analytic orientation of philosophers in the Anglo-American-Australian world to those of nonanalytic continental European philosophers. This appendix is addressed mainly to such readers. I believe that it may interest other readers as well.

The impression is mistaken. Of course, I believe that philosophy should be rational. Moreover, I am convinced that the insights of some analytic philosophers (which are often ignored by philosophical counselors) may be as relevant to dialogues with counselees as the ideas of philosophers of other orientations. The existentialists and phenomenologists are more concerned than the analytic philosophers with lived experiences; Epictetus, Spinoza, Schopenhauer, Kierkegaard, and Nietzsche are clearly more interested in attitudes toward the hazards of life. Socrates, Aristotle, Epicurus, Montaigne, and Erasmus focus more on questions of happiness, virtue and the good life; Saint Augustine, Pascal, Kierkegaard, Bergson and Heidegger pay more attention to aspects of experience to which conceptual explorations seem irrelevant, and seem to be closer to the Buddhist opinion that rational considerations are insufficient or inadequate for coping with human suffering or existential anxieties. But this is a kind of a category mistake: Whatever is personally "really important" in the eyes of the so-called analytic philosopher, he or she prefers to deal with it *philosophically* on a logical, methodological, or linguistic *meta-philosophical level*—or explain on that level why it is not a matter that one "can talk (philosophically) about."

Furthermore, I think that for some purposes, for example, *methodological and educational* ones, the *clear style* of some analytic philosophers in the English-speaking academic *milieu* (logical positivists, pragmatists, philosophers of ordinary language and those who call themselves philosophers of the common sense) is preferable to the complicated formulations of many past German speaking philosophers (like Kant, Hegel, Marx, Husserl, Heidegger and even Gadamer, Jaspers or Habermas). It is also preferable (here again—irrespectively of the importance of the message) to the nebulous linguistic acrobatics of some contemporary French philosophers, who have abandoned the "Cartesian clarity" of their ancestors.

In some chapters I deal with philosophy and counseling mainly on the *meta-philosophical level*, and discussions on that level are always rational, and should be as clear as possible. However, this does not mean that my dialogues *with the counselees*, which takes place mostly *on other levels of philosophizing*, are on issues that interest analytic philosophers. It also does not mean that the options I may suggest as alternatives to the counselees' initial assumptions are always borrowed from that philosophical tradition, or from the so-called continental rationalist tradition, or from philosophical texts. It certainly does not mean that I believe that rationality is reducible to some logical calculi, algorithms for meaning analysis, commonsensical obviousness, or methodological considerations of positivist philosophers.

Levels and Kinds of Rationality

My approach is "biased" by epistemology; like most other philosophers, I am suspicious of unjustified claims to knowledge. Some philosophers however *seem* to give priority to other issues. Aristotle, for example, attacked Plato's claim that the good management of political issues is a matter of theoretical *episteme*. He maintained that in temporal and changeable fields, like the field of politics, which might be involved with contrasting wishes and a variety of opinions—*sophrosyne*—practical prudence—is more useful. Hegel, who believed that spiritual processes take place in nature as well as in individual minds and general history, seemed to prefer analyses of the "thinking" process" to epistemology. He attacked metaphysical agnostics for their reliance on the empiricism and "formal logic" of the "positive" sciences, and insisted that only "dialectical logic" pushes the development of Reason in nature, history and the individual mind, and only it leads to the higher and more comprehensive kind of knowledge—the "philosophical *science* of the Spirit" and its progress toward self-consciousness. Neither Bergson nor Whitehead believed in Hegelian dialectics, but, like Hegel, they criticized some of the philosophical presuppositions of the then-prevalent theories of knowledge. To Bergson and Whitehead, those theories, which were supposed to discover the mental basis, or underlying philosophical principles, of any scientific knowledge, actually just reflected current (Newtonian) scientific conceptions. Both believed in philosophical "quantic leaps" into a new conception of reality, or of science, or of the exploring subject's mind. Whitehead believed that such leaps are enabled by a special kind of rationality—a "creative reason"—while Bergson spoke of "philosophical creative intuitions." Both aimed at understanding which does justice to more aspects of "concrete reality." Marx, in another vein, claimed that philosophy can explain history only retrospectively, and that its theories as well as scientific explanations, are ideologically distorted. He claimed to have laid the basis for a new kind of scientific knowledge, a "dialectical materialism," which can discover the "laws of movement" of history, predict the creation of conditions for historical change and guide the revolutionary vanguard. William James and Heidegger liked neither Marx's "materialism" nor his "dialectics," let alone his political ideals, but shared his practical orientation, and believed that a scientific attitude to the world, whatever are its preconceptions, is only one of the modes of experiencing the world (or being in the world), and not necessarily the wisest or the most meaningful mode. In some of the other modes, other truths (or at least the truth about Truth) are revealed, and if one follows Heidegger's logic, the "being of Being," or the "Being of beings," is better understood. To this partial list one can add Averroes, Maimonides, and Saint Aquinas, who believed that certain metaphysical issues are beyond the capacity of humans to comprehend, but one should have faith that the superior Intellect of God is capable of understanding the enigmatic revealed truths, which are recorded in the holy scriptures of their respective religions, and dissolve all their apparent paradoxes. Both Saint Augustine and Pascal can be added to this list, despite their many differences. Both were convinced that no human knowledge—whether philosophical and whether medical or psychological—can cure humans of their sinful and unhappy nature, and both insisted on the need for Divine Grace. Both believed that Grace follows from Divine Love and Will rather than Intellect, and considered such an assertion a matter of faith rather than knowledge. Both believed that the test for one's faith is one's "love for Jesus" and one's living according to the practical implications of that love rather than one's *arguments* in favor of such an attitude. Yet, whether or not their positions relied on their mystical experiences, their conversations with spiritual guides or their psychological biographies, they claimed to *know* at least one thing: having faith in those Christian dogmas with regards to possible salvation in the future are *already helpful to the faithful in his present life*. Briefly then, all these *seemingly* not epistemology-minded philosophers were in fact epistemologically active. They were suspicious of certain conceptions of knowledge and suggested alternative sources of *knowledge* as *more reliable* than others, for certain *purposes*.

Whatever were their specific opinions and arguments, and whatever are the opinions of other philosophers about them, all those philosophers were *reasoning*, on a *rational meta-level*, in favor of their not necessarily rational positions, and have thus contributed, each in his own way, to the philosophical understanding of certain facets of knowledge. It is perhaps clearest in the case of Pascal, a mathematician and scientist with an excellent "esprit de géométrie," who had a lot to say in praise of the more intuitive "esprit de finesse" in the domain of human affairs, but who also insisted on the need, in matters or religious faith, to accept the *authority of others*—as historical witnesses of past events (or Divine revelations as recorders in the Holy Scriptures) or as "inspired" interpreters of revealed truths—as well as listen to whispers of the "heart." His religious feelings and experiences had led Pascal to declare in his *Memorandum*[1] that his God is the "God of Abraham, Isaac and Jacob," and not the "God of philosophers." Yet he calculated, according to the logic of the mathematical theory of probability, that it is worthwhile to believe in an afterlife and to behave accordingly: even if the degree of certainty is minimal, [and the price of nonrationality is very high for blind rationalists], the utility of such faith is greater than that of its negation, as the expected value of the prize—infinite happiness in the eternity of paradise [for those who, thanks to Divine Grace, already have that face]—is infinite. Well, on the meta-level, where rationality is allowed to acknowledge its limits, some "esprit d'ironie" is also permissible. I may perhaps add to the list the philosopher to whom I owe the idea of rationality acknowledging its limits, Kierkegaard. Although he was interested in *meaningfulness* and not in another kind of understanding, he too sometimes spoke, in his idiosyncratic ironic style, on a rational meta-level.

Arguing on a rational meta-level for an attitude that is not necessarily rational on a lower level is sometimes paradoxical, but it is often coherent. There is no paradox in a rational decision not to waste one's limited resources on meticulous utilitarian calculations, in light of ambiguous, uncertain and insufficient data, when the issue at stake is unimportant in the eyes of the decision maker, or, on the contrary, when it is much more meaningful for him than any utilitarian considerations that might occur to him once he has decided to decide. Therefore, psychologists investigating human rationality sometimes recommend following one's intuition or just guessing rather than getting entangled in time-consuming deliberations with insufficient information.[2] Similarly, the philosophical counselor may rationally decide, on the strategic meta-level, to suggest to the hesitant counselee a variety of nonrational options instead of remaining "stuck" in their insoluble choosing dilemmas, like the starving Buridan's ass in front of the two piles of hay.

Unlike some advice-givers, I do not suggest to the "ass" alternative solutions on the concrete problem level, such as arbitrarily picking one pile or following his sense of smell. Nor do I suggest that he stop seeking the best choice. He is not really an ass, and if he is not in immediate danger, I invite him to take a bit of distance for a while, and deal with his specific dilemmas on a higher level: to think of them as a particular instance of a general philosophical dilemma. I tell him that there are alternative ways to deal with it. My own choices of alternatives depend on the situations as well as my beliefs about the counselee. I may suggest that he explore whether to treat his difficulty like Plato (insisting on the "theoretically best solution") or like Aristotle ("being satisfied with a reasonable practical solution"), or, alternatively, I may confront him with the choice between Spinoza's approach ("do not be an ass . . . a rational man does not hang himself"[3]) and one of Pascal's ideas (either "it is not a moment for a geometric mood, have faith in God's Grace and trust your intuitive guess" or "be rational: however big is the expected value of the best choice, do not forget to take into account the chances of not surviving to enjoy it"). Although my Hegelian approach—relating to the specific case as a "concrete universal"—may seem incompatible with Sartre's conviction that choices are always made in specific situations, and there are no universal principles, values or formulas that can dictate them, I may suggest the exploration of two different opinions of Sartre. One of them is the one just mentioned, and the other attributes to the hesitant "donkey" a "mauvaise foi": he deceives himself in believing that his problem is the difficulty in finding the best choice, while actually he is trying to avoid the responsibility of making any choice (and as not deciding is itself a matter of choice; he, and not "the circumstances," is responsible for his own starvation). I may also invite the counselee to explore his dilemma in light of the difference between Sartre's view with regard to freedom and responsibility and, say, Nietzsche's attitude toward the courage to dare and make mistakes. I may, when relevant, invite him to consider the existentialist option of an "authentic" choice versus Hume's recommendation to trust the wisdom of the dominant custom. (When talking to counselees I try to present less academic candidates, and use real or fictional paradigmatic cases within their personal and cultural horizons.) In any case, I do not pretend to know what "really" motivates the assumed "procrastination." Whatever are my assumptions, I encourage the counselee to start the process of *self-exploration* by suggesting that *he* examine several philosophical options, some of which may correspond to my assumed understanding of his initial attitude, while others might suggest alternatives. Thus, when we come back from the general to the particular case, and he deliberately chooses to follow the nonrational sense of smell or the unexamined custom of "donkeys," he is still choosing on a rational practical level, as the choice to rely on smelling is not made by smelling, and the choice to imitate other donkeys is not just imitating.

Wisdom

Wisdom, if we ignore the mystical meanings that some thinkers seek to give it, is like irony and humor; it is related to the ability to navigate back and forth between different levels of rationality, different attitudes to reality and different frames of reference. It is also related, unlike irony and humor, to the ability to appreciate the reliability and relevance of available resources and administrate their allocation to different uses, practical as well as theoretical, in light of certain values and for the sake of preferred ideals.[4] Briefly, it is related to the morally good, as we tend to distinguish between the "wisdom" of the just and the "cunning" of the wicked even when they demonstrate the same cognitive and emotional abilities. In the same way we tend to distinguish between the "rhetoric" of a speaker whom we consider honest and benevolent, and the "demagogy" of the one who seems to us a malignant liar although both seem to be skilled persuaders.

I owe the last distinction to Aristotle and Pascal. Those who speak of "wisdom" in a mystical mood are not necessarily "demagogues," but by using the term as a rhetorical device they claim to have had a certain "lived experience"—an "intellectual intuition," hearing an "inner voice," experiencing "Divine revelation," and the like, which gives them special access to sources of knowledge or understanding that "merely intellectual" philosophers do not have. However, no rationalist philosopher is "merely intellectual," and as Pascal has wisely argued, philosophizing does not lead to revelations and faith, and a special subjective experience is not a sufficient reason for making claims to *philosophical* knowledge or understanding. From that point of view, philosophical counselors (and psychologists) who promise quasi-mystical *experiences* of "wisdom" can be suspected of conceptual confusion no less than political demagogues.

Intuition

The term 'intuition' has nowadays one common *intuitive* meaning. It is to *somehow know* that so-and-so is the case, or how to do this or that, *without* the subject's *knowing how* he knows it.

Various thinkers have various theories about it. When the psychologist of rational behavior speaks of an "intuitive decision," he assumes that there are innate behavioral tendencies common to the individual's species. They are supposed to be acquired in evolutionary processes, as the best reaction—on the average of a great number of cases—for the survival of the species (or its genes), and their activation is supposed to be based on simple nonconscious cognitive processes. Biologically, intuitive choices are not necessarily the best for the survival of a specific individual. Neither are they, statistically, the best choices in the particular cases where conscious, situation-specific considerations and more complicated calculation may lead to a better choice. But, from the perspective of such a psychologist, they are neither arbitrary guesses nor enlightened insights. When Bergson speaks of "philosophical intuition" he means an insight that leads one to ask questions and look for solutions "outside of the box" of the dominant philosophical view. He believes that is one of the forms of the "élan vital" and/or the "creative energy" that is also responsible for biological evolution, but he does not pretend to explain how novelties occur, or how to promote them. Bergson also talked of the "immediate data of consciousness" in contrast to the empiricists' supposedly elementary "data" in "spatialized time" which, to his mind, are "mediated," that is, already elaborated by notions borrowed from physical mechanics and other irrelevant fields. Some philosophers believe accordingly that phenomenology, which, like Bergson (2001), is concerned with "inner time" and tries to explore experiences independently of "mechanistic" scientific psychology, deals with "immediate data." Therefore, they interpret "intuition" as Descartes's "immediate seeing." It is true that earlier Husserl (1982) *hoped* to arrive at "intuition of essences" [*Wesensschau*], but he expected it to be the fruit of meticulous phenomenological exercises and abstractions. In any case, Husserl aims during his entire intellectual career were very different from the program about which I recently heard, of someone who suggests that we explore "tasting as such" an object "as such" (the person spoke of the experience of eating a tomato, uncooked, without salt or salad). The early Husserl was interested, like Plato, in the "essences" of "ideas" (or meanings") that have *philosophical importance*. Although he would later turn from mathematical objects, scientific concepts, the "transcendental subject" and his "cogitations" of "intentional objects" to "meanings" that are relevant on the intersubjective level of everyday life [*Umwelt*], I believe that he, like Plato, would differentiate between the general issues and concrete cases. Plato (if I remember correctly—in *Theaetetus*) distinguished between, movement or time, change or matter, on the one hand, and mud, on the other hand: In his conceptual scheme it meant the difference between being sure that there is an eternal Idea of the former, but an inability to decide whether it is reasonable to believe that there is an eternal Idea of the latter. Husserl believed that phenomenological studies can answer many philosophical questions by dealing with the perception-use of an object even if that object in the case study is just a tomato; but the question "what is the immediately seen "tomato-ness" of a tomato for the eater who respects the tomato's uniqueness as a being whose truth is always just emerging" was not among them. But, whether "seeing," "hearing" or "savoring," this is a wrong interpretation of Husserl's methodology, which does not consist in "intuiting immediate data," but rather involves gradual "reductions" (and other explorative acts) from regular "gross" experiences, with all the "mixtures" and "foreign" influences that might intervene in their formation (to one of those influences, the "emotional tone," I shall return in the next subsection). It is also a misinterpretation of Bergson (2001), who was attending to the "immediate data" in order to argue that their qualities or meanings are constantly changing during the experience of them in "non-spatialized time"). The psychologist Jung perhaps also influences those philosophers. Jung spoke of "intuition" as an alternative to the more "intellectualized" sense perception. He believed that it is free of "conventional" formulas and theories and may therefore give direct access to unconscious truths (an oxymoron from Bergson's as well as Husserl's perspectives) with regards to the "true self," and with it to the alleged inherited universal or cultural "archetypes." Sometimes, depending on Jung's religious mood and some of his less holy concerns, one may gain access to the "voice of God" (see Appendix C). Pascal, whose religiosity was very different from that of Jung, had "outside-the-box" religious experiences, and his ability to think "creatively" has been demonstrated in his discoveries and inventions in mathematics, physics and related domains. He did not think of intuition as immediate "seeing" or semi-instinctive reaction and understood the term "intuitive knowledge" to mean the ability to think in the "wide" rather than the "deep" way. That is, he thought of intuitive knowledge as the fruit of *tacit* inferences from many common, non-systematic, and unexamined presuppositions rather than explicit deductions, made with "geometrical" rigor, from one assumption (or one system of clear and coherent assumptions). Pascal did not claim that it was a "deeper," "wider," or "higher" alternative to "mathematical" knowledge; he thought that in certain fields thinking "mathematically" is irrelevant or insufficient. The notion of mathematics has changed somewhat since Pascal's time, and it is applicable, to a certain extent, in the domain of human affairs, as is done, for example, by psychologists inquiring about human rationality, but one still needs a lot of Pascal's intuitive thinking to understand people or social facts.

The Jungian idea of attending to intuitions and dreams might be as the diagonal opposite to the Platonic conception of "intellectual intuition" of the ensemble of the eternal Forms, which the accomplished philosopher (if there is any) is expected to experience at the end of his philosophical ascent through rational dialectic. In fact, it is a variation on a theme of perfect non-empirical knowledge, where the most personal (and the most tribal) replaces the universal, the unconscious replaces the celestial, the "true self" and his "conscience" replaces the "Idea of the good" and the inherited "archetypes" replace the other Ideas (which according to Plato are celestial and yet innate in the soul). The way from the Platonic pole to the Jungian pole could pass through religious empiricism, which assumed, like Berkeley, that after death, when the soul is liberated from the "eyes of sinful flesh" and the dependency on empirical information, the Just or Graced can "see" the eternal Forms directly with "the eyes of the spirit." It could pass through German Idealism. It could pass through mystic elaborations of Neo-Platonic, Gnostic, Cabbalistic and Theosophic ideas. Whatever was Jung's actual way, he followed the theosophic thinkers and added some Indian notions, taken out, like their other notions, from their original contexts and the conceptual maps within which they make sense. The fusion of notions of different cultures can be sometimes interesting, fruitful, and influential; syncretic religions (which probably means all religions) excel in it. But before adopting "Far-eastern" conceptions of what "Europeans" call intuition into *philosophical* theories of knowledge, ask an Indian man what he thinks about what the "Westerners" call exercising yoga and ask a Chinese man his opinion of tai chi in American spas—and contemporary Western philosophers about Plato's idea of contemplating the world of *eternal* Ideas or Descartes's "intuitive *evidence*" with regards to "innate ideas" or Locke's reliance on directly experienced "simple ideas."

When I suggest to a counselee the option of relying on his intuition rather than trying to calculate the best option, I am talking to him like a modern Aristotelian, somewhere between Pascal and the above-mentioned psychologist. When I try to encourage the counselee to "get out of the box," as Bergson would have liked, I am not inviting him to think "intuitively." I am rather using techniques that are supposed to promote "creative" thinking. I prefer presenting the counselee with different philosophical approaches to the psychologists' promotion of associative thinking, or "brain storming" with a variety of unrelated ideas or interpretations, in Jung's style, of the counselee's dreams. I believe that my way involves the counselee in a rational self-exploration, which deals with his beliefs and values. Yet I may sometimes get information about the counselee by listening to his "intuitive," in the sense of nonreflective answers to my questions; I also learn from the nonvoluntary external expressions in his "body language." Sometimes he himself may know himself and his preferences a little better by attending to the proprio-sensations of his body, the "gut feelings," "the shoulders freed from the burden," the "whispering of the heart." Sometimes relying on the "intuitions" of his experienced spouse is wiser than listening to the opinions of those who, thanks to their degree in abstract knowledge and formal training, are supposed to be the experts. Sometimes his "insights" seem to me more "illuminated," and in any case more relevant, than the analyses of professional philosophers.

Emotions. Moods, Feelings, Sentiments, and "Spiritual Health"

Darwin believed that emotional *expressions* have survival advantage. They provide information to others about oneself and the environment: pain and signification of danger, pleasure and information about food, surprise and announcement of unexpected changes, anger and a threat of aggression. Darwin was perhaps aware that the physiological changes perceived by others as bodily expressions, which are reflected in all kinds of physiological tests, are often subjectively felt as inner states or occurrences in one's *body*. Some phenomenologists (I think of Merleau-Ponty and Nussbaum) and some philosophers of language who deal with the issue of "other minds," are aware that it is sometimes the problem of *not feeling the other's body with the other's body*. I have in mind psychologists and phenomenologists exploring emotions as well as Wittgenstein, Austin, or Wisdom arguing with partisans of introspection. Their observations have taught that, like any other *felt sensations*, "*proprio-sensations*" may, as in the famous Duck-rabbit optical illusion, be perceived differently on different occasions. Sometimes they are *perceived as* vague *mood*, and at other times as "feeling an emotion." The same proprio-sensations may be felt on one occasion as a *certain emotion toward a certain object* and on another occasion *as a feeling of different emotions toward the same or other objects*. The way in which they are *perceived* depends on context, mood, and perspective, as well as on past experiences and personal wishes and future expectations, and hints from others. In all cases it is a matter of *subjective interpretation* of the experience and not an immediate datum. The recommendations to attend to "gut feelings" or listen to the "heart" in contexts of difficult choices, where rational considerations are insufficient, presuppose that one does not know precisely what ones prefers, and the bodily feelings interpreted as attraction, repulsion, fear, or joy, which are raised by imagining the alternative options, may indicate to oneself what one "really wishes" or "does not really want." One may feel such inner experience as a "deeper" truth than is indicated to others by one's body "language." As information, it is often not more reliable, yet it is personal, and more relevant to one's ability to decide.

Changing Moods and Emotions

My interest, as a philosophical counselor, in emotions and moods, is not necessarily related to the clarification of "real" wishes or the detection of denied fears in contexts of difficult decisions. It may be related to the aim of changing the counselee's state of mind.

Many things can change a person's state of mind. Aristotle and some others believe that active expression of emotions, like crying, yelling, or laughing, "purges out" something (Freud would say that it purges the "energy charged in emotions"). Accordingly, there are some psychotherapists who encourage their patients to yell in order to "purge out" their pains or angers. Others, relying (mostly unknowingly) on other philosophers, for example Dewey (interpreting William James), encourages apathic or depressed patients to laugh; they believe that the corporeal behavior is the cause rather than the effect or expression of the state of mind. Both James (See Barrett, 2017, 161–62[5]) and Aristotle had in mind more sophisticated elaborations and applications of their insights. Aristotle himself applied his idea in his debate with Plato about the place of the arts, and in particular theatrical performances, in the good state. In *Poetics*, he explained that when the audience is actively experiencing the protagonists' fear or anger, the "excess" of those emotions is "purged-out," and therefore citizens who are allowed to enjoy theatrical performances are emotionally more moderate in their behavior. This might remind us of the ethologist Konrad Lorenz, who recommended (1966) discharging the excessive aggression of humans in sport, since nowadays most humans do little hunting and engage only occasionally in wars. However, Aristotle spoke of emotions not just as "drive energy" within the animated subject, but also as object-directed thoughts. He believed that the audience's identification with the protagonists involves *the ability to imagine the object-directed thinking of others*, even if those others are just mythological or fictive persons. Freud, whose teacher of philosophy admired Aristotle, borrowed from the latter the often-missed point of his book about jokes: the *corporeal* event of *laughter* not the *opinion* that the story or situation is funny—is one of the forms of a pleasant partial "discharge of the energy" of (repressed sexual or) aggressive wishes. His major idea regarding psychoanalytic treatment is also Aristotelian, albeit ironically. The analyzed subject is supposed to "work through" the obstructive emotional "memory traces" of his relations to the past objects of his wishes and emotions under the artificial and fictive conditions of the "transference." The analyst is the "object" that substitutes for the analysand's past objects, yet the atmosphere in the clinic is more moderate than the past dramas as they were imagined or interpreted by the child. However, the important thing, in Freud's eyes, is the ability to *reinterpret* the child's memories in an "adult way," a change that does not occur quickly, like the "catharsis" of the audience in the Athenian theatre but is supposed to happen slowly. I am not asking whether specific ideas discussed by Aristotle in his *Nicomachean Ethics* are also reflected in Freud's approach. *Nicomachean Ethics* (like Spinoza's *Ethics*) is addressed to a small elite, and is concerned with the character formation of the wise person. Freud, despite his talk about cures, was also interested in character formation (See Appendix C for more remarks about Freud). However, according to my conception of philosophy, philosophical counselors should not try to form character, and according to my acquaintance with the field s of education and the experience of counseling—they *cannot* do so even if they believe that they should and have all the time in the world. Yet I share Freud's conviction that philosophical ideas and reinterpretations of experience really *matter and may be relevant to "ordinary people*." I also share his realism: philosophers as well as psychoanalysts and philosophical counselors are not "extra-ordinary" persons.

My counselees, whether or not they are themselves professional philosophers or psychologists, sometimes complain about their emotional difficulties. Sometimes they are "stuck" in professional dilemmas or moral conflicts, and in consequence are in an emotional state of mind that obstructs their solution. So the question of how states of mind can be changed may still be relevant. The active exercises mentioned above, as well as psycho-dramas, have no more room in a philosophical *dialogue* than offering alcohol, psychiatric drugs, or meditation as mood-changers. (I mention them in order to express again my disagreement with the claim of some philosophers that bodily changes are irrelevant to the mental.)

Listening to the counselee's complaints and trying to understand them, which sometimes is done more effectively by friends than by counselors, may attenuate acute states and is, to my mind, an indispensable part of the counseling process. Good listening can create interpersonal "rapport" and a reduction in the counselee's feeling of loneliness; most importantly, a good listener can encourage and enable the agitated person to probe his mood, attempt to describe his emotions and explain them, and thus create some distance from himself as an-excited-being.

Distraction of the sufferer's attention is another way to attempt to change his mood, and as with listening, others may do it more efficiently than philosophical counselors or anyone relying only on verbal means. Some philosophical counselors would disagree: They believe they have the special talents needed to persuade the counselee and, inspired perhaps by the Stoics, they claim to be able, in a two-hour conversation, to reduce to the minimum the range of issues that it is *rational* and *worthwhile* to worry about, and thereby move the counselee's mind away from the irrelevant things that have been preoccupying him. Other, more religiously minded, and perhaps inspired by Buddhist traditions, use their persuasive gifts to encourage people to join activities that will enable them to concentrate on an object that is comprehensive, sublime or infinitely wide. Having such an "oceanic" experience is supposed to immediately "trivialize" all possible human concerns. In both cases they are inspired by traditions which presuppose that the desired end cannot be obtained quickly or easily. Many philosophers do not share the ideals of those traditions, and some even believe that, say, talking about a football game, is more effective in the short term, and sometimes it is enough for enabling a conversation with an agitated counselee.

The counselors we have been discussing probably have other abilities. But whatever their other abilities are, they are supposed to have, as philosophers, the skill to raise the level of discussion from the personal and particular to the philosophical and general, or at least to analogical cases in other domains. The ascent to a philosophical level of discussion must not be done by conceptual analyses; it can be done in the ways of bibliotherapists and joke-tellers, for example, by analogies to similar difficulties in fictional contexts, where there is room for imaginary and funny solutions and movements between different domains of meanings as well as different levels of rationality. In brief, the philosophical counselor should be able to turn the counselee's attention from the immediacy of his specific emotionally laden concern to something less stressful without demeaning his human worries as "stupid" or "petty," or hypocritically pretensions to be, "extra-ordinarily," beyond such worries.

Only when the mood of the counselee enables him to take part in a rational exploration can the counselor begin the essentially *philosophical* job in the domain of changing emotions: challenging the *cognitive aspects* of his emotions. This is done by examining the counselee's interpretation of his situation and exploring alternative interpretations.

Many psychotherapists, including those who do not think of themselves as cognitivists, try to change emotions (and behavior) by such examinations and explorations of the cognitive aspects. They probe the causes or motives which might explain them (philosophers prefer to talk about the *reasons* that seem to *justify* them), alternative interpretations of the problem, situation, and alternative reactions and solutions. However, many of them, mainly psychoanalysts and dynamic psychotherapists, believe that the beliefs and attitudes at the basis of the counselee's initial unconscious interpretation were themselves created unconsciously, under conditions of intensive emotional involvement and the intervention of "unnatural" associative thinking. They are convinced that changes in interpretations will not occur unless the same kind of associative thinking and intense emotional involvement are promoted by the treatment and create unconscious as well as conscious changes. Philosophers as well as cognitive psychologists (under a grand variety of titles) tend not to share these untestable beliefs about the unconscious origin of the counselee's initial interpretations, or the convictions regarding possible changes. The various schools of cognitively oriented psychotherapy have their respective theories about the origin of the patient's allegedly mistaken initial interpretations and corresponding emotions, and those theories are often inspired by philosophers. But different philosophers have different opinions, and although some philosophers tend to mark every emotional reaction as nonrational, it is not philosophically obvious that the counselee's initial interpretation and therefore his emotional reaction is logically or factually erroneous. The philosophical question is whether there are alternative interpretations and emotional behaviors that are preferable, according to considerations on higher levels and from other perspectives—practical or philosophical, moral or religious, individual or collective, short term or long term.

Since ancient times philosophers, in a great variety of frameworks, have elaborated theories about the *meaning* of specific emotions, their value and "right measure." They have discussed the place that emotionality in general should have in the life of the wise. One can find such discussions as part of conceptual investigations of virtues, the worthy life, happiness, and in modern times in considerations of rationality, in analyses of moral criteria and in reflections about the meaning of life. One can also find them in explorations of mind-body interactions, debates about the reliability of introspective studies and discussions about the possibility of self- and other understanding.

Dealing with Emotions Does Not Necessarily Mean Trying to Change Them

The Importance of Emotions

Some modern philosophers made their most insightful, or at least impressive, statements regarding emotions in claims about the allegedly hidden or unconscious emotions; this was sometimes done in the contexts of their criticism of the dominant norms or the allegedly prevalent *Zeitgeist* in their respective societies, as in Nietzsche's onslaught on "Judeo-Christian" compassion for the weak, allegedly motivated by despise, or "liberal democratic" ideals of solidarity, which to his mind are motivated by resentment and envy of the strong, or the Marxist onslaught on the "false consciousness" and hypocrisy of the "bourgeoisie." They recommended alternative moral views, which praise other attitudes and promote emotions that the "conventions" or "class consciousness" allegedly condemn. In Appendix C I discuss their impact on some depth psychologists, who believe in unconscious motivation. Others, philosophers as well as psychologists and sociologists, who did not accept that notion of "depth," and did not share all the new moral ideals, reacted by dedicating themselves to the study of emotions. Some of them, for example existentialists, claimed to have detected other wrong attitudes and other, not "unconscious," ways of self-deceptions, and instead of recommending the promotion of specific alternative specific emotions, discussed the possibility of living an "authentic" life. Others tried to make "value-free" studies, whether by systematic introspective phenomenological explorations like Husserl and some of his followers, and whether, like Dilthei or Weber, by empirical, yet "understanding" [*verstehende*] studies of emotion-laden behaviors, which aim at understanding the logic of others from their subjective, though culturally and socially depended, point of view. Yet, despite their hope to protect their moral positions by value-free studies, they were "biased" by their opinions about the *importance* that should be given in modern life to this aspect of the human condition. Some philosophical counselors prefer to relate to the emotions of the counselee in light of one specific theory from that rich collection. I prefer to learn from the tacit controversies among the authors of these studies, and believe that philosophical counseling should confront counselees with opposite theories and encourage them to explore and arrive at their own conclusions.

The opinions of philosophically minded artists are also relevant. It is worthwhile to view paintings of Edvard Munch or Edward Hopper or watch movies by Antonioni, for example, in order to better understand anxiety and melancholy. When one wants to learn about the complexity of envy, Shakespeare—and not only Spinoza, Hegel, Nietzsche, or Melanie Klein—is worth reading. When one wants to learn about the vicissitudes of love, one should listen to Proust and not only to Plato, Saint Augustine, or Freud. The reflections of protagonists or narrators in "classic" literature as well as popular tales about *the proper attitude to such emotions* may be as instructive as those of academic philosophers, and often more interesting.

"How Would You Deal with Envy?"

I was once asked to illustrate my approach "in the case of envy" in a workshop. I refused. There are no "cases of envy," there are only *cases of persons* who are concerned with envy, or seem to be envious without knowing it. One man may perceive his attitude to his brother as envy, and it bothers him because he has been taught that envy is a sin. Another, whose brother is considered smarter than him, complains that despite his Epicurean and other spiritual exercises, he still feels pangs in his heart when his brother is successful. One counselee says that he would not have chosen his profession, which he hates, if he had not been trying to prove that he is smarter than his brother. Another counselee is proud of his brother's success, but his description of his interactions with his brother raises *my suspicion* that he also gloats over his brother's failures. One counselee criticizes his brother for spoiling his children and is angry at his wife, who insinuates that he cannot bear the fact that his brother is nicer and more tolerant than him. Another believes that his parents' unfair preference for his brother justifies his resentment, yet he is not sure with whom or how he should "settle the account." One counselee sits in prison for having "settled the account" by violence and defends himself by saying that it was not him, but his envy, which had "blinded him," while another prisoner denies having been motivated by envy and insists that his aggression against his richer brother was a matter of justice. One counselee claims that a socialist worldview expresses the "resentment of the mediocre many toward the gifted few." Another says he opposes the integration of immigrant children into classes of native children because this might incite the former's envy and slow down their academic progress. Since these counselees are bothered by different issues, they raise different sets of questions in the counselor's mind.

In some cases the counselor might suggest alternative interpretations of the situation as presented. In some he might challenge the shame or guilt that the counselee experiences when he feels envious, and raise the question whether envy is natural, or whether it is always bad. Sometimes the question is the counselee's self-acceptance despite his feelings, and sometimes the issue is his ability to control himself and not let his feelings dictate his behavior. Sometimes his problem is a matter of avoiding responsibility, perhaps by self-deception, and sometimes the issue is his overt disdain for any moral considerations. Sometime the question is whether the counselee's real concern is his envy or something else—the opinions of other persons about him or his own personal confusions about his true wishes.

My selection of examples shows that in many cases the issue is not changing a specific emotion. The selection corresponds with a great variety of themes that have been discussed by philosophers since ancient times, and illustrates some of the many approaches to emotions in the Western philosophical tradition. I add to them some more basic questions with regards to emotions:

How much mental activity *should* be dedicated to the fact that one *sometimes* experiences envy? Should one spend years in psychoanalytic analyses in an attempt to discover the roots of one's envy or to become immune to its impact? Is it all right to ignore sometimes one's feelings, as philosophers like Kant would recommend—or does ignoring them mean, as some romantics would say, one is denying parts of one's "true self?" Is not there a third possibility, as implied by Jung, of acknowledging the "negative feeling" of envy but being aware of one's having also "positive feelings" (such as the relevant empathy for the parent who prefers the envied brother, or the irrelevant love of nature) and letting those different "parts" of "self" have an inner conversation? Is it a psychological issue, a matter of conversation between "parts" of "self," or a philosophical issue, and a matter for moral discussion? Is hiding one's feelings is always hypocrisy, and will it lead necessarily to further problem, as Nietzsche seems to suggest and some psychologists aggressively insist? Sometimes the question is whether other emotions are more important to explore, and sometimes the question is what is the purpose of exploring emotions. Should the exploration always be for the sake of one's self-empowering, as implied by Spinoza or Nietzsche or one's self-control, as suggested by the Stoic or one's inner harmony as suggested by Plato—or for the well-being of others and for more harmonious coexistence with them? Maybe for the sake of others as well as one's morality one should try sometimes to overcome or ignore one's envy, but, in contrast to Spinoza's and Nietzsche's teaching, never overcome or ignore one's moral remorse for having done wrong to envied individuals or groups?

Existential "Malaise" and Mental "Sickness"

Philosophers who deal with the human condition often focus on analyses of existential "malaise":—"death anxiety," "insecurity," "meaninglessness," "hopelessness," "self-alienation," or "loneliness." Sometimes they focus on irresoluble conflicts—between dreams and reality, for example, or between wishes and norms, the self and others, and so on, and the "wrong ways" in which people tend to deal with such inevitable dilemmas. Sometimes those philosophers also propose the "right way" to deal with them. As I argue in Appendix C, the psycho-analytic approach of Freud, no less than those of the rebels Jung and Adler, were inspired by such questions. In particular, each of them responded to Nietzsche's provocations (and Marxist counter-challenges) according to his own interpretation and his own concerns and values. Some psychoanalysts dissatisfied with the orthodox theories and not always aware of their philosophical roots, decided to "finally" introduce philosophy to therapy—that is, to borrow ideas from phenomenologists and existentialists. Some, following Kierkegaard, concentrate on death anxiety and meaninglessness. Others are intrigued by Sartre's ideas about the burden of freedom or De Beauvoir's idea of moral ambiguity. Some are inspired by Buber's version of alienation, and some introduce their own interpretations of an aspect of Heidegger's theories. Many innovators agreed with Jung and Adler that difficulties in coping with existential issues and the accompanying moods and emotions, however disturbing, are not "neuroses." Nevertheless, the rhetoric of "sickness," which seems to be occasioned by the medical background of some psychotherapists and the psychiatric tendency to classify the problems they treat as "mental illnesses" or "disturbances" led some to *misinterpret* the philosophical claims.[6]

The most conspicuous *misconception* is the interpretation of existential "malaise" as the *cause* of "mental illness"—whereas the philosophers conceive of it as the "(permanent) human condition." Sometimes, when those philosophers use the rhetoric of "sickness" they are describing the awareness of it (like the nausea felt by some of Sartre's protagonists), they do so in order to criticize the "wrong" ways of coping with it, that is, ways which are *philosophically*, *spiritually* or *morally* inadequate. Even those who propose a kind of "philosophical psychoanalysis" expect it to provide a better understanding of the "human condition," not a cure for psychological suffering. Indeed, most of them do not assume that those who cope in the "wrong" way suffer *psychologically* more than those who cope in the "right" way, or have, according to clinical or diagnostic criteria, more *psychological disturbance*.[7] For Kierkegaard and some of his followers, for example, life crises are not mental pathologies, with causal etiology and psychotherapeutic remedies. Instead, they are *occasions for radical changes*—which transcend the limits of a person's existing conceptions, values, and horizons. (It should be noted that the issuing transformations, which enable the person to live more *meaningfully*, do not protect him against further crises, nor guarantee more than temporary happiness or peace of mind.) Heidegger's "authentic" person has perhaps a deeper sense of inner integrity and self-determination. He is perhaps more resolute, more ready to accept the common "destiny" of his community. (Saying that the philosophers' stance is *moral* and not *medical* does not mean that it is necessarily morally *good*. Thus, some psychologists assume that one of the criteria for "mature sanity" is the patient's ability to go further than Heidegger, and, as most universalist philosophers insist, assume responsibility for harm done to others by himself or his community, even if those others are from a different, "strange," community. At least some of Heidegger's critics not only accuse Heidegger for failing personally to assume such a responsibility, they also wonder whether his conception of "authenticity" is sufficient to enable one to assume responsibility more readily than, say, Camus's deranged "stranger.")

The following example of a *mistaken* psychoanalytic application of existentialist insights is relevant to what Heidegger calls *Befindlichkeit*. I learned about the application from a reader who criticized "the rationalistic ignorance of that aspect of human experience." (I do not mention the name of the psychoanalyst because I am not sure that I myself am not misunderstanding him.) The German term 'Befindlichkeit' is often translated as 'mood,' but in the very literary sense that Heidegger uses words it is, as I found in some Heideggerian lexicon, "the [mental and spiritual] state in which one finds oneself (or exists) [in the world]." This may, of course, mean many things: emotionally laden opinions and attitudes, feelings and temperament as well as moods. I believe Heidegger is elaborating the idea of the "emotional tone" that accompanies all our conscious experiences, an idea which had already been mentioned by Husserl. Husserl tended to put that "tone" in parenthesis *in analyses whose purpose was conceptual clarifications*. Heidegger opposed both conceptual clarifications and analyses that are done from the perspective of an "ex-mondial" mind that observes the world. Therefore he insisted on the meaning of the '*befinden*' [to be in some place or exist] part of the '*Befindlichkeit*' which replaces the "emotional tone." I am not an expert in the details of Heideggerian phenomenology, but according to what I know about what he said with regard to death anxiety—the ability to *choose* between flight from the awareness of one's personal finitude and the courage to confront it (and the difference that it is supposed to make)—I do not think he assumed that persons are always in the same state of mind, or that each has a "basic *mood*" that is his specific *mode* of existing in the world. I therefore believe that the "existentialist psychoanalyst" who thinks that not being aware of one's "basic mood" and living accordingly is the *cause* of mental illness, misunderstands Heidegger, and confuses Heidegger's notion of "*Befindlichkeit*" with his own misunderstanding of Jung's notion of Self. Of course, psychoanalysts may develop their own theories; but the conviction that their task is to help the analysand find the right words for describing his mood, and thereby enable him to become both sane and authentic, is too original. In fact, even the most uncritical romantic, who believes that one should fully live his emotions, and the most religiously minded individualist, who thinks that one should "realize" his "true self" as if this were a mission dictated especially for him by the gods, would not say that being authentic is living according to one's emotional state of mind. However, it seems that among contemporary phenomenologists there are some who, unlike Husserl or Heidegger, Merleau-Ponty or Schutz, Scheler or Jaspers, believe that phenomenological studies are not methods to explore possible answers to *philosophical questions*, but are ways of *experiencing* modes of existing in the world. For those phenomenologists living in accordance with one's true "mood" rather than exploring whether, when and why being in that mood is adequate, may seem as philosophically inspired psychoanalysis.[8] I have already admitted that I do not have a copyright on the use of the word 'philosophy.'

There are philosophical counselors who talk of some ways of thinking as "philosophical pathologies," some who propose "philosophical diagnostics," and some who try to promote a concept of "philosophical health." According to my conception of philosophy, one should examine when a certain way of thinking is adequate and when it is not, rather than diagnose "thinking pathologies." One should not define philosophical opinions as "unhealthy" just because one prefers other opinions. According to my conception of philosophical counseling, counselors do not need such concepts in order to do a proper job. According to my *historical* knowledge, such professionally superfluous and philosophically confused tools can nevertheless be efficient—in the hands of oppressive groups and tyrannic institutes.[9]

Notes

1. I hardly mention Pascal in the other chapters, so I give references here, and by doing so at length, I hope to demonstrate why I do not do this with the other examples. My claims are based on the interpretation of several texts. I chose an old version (1901) of an English translation of Pascal's posthumous book, Pensée [1670], because it is accessible online as a pdf text, and includes the Memorandum, under the title "Pascal's Profession of Faith" in the translator's Introduction. Authors writing about Pascal normally refer to numbered fragments in the original French, but the English translator and editor preferred to reorganize the text by chapters. He also modified—I would say "improved"—the book's ideas, and interpreted 'esprit de géométrie' as 'mathematical mind' and 'esprits de finesse' as 'practical mind' which, it seems to me, misses the finesse of Pascal's idea of "finesse"—something between "practical" and what is nowadays called "social and emotional intelligence." This interpretation misses the aspect of "sociable" and "poetic" skill of conversing politely and pleasantly but superficially, on the basis of common unexamined assumptions which are neither clear nor necessarily coherent. Pascal compares the two "minds," or rather moods or ways of thinking, in Pascal (1901, 223–24). The Memorandum is cited in the same book (ibid., 10), as are the remarks about the relevance of "heart" rather than "reason" to matters of faith (ibid., 69–75). The same chapter—"On the Need of Seeking Truth"—also includes the argument offered referred to as the

"wager"—the "proof" by probability calculations—as well as the explanation of its uselessness (ibid., 71–72). Pascal's attitude to authority is discussed in "Preface to the Treatise on Vacuum," which is included in Pascal (1910, 444–51). According to his biographers, for example Bishop (1936), he accepted as authoritative the "inspired" interpretation of the revealed truths by Saint Augustine, as the latter was, in his turn, interpreted by the seventeenth-century Jansenists. Pascal's philosophical texts are worth reading even if one does not share his religious convictions (and is not interested in the sources of my interpretation): the depth of his insights, the width of his horizons, the wisdom of his analyses and the wit of his paradoxical remarks are efficient antidotes against all kinds of dogmatism and narrow-mindedness. Philosophical counselors as well as their counselees can find in those texts many ideas that are relevant to their concerns.

2. Other psychologists, who believe in a wise, whispering "true self," recommend listening to one's "inner voice" rather than leaving the decision up to the "intellectual calculations" of the "conventionalist ego." I believe that their arguments are somewhat confused, but they are still arguing, and not citing "inner voices."

3. (Spinoza, 1954, book 2, proposition 49 explanatory note): It demonstrates that even philosophers with pretentions to philosophizing in the most rigorous "esprit de géométrie" and behave in the politest ways may express rudely insights of their "esprit de finesse."

4. Some German philosophers might be shocked by my apparent "instrumentalist rationality." I believe that their interpretation of any end-directed thinking as "instrumental" reflects a confusion between Kant's conception of morality (treating other persons as "ends in themselves," and not "only as means"), his non-consequential criteria for the morality of an action, his conception of aesthetic pleasure as not motivated by "interests" and the Aristotelian notion of an activity that is performed for its own sake. As Freud well understood, the last-mentioned activity, which is, indeed, not instrumental, may be neither moral nor aesthetic: His paradigm or such activity is the baby's allegedly "auto-erotic" behavior. On the other hand, wondering whether to send a colleague an invitation to discuss morally the importance of "non-instrumental reasoning" is end-directed thinking. Would they consider it instrumental?

5. Barrett offers (to my mind) a more accurate interpretation of James's idea than the version known as the James-Lange theory of emotion (which was elaborated by John Dewey).

6. I am not speaking of Lacan, who did not reject but rather reinterpreted Freudian theory considering his own philosophical conceptions.

7. I am not talking about exceptions like Albert Camus, who spoke of the possibility of being a "happy Sisyphus" (Camus, 2018), which presupposes that many are not happy with their Sisyphean life; nor am I talking about Camus's rebels, whose situation presupposes that many are discontent yet do not revolt; nor about Dr. Rieux, the protagonist of *The Plague* (Camus, 1991), whose choice to act morally despite the "absurdity" of existence gives meaning to his life (or about the meaningless and

purposeless life or the indifferent and amoral outsider Meurceault (Camus, 2012). I am also not talking about Jaspers, whose prior career as psychiatrist and interest in "understanding psychology" (of living persons, not of constructs like "Dasein"), did not allow him to make the sharp distinctions that Heidegger, for example, makes between the "psychological" and the "existential," (or the "inauthentic" and the "authentic").

8. Maybe it is just nonrationality, which is perhaps better than the irrational way of introducing of practical philosophy to students at a Japanese school of business. I refer to a reading, imposed by the teacher, of a meta-meta-philosophical book about Western philosophical tradition. One student concluded from it that reading, say, Descartes, is theoretical philosophy, while being Descartes is practical philosophy. (The book in question is the controversial *What Is Philosophy?* [Deleuze and Guattari, 1994], which does not relate to practical philosophy, but speaks of the ultra-theoretical activity of the philosopher such as Descartes pretending to be a skeptic).

9. I relate to that issue in the last section of chapter 5.

Appendix B

Philosophical Controversies

Philosophical controversies pervade not only every domain of philosophy, but also every camp. In this appendix, I relate only to controversies which are relevant to the clarification of my approach to philosophical counseling. My choice gives to my discussion a sort of epistemological bias: Some philosophers might condemn it, as "true philosophy" should not give to questions of knowledge and rationality such importance. But this criticism relies on tacit presuppositions which are no less epistemological than the explicit positions of philosophers who think that such questions are the central themes of any serious philosophy. I include some of their positions in my *very partial survey* and rather *superficial* tour of the debates about the possibility of putting an end to philosophical debates. Limited space obliges me to omit the names and ideas of many interesting and challenging participants. Finally, my limited acquaintance with controversies in other cultural traditions obliges me to limit my discussion to Western philosophy.

Controversies in the Greco-Roman World

The story as I know it starts with disagreements among pre-Socratic philosophers about the nature of the physical world, the true and the apparent reality, universalism and pluralism, human virtues and vices, good and bad states, knowledge and belief, skepticism and relativism, and reasoning and persuasion. Socrates, encountering the Sophists' disagreements, believed he could overcome them through logical dialogues in which latent contradictions and fallacies are exposed and "aborted" and "birth" is given to "true opinions" or knowledge. His disciple, Plato, went further in the same direction and tried to offer ultimate solutions to other disagreements as well, for example, that between Parmenides and Heraclitus about the nature of the domain of "eternal being" and that of becoming and passing away of "phenomena." He added to the Socratic attempts to arrive logically at the "true" definitions of what would later be called concepts, the quest for understanding the "true" logical relations between them , and, as the final answer to pluralists and relativists, sought to anchor each "true"—that is, logically tested δόζα" doxa, opinion or mental concept—in an εἶδος [Idos] or ἰδέα [Idea]—form—which was said to exist independently of perceptible events and human thinking in the eternal, unperceivable and unchangeable "world of Ideas" but also to be innate although "forgotten" in the human soul. The Idea or Form can be "re-called" by means of logical dialogues which gradually lead to them and thus to truth. Plato elaborated for that purpose the *dialectical way* of exploring opposite possible answers to a guiding question by purging the answers that are based on contradictory assumptions, or imply contradictory consequences. States of ἀπορία [aporia]—"impasse," when both of the opposite answers are found inadequate, are overcome by starting a new series of questions, exploring a new pair of opposite positions that appear to be free from of the errors of the former pair. In this way perplexities, doubts, and above all, controversies are supposed to gradually disappear.

In order to be sure that thc discursive processes lead eventually to full correspondence with the World of Ideas and enable an understanding of the internal relations between those Ideas, Plato needed a further step, a "post-dialectical" θεωρία [theoria]—intellectual intuition- which is supposed to enable the philosopher to have a σύνοψις [synopsis]—a comprehensive view—of the realm of Ideas. Plato compared this to getting out of a cave, (where one could see only the shadows of objects illuminated only by a local fire) and seeing the "real things" outside, in the "true light" of the "real sun" (Plato, 1997, *Republic*, 514a–520a). Plato believed that this process leads to a certain and perfect ἐπιστήμη [episteme]—knowledge. Therefore it also leads to an agreement among all "full-fledged" philosophers, who, thanks to their perfect knowledge, will also be able to identify the truly good and prefer it to lesser goods. Thus, they become both morally virtuous and happy. That would put an end to moral disputes and ethical disagreements about virtue and the good life.

Notwithstanding the philosophers' final achievements, Plato was sure that most people are not able even to start the process and share that knowledge. He therefore believed (as described in the allegory of the chariot) that their souls do not always control the horses of rational and irrational desires and emotions (Plato, 1997, Phaedrus. 246a–254e). Their political opinions are biased and divergent, and their taking part in political activities dooms the state to instability. The practical overcoming of political controversies and the constitution of a stable regime in a happy and just state can, he believed, be achieved only under the rule of a perfect philosopher-king. As he will not be biased by personal passions or interests, the philosopher-king will organize the state according to relations in the world of Ideas; he will put every person in the place and role that fits him or her, and take care that proper education and careful censorship prevent the bad influences of art, myths, poetry, drama, or "sophistic" demagogy. (Plato, 1977, *Republic*).

Some philosophers interpret the whole Western history of ideas as endnotes to Plato's philosophy (Whitehead, 1997a). Be that as it may be, Plato raised disagreements even among his immediate disciples. The best known of them, who was eventually as influential as his teacher, is Aristotle. Like Plato, Aristotle believed, in the eternal Forms, but while Plato believed that they all exist in a separate realm, and that physical things and human thoughts "imitate" them in some degree of imperfection, Aristotle believed (Aristotle, 2009, *Metaphysics*) that all of them but one—the Pure Form, (which is also the "unmovable mover" the "thought thinking itself" and God)—exist only potentially, and are made actual when they are materially embodied, according to its natural τέλος [telos]—end or goal—(or, in the case of a human artifact, the purpose of the maker), if the right "efficient" cause is present and hazardous disturbances do not intervene. This means not only that knowledge of the Forms is insufficient for understanding events and processes in the concrete world, but also that the advance of the philosopher toward knowledge, virtue, and happiness, is a process which depends not only on the Forms that the philosophers explore, but on the three other "causes"—besides hazard interventions: matter, telos and efficient factors operating on the knower's body and soul as well as influencing the concrete objects or events that he seeks to know. Thus, while Plato's model of knowledge—episteme—was geometry (Plato, 1997, *Meno*) and he was interested in ideal figures rather than their concrete imperfect "imitations" in objects, Aristotle's model was his conception of biological growth and human activity as teleological processes that are not necessarily successful. Their products always have "accidental" features that are not part of their "formal" essence. It also means that Aristotle's conception of the acquisition of knowledge, which does not start in the way assumed by Plato—perception of empirical objects whose "form," despite its imperfection, reminds the soul of the innate ideal Form—but by abstraction of perceived qualities and their comparisons, grouping, and generalization into increasingly general concepts (Aristotle, 2009, *On the Soul*). This does not guarantee that human concepts resemble the ideal Forms; that is, it does not promise certain knowledge deserving of the title "episteme" and is not just a matter of reasonable "doxas." Moreover, although Aristotle did not think that the truth of opinions depends on the knower's time and place or language, he was aware that logic as he conceived it does not apply to sentences that relate to the future (the sentence "tomorrow there will be a sea battle in Salamis" is today neither necessarily true nor false (ibid., *On Interpretation*), and the ways in which we talk about existing things (the "categories") are the ways in which we think beings exists (ibid., *Metaphysics*). He also thought that knowing how to handle wisely our practical life is a matter of φρόνησις [phronesis]—prudence, mindfulness to details—and not the general episteme (ibid., *Nicomachean Ethics)*. Finally, he thought that the human personality, having "vegetative" and "animal" aspects besides the "rational" one (ibid., *On the Soul*) allows our desires, emotions, and personal interests to interfere with our rational deliberations, which means that even the wisest are not perfectly immune to irrational influences (ibid., *Rhetoric*). Therefore the political opinions, even of philosophers, are a matter of debate, and the best political regime is not that of a philosopher-king who is supposed to have the necessary episteme for ruling and handling state affairs correctly, but a regime that gives room to debates about political issues (ibid., *Politics)* and allows art, poetry and drama, which indeed evoke desires and emotions, enable the κάθαρσις, [katharsis]—purification—of excess emotions (such as anger and fear) (ibid., *Poetics*). Aristotle believed that the intellectual part of the human soul is eternal (ibid., *On the Soul*) and some say that he believed that it joins after death, as an "active intellect," the "thought that is thinking itself." Whatever were his beliefs about the afterlife, it can be interpreted as a polite way of saying that philosophers, as whole persons of flesh and blood, are still in the cave, moved by their desires and emotions, failing sometimes to behave according to their best judgment, and do not share with any God any comprehensive intellectual view.

Writing those words, I am surprised to discover to what extent I am an Aristotelian, despite the fact the Platonism always seemed to me, in some respects, much more inspiring. Even Aristotle's way of starting the dialectical exploration (Aristotle, *Nicomachean Ethics*), or the rhetorical exposition (ibid., *Rhetoric*) from "endoxa," i.e., reputable opinions, whether of "experts" or just experienced and commonsensical "Idiotes," appeals to me. My conversation with a counselee is not "dialectical," but when I challenge an opinion or attitude that seems to me obstructive, I suggest, as would Aristotle, that he explore several alternative reputable opinions.

Skepticism is also a way to put an end to controversies, and that was the position of Pyrrho and later Pyrrhonists who referred to him as the founder. They recommended the attitude of ἐποχή [epokhē]—lit. cessation—that is, suspension of judgment with regard to theories, because they believed that no theory can be proven, and one cannot logically decide which theory is better. Suspension of judgment enables the adoption of the attitudes of ἀταραξία [ataraxia]—lit. not being troubled—which meant having an equanimous attitude toward theories of any kind, whether of nature, eternity, or the state or the soul, and also toward beliefs regarding future dangers and beliefs that raise regrets about the past. They believed that philosophy should be practical and, for guarding one's equanimous mood—recommended. Some added, as did Hume in the eighteenth century, reliance on common customs and norms instead of looking for rational rules or criteria, a search which would be in vain. Ataraxia should enable one to achieve εὐδαιμονία [eu̯dai̯monía]—lit. the good spirit—which meant well-being in the sense of living a worthy life[1] in the light of the ideal of virtue (Vogt, 2018).

An alternative attitude of practical philosophers, who aimed at *eudaimonia* and believed that ataraxia is needed in order to achieve it, preferred a different attitude to theories and debates about them. They favored the adoption, rather dogmatically, of a deterministic conception of nature, like the atomistic theory of Democritus, according to which "being in harmony with nature" meant accepting with an equanimous mood anything that nature or fate gives or takes away. For the Epicureans that meant being content with what one has, however little it is, though still challenging existing social norms or customs that fail to fit their moral ideals (Konstan, 2018). For the Stoic, who accepted the existing order as part of nature, harmony with nature also meant being indifferent to unworthy desires, and being bothered only by what is under one's control: oneself, that is, one's thoughts and one's desires, feelings and actions. They fostered exercises for the formation of character according to their conception of virtue, their view of a worthy life was more ascetic than that of the Epicureans who, though they might be content with good luck and comfort, understood that one does not really need the "superfluous things" that attract and bother fools (Baltzly, 2018).

Some philosophical counselors believe, like the skeptics, that philosophical theories are not worth being bothered about and that the practical philosopher should, like the Epicureans, practice parrhesia and "problematize" bad habits, customs, or attitudes. Others share a disdain for theories, but believe, with the Stoics, that practical philosophy should foster in the counselee an attitude of ataraxia toward desires that are not really important or worthy and learn to not allow himself to be troubled by things that he cannot change. Yet beneath the indifference to explicit philosophical theories hide the biases of tacit philosophical beliefs, for the questions of what is "not really important" and what "one cannot change" were matters of debate even between Epicureans and Stoics. Even when the rationality or will of a monotheistic God replaced the "Nature" with which one should live "in harmony," and God's Laws were supposed to direct the believers, Epicurean and Stoic ideals still had an impact (without the terminology and without acknowledgment) on religions that developed in areas that were open to Greco-Roman influences. One can find them in various Jewish, Christian, and Muslim ideals of the virtuous person. However, with their very different presupposed beliefs, those religions developed very different conceptions of what is "not really important" and what "one cannot change," with many debates within and between the groups. Moreover, those religions have additional ideals that are not always compatible with the ancient Greco-Roman ones, and they too have their impact on contemporary counselees, if not directly than through their echoes in modern secular worldviews. That is why some philosophical counselors believe that they should not try to convince the counselee to share their ideals, whether Stoic, Nietzschean, Marxist, or Buddhist. Instead, they expose him to a variety of possibilities beyond his current cultural horizon, and invite him to explore philosophically which beliefs seem to him more reasonable, and which ideals seem to him worthier.

I related to the theories of the ancients because many of their themes and debates recur in later generations and are still not settled, although they have changed their form: Platonic "forgotten" ideas became "innate ideas," developed to "transcendental conditions of possibility," changed to culturally dependent or scientifically more advanced "a priori," and appear nowadays as "genetically inherited patterns with evolutionary advantages" or "rule-governed algorithms" in computer simulations of an alleged innate human rationality. The Aristotelian conception of knowledge reappeared as empiricism or associationism and it reappears nowadays in the forms of "connectivism" or statistical elaboration of data in computer simulations of learning. The philosopher-king will reappear as the wise Hobbesian sovereign, the inspired totalitarian ruler, or the reliable technocrat and so forth. Skeptics, relativists, and pluralists reappear anew in each era, although sometimes they do not dare to do so overtly.

The Revealed Truths

In the Middle Ages, when the privilege of comprehensive knowledge was believed to be reserved to an omniscient single personal God, and philosophy was mobilized in the service of religion, some thinkers believed that *Divine truths*—which were said to be encoded in the Holy Scriptures—*should have the last word in philosophical controversies*. This did not, however, prevent controversies even within the confines imposed by authoritative institutions and their exclusion and persecution of heretics. There were debates about the relation between God's reason, power and will, his omniscience, predestination, and providence, free will and responsibility. There were also debates about man's cognitive ability, whether he can perceive, with his eyes of flesh and blood, only sensible things or whether he can also "see intellectually" the Forms or the Divine light even before their death and salvation. These debates echoed Plato and Aristotle's disagreements, while their dialectical legacy left traces in theological controversies and in debates among authorized interpreters of the Laws or in authorized tribunals for judging the disobedient. Some Neo-Platonic, Epicurean, and Stoic ideals are echoed in the ideas of the founders of Christian monastic orders, in the practices recommended to monks and hermits, and in stories about formal or informal saints in the three monotheistic religions. Fideists, believing that religious faith is above and beyond philosophical speculation, resembled the sceptics. There were also true sceptics within those cultural groups, but they preferred to stay silent until the Renaissance, when courageous persons like Montaigne and Shakespeare openly expressed their ideas and doubts.

Philosophical counselors whose counselees have various cultural backgrounds should be aware that in all monotheistic and probably other religions, traditions speak in more than one voice. When they or their counselees belong to religious groups in which the verdict of revealed truths or the opinions of authoritative interpreters prevail, they may sometimes need to adopt the evasive wisdom of medieval philosophers, or the irony of Renaissance writers, in order to make room for the counselee's independent thinking.

Controversies in Modern Philosophy

The Introspective Method

In the seventeenth century, the authority of religious dogmas and institutes was not just a matter of intellectual debate but also the cause of political struggles and real wars. New conceptions in mathematics and physics empowered demands to rely on human reason and observation, and a new method for overcoming controversies and inner conflicts came to the fore: The solitary *introspective analysis of "ideas" in the mind of the philosophizing person* (following, in this respect Saint Augustine [2006]) and *the application of a method* (some following Euclides and others—a new and revised version of Aristotle's *Organon* [Bacon, 2004]). God somehow remained relevant, and faith in him, abstracted from specific religious dogmas except for his perfection and infinite benevolence, was still the guarantee for the truth of some ideas, which were supposed to be innate, and justified the reliance on logical inferences. Some philosophers needed God to explain connections that the new method could not explain, such as the connection between the mental and the physical, and between ideas which were "in" the philosopher's mind and in the reality "outside" his mind, that of physical objects and that of other minds. The method consisted of two things: first, *finding within the contents of the mind elements whose truth was evident*, and second, finding a reliable way for *combining these elements with logical certainty, into more complex truths*, and discarding combinations that were impossible, uncertain, or confused. René Descartes, with his "geometrical mind," believed that the basic elements that are beyond doubt must be ideas that are innate in every rational mind. The reliable way of combining them is equally innate and logical, and the evident combinations, which are metaphysical principles at the base of science, are theorems. (Descartes, [1637], 1999). This seemed applicable also to self-understanding and moral conduct[2]. Descartes, like Spinoza (Spinoza, 1954) was convinced that everybody who made the effort would arrive at the same philosophical conclusions.

However, he was soon faced with a counter-method in the work of John Locke. Locke was a practically oriented thinker, and, in contrast to Descartes, thought that the *basic "ideas" were either sense data* or psychological data of *the mind reflecting the experiencing of those data and its feeling of pleasure and pain while experiencing them*. Their combinations were the result of "*associations of ideas*." His method consisted in *determining which combinations can be the basis for fixed rules, concepts or linguistic terms, which are just "natural," that is., inductive generalizations* that are for the time being empirically true, and which are "unnatural," combinations of ideas that do not any more, or can never, appear together in experience (Locke, [1670], 1975). One of the purposes of Locke's method was to sweep the mind clean of "unnatural associations" that are responsible for metaphysics, mistaken political or educational conceptions and other kinds of stupidity and madness (ibid., Ch. XXXIII). This approach, which would lead later empiricists to rejection of all religious beliefs, led Locke to a more or less supportive attitude to religious tolerance.[3]

The belief that irrelevant associations of ideas are the source of logical errors and fallacies goes back to Aristotle, who was also aware of the power of habits. But Locke, conceiving one kind of "unnatural association" as obsolete habits that interfere with the ability to pay attention to present situations and behave appropriately, can be considered the ancestor of behaviorist psychology as well as psychiatry and psychoanalysis. He is also the grandfather of the idea of psychological "projection," although psychologists needed poets like Shakespeare, or philosophers like Hegel or Nietzsche, to replace the mental connections that are projected onto the physical world by the negative intentions or traits that are projected onto other persons. Some philosophical counselors share Locke's views, as well as those of the ancient philosophers, in their understanding of projection and in their conviction that the counselee needs their help because of his failure to think logically and avoid "unnatural" associations. They seem, however, to lack the Aristotelian and Lockean understanding of the role of uncertainty and emotional ambiguity in the human predicament.

The competing methods gave a new form to the old controversy between Plato and Aristotle, and between the mediaeval rationalists and empiricists. But they did not calm down the skeptics, notably Hume (1930) or the relativists and pluralists. The new worldviews that were supposed to be enlightened by "reason"—the determinism of a mechanical nature and the relevance of general consensus in human affairs, intrigued those who, like Pascal, believed that not everything can be clear to reason (Pascal, 1901) or, like the Romantics, were interested in the "sentimental" or "passionate" quality of life, rather than the truth value of grand theories. They raised new debates about new questions, such as the relation between "the God of the philosophers" and the "God of religion" (ibid., 10) or the fate of man and his freedom, individuality, or creativity.

The Transcendental Exploration

Toward the end of the eighteenth century, after a long period of debate between rationalists and empiricists about the reliability of science and the validity of metaphysics, and in the face of debates between partisans of Enlightenment ideals and their conservative opponents, growing interest in biological processes and interest-oriented human activity and still more debates about the role of reason, desires and sentiments in religious, moral, and artistic judgments, the method of selecting inner "ideas" and examining the mind's "rational constructions" in order to put an end to controversies was replaced by a new method: "transcendental analysis." According to Kant's "Copernican revolution," human Reason is not waiting for inner experiences or revelation to tell it the truth; Reason is asking its own questions, and it is the role of the "critical philosopher" to explore how some of them can be answered, and others cannot. Accordingly, Kant designed a new approach—*a "transcendental" exploration.* Its purpose was to determine which of the questions can be answered and how, and to explore the various tools with which it constructs "phenomenal" objects, conceives "noumenal" entities or creates "ideals" and makes, respectively, epistemological, practical, artistic, or teleological judgments. Valid and invalid judgments, universally valid and not universally valid statements, should be distinguished. The method consisted of "*reductions*" from the linguistic to the logical level and from there *to a "transcendental" one*, that of the "*synthetic*," not purely logical, *but innate or pre-given ("a priori") tools of Reason*, and a critical examination of their valid application. It was supposed to found *once and for all* the validity of mathematics and physics; discard *forever* any metaphysics, yet limit the domain of determinism; distinguish *sharply* between utilitarian and moral decisions; explain the possibility of freedom and the initiation of moral actions; support some ideals of the Enlightenment with regard to future individual and political rationality; decide *definitely* about the role of feelings and reason in aesthetic pleasures; and judge to what extent religious hopes for an afterlife and political hopes for eternal peace in this world can be *rationally justifiable*. It also enabled Kant to found philosophically his pessimism: discard all philosophical as well as religious attempts to liberate humans from the basic conflicts between their dual nature as "phenomenal" (including their "animal desires" and "egoistic and greedy" interests) and "noumenal" beings (including their self-imposed limitations by alliances and contracts with others) yet stay with the psychological frustrations (and pave the road to Freudian pessimism).[4]

The Problems of the Self

Kant's most important indirect impact was through the reactions of some of his contemporaries to his idea, discussed in (Kant, 1999a) of what he called the "transcendental unity of the apperception, "and "the consciousness of the I that accompanies all my representations." In his discussions of the subject, he was probably trying to answer Hume's denial of the idea that the existence of an experiencing subject can be inferred or constructed as a Cartesian "thinking substance" from the data of experience (Hume, 1930, Vol I, 239–52). Kant distinguished that awareness from "self-knowledge," where the experiencing subject relates to himself, or to his "inner experience" as a phenomenon, that is, as an object of experience (Kant, 1974).[5]

However, his involvement in the perspective of the nonempirical "transcendental I" was too much for his empiricist contemporaries, and too little from the point of view of many of the others, since that "I" was detached not only from both God and the real world, but also from the inner worlds of concrete persons and the place of religion, myth, or poetry in their lives. This opened a new theme for discussion: Subjectivity or selfhood: the possibility and meaning of self-knowledge, the possibility to identify and understand the other as a "subject" or to explain interactions between "subjects."

The German Idealists Schelling, Hegel, and Fichte, offered a pantheistic vision, combining ideas derived from Neo-Platonic traditions, on the one hand, and Spinoza, on the other hand. Instead of Spinoza's single Substance, which is God and Nature, "from the perspective of eternity," while the mental and the physical are just two of his infinite aspects, the German Idealists posit the conscious "Ich" [I] (or the "Geist" [Spirit or Mind]) in a dynamic temporal story. It starts like the Neo-Platonic "One," an "absolute" but single being, that creates the "multiplicity" by "throwing" itself into the "Not-I," nonconscious nature. It finds itself again in a process in which conscious humans become gradually self-conscious and recognize the God in themselves (or themselves as part of a pantheistic world), understand their history as a realization of a Divine plan, and realize that the apparently irrational aspects of their culture are "unconscious" or implicit expressions of the spiritual truths that philosophy seeks to make "self-conscious" or explicit. Thus, not only the personal "I" but also the "collective I," not only the "consciousness" but also the "unconsciousness," personal and collective, were introduced to the philosophical discourse. Later, changes were made by some of the German Idealists and other German philosophers that rejected their view altogether. The "One" was replaced by "Energy," unconscious "Will," "Instincts," or "Drives." The self-alienation of the "I" was replaced by "forgetfulness" of one's self and one's "true" group identity—ethnic, national, or class-related—or "repression" of one's socially unacceptable aspects and a "projection" of them onto others (in the Marxist version, this is "class false-consciousness").

Depth psychologists owe many of their ideas to that rich but confusing arsenal, although their selections and interpretations were different enough to create the famous disputes between Freud, Jung, and Adler and their rebellious followers. One should therefore mistrust the attempts to reduce them to psychological explanations. Confusions or disagreements about philosophical issues are not reducible to such explanations. Some postmodern philosophers also flirt with ideas borrowed from that arsenal.

The "subjectivist" opponents of Hegel put the stress on individual "subjectivity," and a split were created between those that put the stress on personal particularity, self-realization, and authenticity and those that tried, like the phenomenologists, or sociologist like Georg Simmel and Max Weber, to turn the "subjective experience" into the base of common, social as well as physical, objective reality. This split created, on its turn, further disagreements between believers in the possibility of self-knowledge and those who believe that persons can be conceived as knowable only from the perspective of others; between those who assume that self-knowledge is possible thanks to subjective explorations of conscious experiences and those who believe that it is involved with deciphering personal unconscious messages or discovering cultural subconscious influences; between those who insist that the "subject" or "self" is not a knowable being because of its spiritual nature, and those who explain that it is a psychosocial construct, and self-identity is a matter of social classification by others or ideological self-identification with a certain group. Sociologists would go further and speak of multiple selves, and add self-presentations to self-images, denying the idea that behind them exist a definite "true self."

Let "History" Decide

Some nineteenth-century philosophers, aware, on the one hand, of the difference between the Enlightenment's and Kant's conception of reason and ideals of rationality and the terrors of the French revolution and the atrocities of the Napoleonic wars and inspired, on the other, by ideas of biological evolution and hopes for a sociopolitical one, developed ideas of overcoming philosophical controversies in a new way. Instead of assuming the atemporality of reason and looking for its traces in the philosopher's "subjective" consciousness, they advocated *following the development of rationality in the "objective" cultural, social, and political realm.* The practically oriented *positivist* Auguste Comte conceived rationality as a tool for survival and believed that humanity in all its phases tries to understand the world and its dangers and find efficient ways to cope with them. The evolution of reason, he explained, consists in the development of clearer and empirically provable ways of thinking and more efficient practical techniques. He assumed that each new historical phase starts with the awareness of challenges that the existing approaches cannot deal with satisfactorily and the creation of new ones. As the new approaches are followed, the approaches of the former phase are gradually more or less abandoned. The thinking in the "metaphysical" phases, in which people speculated about general principles and created theories and techniques according to them, was more efficient than the "theological" thinking of the primitive phases, and therefore their beliefs, including religious beliefs, their magic and rituals, became obsolete. The present, "positive," way of thinking, is based on seeking knowledge that is gained from systematic studies of empirical facts in order to discover laws, and practical techniques that apply such knowledge. It is more efficient than philosophy with its endless debates about the advantages of alternative principles in the fields of metaphysics, ontology, epistemology, morality, politics and so on, and is the only hope to come closer and closer to the knowledge of reality. *The last word will be given to natural and social sciences and the respective engineering of practical plans* (Comte, 1961; Bourdeau, 2006).

Behaviorists, denying the reliability of any introspective research, embraced that position in the twentieth century, and added behaviorist psychology and its practical application to the positivist hope of scientifically reshaping human reality. Yet this was not the end of controversies but the start of new ones.

In contrast, Hegel and his followers (the rationalist among the *anti-positivists*) believed that philosophy provides a rational knowledge on a higher level than science. Hegel believed that myths, religious beliefs and rituals as well as literature and the arts express the philosophical truths or conflicts of their respective eras in nonphilosophical ways, but believe that only their explicit expression in conceptual forms enables awareness and self-awareness. Instead of ending "futile debates" by the triumph of scientific thinking, he believed that *dialectical logic*, reinterpretation and re-integration of the oppositions in existing material conflicts as well as ideational controversies in a synthesis on a higher level (in which they are both accepted, but as partial aspects) *was a process that started with the creation of the world. In its final step "the full realization of Reason" would culminate in a comprehensive, contradiction-free social reality as well as philosophical theory* (Hegel, 2018, 2004).[6]

Hegel shared with Comte the belief that the development of the species is repeated in the development of each individual; therefore, like Comte, he expected that at the final stage not only political conflicts but also many individual conflicts would be overcome. Yet both were aware that most of the world has not yet arrived at the final stage and that some residues of primitive ways of thinking may nevertheless persist even in the most evolved societies.

The impact of these ideas is still echoed in all the psychotherapeutic theories that assume that individuals evolve according to a given schema of development from birth to maturity or old age, and that the sources of their "psychological problems" are unsolved conflicts in earlier stages of their cognitive, affective, social, and moral development. (Psychoanalysts added sexual development to the story.) They tend to assume that the mature and sane individual has also arrived at the most reasonable philosophical position (i.e., their own).

The conflict between positivists and Hegelians in their changing forms is still going on, although both positions were criticized from a variety of directions, including opponents who concentrated on the logical flaws in those theories. They were attacked by anti-positivists who believed that the alleged progress of Reason was one-sided or even distorted, and was accompanied by the loss of other venues to truth, wisdom or inner personal power. This camp contained conservatives and partisans of religious or nationalist causes as well as philosophers who paid attention to the unconscious aspects of reality and self.[7]

Jungian psychotherapists follow this camp. Jung did not share the Enlightenment assumptions and ideals that were common to both Comte and Hegel, but rather those of the counter-Enlightenment in the German style, starting with the later Schelling and ending with Nietzsche, and making, under the impact of Schopenhauer, a long mental tour in Indian symbolic territories. A Jungian treatment is supposed to free patients from involvement in "pointless intellectual disputes," accept rather than fight conflicting aspects of personality and reality, and lead the patients to "deeper, spiritual truths" and awareness of their unconscious, personal, "selves."[8] (Jung was probably also influenced by the ideas of the theosophic movement, particularly those about connections between "Germanic" and Indian mentalities, the great mother and other ideas that were selectively absorbed into the Pan-Germanist ideology.) Others were interested in immediate experience and intuition.[9]

There were also those who mistrusted theories of history as a threat to liberal freedom (Popper, 1957) and those who believed that they were too speculative and ignored the real impact of participating individuals, their intentional actions and reactions and the unintended results of their interactions, like (Mill, 2015) or (Weber, 2010) or the "subjective meanings" of their experiences and behaviors (Dilthey, 2002). Other philosophers felt that they were irrelevant to personal life problems and crises (Unamuno, 2011) or were meaningless in the quest for meaningful living (Kierkegaard, 2014).

Some thinkers claimed that those philosophies were distortive ideologies of the dominant or "alien" groups. Among these were socialists who believed in progress, like (Marx, 2000, chapters 13, 14, 16), "Völkerists," who revolted against modernity and urbanism and aspired to "revive" the allegedly ancient but suppressed cultural heritage of their ethnic group or "race" (Mosse, 1966)[10]. Some radicals, inspired perhaps by the syndicalist (Sorel, 1999), but preferring anarchist or violent Fascist ways, were future-oriented and anti-traditionalists but did not believe in progress in light of Enlightenment's ideals (such as the superiority of logical and explicit thinking, the belief in its universality, and the importance of universal consensus based on the assumption of the basic equality and freedom of all human beings). Finally, there were lovers of alternative theories of history, for example, organic, cyclical, and relativistic theories like that of (Spengler, 2013), who prophesied the decline of Western civilization after a final, long, phase of happy dictatorship. In addition to all those opponents, and the controversies among them, there were other relativists, pluralists, and skeptics. Briefly, instead of putting an end to controversies, the attempt to let "history" decide created many others.

Some Twentieth-Century Attempts to Overcome Philosophical Controversies

Revolutions in the "Hard" Sciences

Evolutionary changes in mathematical logic since the end of the nineteenth century shattered some basic beliefs about mathematics—the model for a priori knowledge, such as the intuitive evidence of basic axioms or the conviction that the truth or falsity of theorems can always be logically demonstrated within the axiomatic system to which they belong. Revolutionary changes in some basic concepts of physics, the model for the "unshakable knowledge" of empirical reality such as time, space, causality, and the belief in the independence of the observed from the observer, had equally devastating effects on philosophy. They demonstrated that even theories in disciplines of the "hard" sciences were imperfect and replaceable by alternative theories. They showed, moreover, that prior philosophical attempts to found mathematics and science on something more basic—experiential data, innate ideas or a priori tools of reason—actually reflected the impact of dominant mathematical and physical concepts on epistemological conceptions, and therefore those analyses were logically fallacious, mistaking the "based" for the "basis," projecting theories about entities in "spatialized" time on the "immediate data of consciousness" in the mental "duration" (Bergson, 2001) and "misplacing the concreteness" of physical as well as psychological reality in abstract theories (Whitehead, 1997a, 52).[11]

Epistemological conceptions were now conceived as irrelevant to the understanding of mathematical logic, and as obstacles to scientific progress, since they could hinder the acceptance of new theories, which transcended their horizon.

Phenomenology

Edmund Husserl's phenomenological plan was a heroic attempt to revive the Kantian project to found mathematics, science, religion, morality, esthetic, or political theories on the structures of human consciousness, which he hoped to do by reliance on "immediate experience," independently of epistemological conceptions and the metaphysical or ontological assumptions underlying physical, psychological or and social theories. He developed, inspired by Henri Bergson and influenced by Franz Brentano, a new kind of conceptual research: *the explorations of the genesis of "meanings."* It consisted of *introspective "transcendental" analyses of the exploring "transcendental" subject's concrete experience relating, in a variety of "intentional acts"* (perceiving, remembering, imagining, expecting, wishing, hoping etc.) *to "intentional objects*" (whatever is perceived, remembered, imagined, expected, wished, hoped for etc.), *while "putting in parentheses,"* (i.e., postponing, irrelevant judgments and abstracting from irrelevant aspects), *and explorations of processes of "giving meaning"* (interpreting the objects as so an so) and more importantly, exploring the processes which enable the "*constitution of meanings*" (the formation of the interpretative notions and concepts). Husserl believed that the new discipline will be able to solve the philosophical as well as the political and religious crises of his time, as those analyses were supposed to solve once and for all three problems: The first one concerned the foundation of the basic structures of experience, where not only "emotionally tuned" (gladly, regretfully, anxiously etc.) perceptions in the present but also "retentions" from the past and "protentions" to the future (in the subject's "inner time") participate in the formation of the *meanings that the subject gives to objects*. The second was a conceptual study of various kinds of objects (physical, social, religious, artistic, etc.) and their modalities of existence (concrete, dreamed, theatrical, ideal, etc.). Husserl did not propose, however, to stay on the subjective level; rather, his purpose was to explore which abstractions and exchanges of perspectives with others enable the formation of a common language and the intersubjective world on the level of common sense as well as on the level of social, religious, scientific or artistic experiences. Hence the third problem that he tried to solve: the "constitution of the meaning" of an "objective world," and exploration of the "transcendental conditions of possibility" of an intersubjective world (Husserl, 1965). The last project was, however, entangled with difficulties to solve the "other minds" problem that bother philosophers since Descartes started his introspective studies: to explain how the thinking subject can "constitute" within his subjective experience the "meaning" of an object that is not just a body but also an experiencing other subject. Without the "other subject," who can corroborate his experiences and add information from perspectives that are inaccessible to him, the exploring subject cannot "constitute" the "meaning" of an "objective world." Husserl had therefore to abandon some his dreams (Husserl, 1936) and returned from the "transcendental" level to that of everyday life, were intersubjective reality is taken for granted. He continued to examine the adequacy of the conceptual schemes of grammar, mathematics, and the empirical sciences, which, according to his analyses, are abstractions on a second level, to the respective first-level abstractions of the commonsensical domains that those sciences purport to explain, and the relations between the first level commonsensical abstractions to the basic, concrete but subjective experiential level. Some of his followers in that direction, for example Maurice Merleau-Ponty (2012), who studied the experiencing of one's own and the other's body, or Alfred Schutz (1967), who studied social interactions, found affinities between their studies and the studies of various kinds of experiences and attitudes by the American pragmatist William James (2012).

Other phenomenologists who made that return, notably (the early) Heidegger, were not interested in the sciences or in the "constitutions of meanings," i.e., or forming of concepts [or "essences"], by a "subject" that apparently resides "outside the world" and perceives "objects" existing within it. They preferred the exploration of the experience of a being that is "being-there" in the world [Dasein], acting on exiting things, feeling, knowing-how (rather than the explicit conceptual schemes of knowing-that), being with others [Mitsein], sharing with them traditions and customs, yet aware of his personal finiteness, and trying anxiously to give existential rather than conceptual meaning to his individual life (Heidegger, 2010). From (the early) Sartre's perspective, influenced by Hegel, the existentialist stance meant a phenomenological exploration of the experience of a being-in-an-interpersonal-world, who is tilted between his self-awareness as a free, undefinable, "being-for-himself" [être-pour-soi], and, himself as a "being-for-the other" [être-pour-autrui], that is, an object in the "regard" of the other, who sometimes tries to reduce him to a definable and predictable being, as if he were an unconscious "being-in-itself" [*être-en-soi*], without freedom of choice or possibility of being unexpectable.

Disagreements among Husserl's "loyal" followers and the "rebellious" existentialists (on the theoretical as well as the political levels) was one of the obstructions that prevented the solution of philosophical "crises" in the phenomenological way. The other obstacle in its way to put an end to controversies was the disdain of both analytic and structuralist philosophers to subjective experiential analyses.

Analytic Philosophy

Both analytic philosophers and positivists *denied the validity of introspective studies* and rejected attempts to base logic and objective knowledge on what they conceived as merely sociological or linguistic contingent facts, reflected in a distorted way on the unreliable psychological level. They sought to *limit philosophy to logical analyses*, and in particular, to analyses of the logically adequate *languages* for dealing with the relevant philosophical issue. They proposed that we discard as pseudo problems *philosophical questions that could not be dealt with in any such language. They considered such problems void of cognitive meaning or just nonsense* (Wittgenstein, 1922; Ayer, 1952). This led them to constitute a new domain of research—the philosophy of language—which was supposed to put an end to traditional introspective as well as metaphysical studies and to their "meaningless" disagreements.

But it soon led to a split between the explorers of "ideal languages" or formal languages from the logician's perspective, and the philosophers of common language, for example John Austin, who criticized metaphysicians for failing to understand how words work (Austin, 1947), and methodologists both failing to understand how communication among scientists works. In this respect Austin and the others joined philosophers who preferred, like Aristotle, commonsensical prudence to "Platonic" systematic knowledge that is supposed to be always true but, as the later Ludwig Wittgenstein (formerly on the sides of the logicians) said, it actually "works" only hypothetically: on ideal "frictionless ground," where walking is impossible (Wittgenstein, 1967). They relied, like Hume, on well-functioning customs or the intuitive "rules of thumb" of the skilled. Unlike some of the logical analytic philosophers, the philosophers of common language were interested in the possibility of communication, in the variety of uses of words, the different functions that may be fulfilled by speech acts, the nature of linguistic rules and the psychological or social impact of linguistic distinctions. Those philosophers did take seriously some of the issues that intrigued the phenomenalists, but they rejected their experiential approach. They not only denied the philosophical validity of the subjective point of view, they claimed that linguistic customs, or, in Wittgenstein's jargon, "language games" that are "played" in one's culture determine the categories in which one thinks of one's experiences, and the distinctions that one makes not only with regards to common objects but also with regards to one's inner world.

The common language philosophers believed to have solved the problem of solipsism, which presupposes the priority of subjective experience and "private language" to a common language in an "intersubjective" world; but they created a new problem: the incommensurability of different "language games" and the danger of relativism or even solipsism on the cultural level. That danger became more accentuated when ideas of philosophers that were influenced by structural linguistic and the application of its categories in anthropology and literary interpretation, like Michel Foucault (Foucault, 1973), mixed its entirely different conception of language with some ideas of the philosophers of common language and combined it with Kuhn's idea (see the subsection "Let us explore science . . ."), following the crisis in the methodology of science, of the incommensurability of different scientific paradigm (Lyotard, 1984).

Methodology of Science

In contrast to all the formers, the logical positivists, who shared the positivistic conviction that science should have the last word, insisted that philosophy should limit itself to a critical study of *the logic of the correct methodology and the appropriate language of science*, and thus form clear criteria for judging which theories are scientific and which should be rejected, accepted or, in cases of competing acceptable theories, preferred to others. It would thus also enable the liberation of science from metaphysical, religious, political biases or any other bias that relies on pseudo-theories or unreliable intuitions, which are irrelevant to science and might hinder the advance toward better knowledge and improved technology. But they failed in their endeavor to formulate the logical rules for unambiguous scientific language. The attempt to find logical criteria for purely "positive" science based on inductions from data (Carnap, 1967) or at least for the exclusion of "irrelevant assumptions" from scientific "nomothetic deductive" theories (Hempel, 1965) involved them with fallacies and paradoxes, and they could not agree about the criteria for acceptance of theories or even for preferences among them. They failed, furthermore, to cope with actual difficulties in physics that were formerly considered typical to the domain of the "soft" human sciences, such as "uncertainty" (i.e., the inevitable use of various, incompatible, theories for the explanation of the behavior of the same objects under different conditions or from different perspectives), "indeterminacy" [of the behavior of individuals] or the "incompleteness" of systems; in other words, the need, in mathematics and computer science, to refer to meta-systems for the checking the truth of theorems).

Let Us Explore Science As It Practically Is

The inner difficulties of the philosophy of science gave birth to a new discipline: socio-historical studies, which explore the actual *activity* of research and communication, and examine under which conditions theories are rejected, accepted, or preferred *in practice*.

Thomas Kuhn (1962) was inspired by the ideas of Whitehead and by the discussion provoked by the Popperian demand to reject any theory, regardless of the percentage of its empirical confirmations, when scientists agree that one of its empirical predictions is contradicted (Popper, 1959).[12] Kuhn suggested the idea of a dominant paradigm, which is not just a successful theory that serves as a model for other theories in other domains, but a whole presupposed conception, whose tacit metaphysical and epistemological assumptions serve as a basis for theoretical claims, and for scientific methodology, observational practices and logical considerations. It determines, moreover, which questions are scientifically meaningful. Kuhn defined "revolution" in science (and other disciplines) as a "paradigm shift." He found that dominant theories are not rejected because their predictions are occasionally falsified. They are held as long as they enable the production of satisfactory answers to new questions. But when that ability is diminished, when it is "infected" with "fatigue" (in Whitehead's terms), the inability of the normal activity to answer questions and solve accumulating "riddles" encourages the creation of alternative theories that transcend the limits of the dominant conception. The alternative theories are incompatible with some of the presuppositions of the dominant conception, and in that sense are revolutionary. The "paradigm shift," the acceptance of a new conception by the community of scientists in the relevant domain, is accompanied by philosophical discussions which eventually enable the scientists to become aware of the presuppositions they took for granted and realize that they are neither necessary nor beyond any doubt, and therefore are replaceable.

Kuhn's conclusions were far reaching. He insisted for a while that new paradigms are "incommensurable" with the old ones, and his claims were criticized by some philosophers and historians and philosophers of science.[13] Although the latter were ready to acknowledge that scientific decisions are enabled thanks to all kinds of presuppositions that were considered irrelevant by the logical positivists, his claims did not cause a complete paradigm shift in the philosophy of science.

They had, however, a great impact on other philosophers.

Postmodernism

Many Ideas, a Little Order

The postmodernists were first influenced by *structuralist* approaches to anthropology and mythology (Lévi-Strauss, 1963a) inspired by ideas of the structural linguist De Saussure, and tried to apply them (and the ideas that "the meaning of a member of a system depends on its place in the system," and the "subjective" opinions of the individuals who members of the system or are using the system are irrelevant to its functioning") in other domains.[14] Thus they challenged the place that modern philosophy accords to the "thinking (or experiencing) subject" or "I," his intentions and understanding. That place was already challenged by the positivist sociologists, who followed Comte, and Freud's psychoanalysis, which was deeply influenced by Comtean ideas, it should be stressed that the postmodernists challenged right from the beginning the Comtean (as well as the Hegelian) evolutionary assumptions, according to which modern ways of thinking, conceptions are practices are more rational than traditional, ancient, or primitive ones. Yet many among them still adhered to Marxist and Freudian ideas. Later they were influenced by the "post-structuralists," who, like Derrida, found the structuralist conception inadequate and "logocentric," and were interested in the "deconstruction" of conceptual clusters rather than "constituting" new ones. Still later, they became 'post-Marxists," "post-ideologists" and so on. Now their views are comprised of what, to my mind, is a mishmash of structural linguistics and other conceptions of language, where "incommensurable" approaches to language, such as semiology and the inquiry of speech acts are melded together and opponents like, for example, Marx with Nietzsche and Hegel and Lévi-Strauss, Heidegger and enemies are best friends. In the formerly opposed analytic camps, "post analytic" philosophers, like Richard Rorty (1989), became pluralist and relativist, and reduced approaches to philosophy, that from the perspectives of their authors, such as Heidegger, Wittgenstein and Dewey, were totally different to the common numerator of "being therapeutic" (Rorty, 1979). Some "post-positivists" philosophers of science, like Feyerabend, support methodological anarchy, and their claim that "everything goes," not only Newton's and Einstein's theories, Christianity, and Islam, but also fascism and communism, totalitarianism, and liberalism, enabled eventually the claim that there is no difference between true and fake "news" or "narratives." Some of the declared postmodernists, like Lyotard, have tried to write a systematic and responsible postmodern philosophy (Lyotard, 1984); some, like Deleuze and Guattari (1994), propose a postmodern theory about the incommensurability of philosophers. Both versions of postmodernism could count as new skeptical versions of the ancient attempt—to put an end to philosophical controversies—unfortunately without the promised ataraxia and eudaimonia.

Yet they did not put an end to any controversy.

Opponents of Postmodernism

Besides the "stubborn" empiricists or naturalists and the "stubborn" rationalists or realists (see note 11), there are other philosophers that oppose the postmodern relativism. For example, thinkers with the legacy of the Frankfurt school, like Habermas, who try to revive Enlightenment ideals by enlarging them to include within its horizons neglected problems and the voices of groups of "others" which earlier philosophers of that camp failed to hear (Honneth et al., 1992).

Despite my agreement with some postmodernist claims and doubts, I am among their opponents because of their problematic influences. For example, post-colonialists and some partisans of the causes of other "others," like feminists and LGBT people, who do not want to be included in a universalist worldview but rather insist on their different "identities" and their different moralities and social values which have been denied or disrespected by colonialists or other oppressors (Homi, 2004). Their "politics of identities," which is based on many fallacies, is socially and morally problematic.[15] Moreover, under the impact of some postmodernist ideas, students, like those of visual arts, for example, are encouraged nowadays by their schools to replace philosophers, as their abstract-minded "philosophy-of-art" teachers tell them that they are not just making in their paintings variations on a theme: they are "exploring concepts," while their politically minded trainers tell them that they are not just learning how to design posters: they are "making philosophical statements." They are also taught that those "statements" should not be criticized artistically, philosophically, or politically, because such criticism would violate their freedom of speech. If we remember the Shakespearean "fools," who had the privilege to criticize without being criticized, we can say that th ose "philosophers," who are making a caricature of philosophy, ask their students to make fools of themselves.

They inspire cynical journalists and politicians to take advantage of that "everything goes" spirit and join the social networks in creating deeper controversies by disagreements about "fake news" and "alternative truths." They also inspire some philosophical counselors with no philosophical background to invent alternative and fake philosophies.

Relevance to Philosophical Counseling

It is possible that some new ideas will break through the impasse created by the cynical or stupid misuse of skepticism, pluralism and relativism, and new ways to overcome controversies will be suggested. However, philosophical counselors, although they do not necessarily have a synoptic view of the philosophical realm, should be aware of the present state-of-the art. Therefore, they should avoid presenting their preferred philosophy as "the" philosophy, be aware of the opinions of its critics, and let the counselee be aware that it is one among several alternative views that are relevant to the issue that bothers him. They should enable him to make—despite all the noises just described—his own philosophical choice, whether among them or whether among other possibilities that occur to him thanks to a horizon-opening philosophical dialogue.

I am among those who are not convinced by Kuhn's idea of the "incommensurability" of paradigms (nor by Foucault's analysis of "*epistemes*" (Foucault, 1973) and the alleged impassable gap between "identity groups." I believe that, as in the case of adherents of religious or political groups, scientific or philosophical researchers share some of their presuppositions with opponents who support alternative theories. The similarity between members of any given group to members of the opposing group may be greater than their similarity to some members of their own group. I agree with some empiricists on the common factual referent of alternative theories or narratives, and with some rationalists about universal elements of rationality. I also believe that most of the concepts presupposed by a theory are "fuzzy," and that most of the concepts presupposed by a revolutionary theory bear some "family resemblance" to most of the presupposed concepts of the old theory. Yet revolutionary theories transcend the limited horizon of the old theory. The fact that revolutions, like controversies, recur, does not mean that they leave us in the same place.

Kuhn succeeded in showing that, at least under some conditions, philosophical controversies are not only unavoidable but also beneficial, and in any case enable awareness of obstructive presuppositions and the possibility of alternative ways of thinking. Such widening of horizons may be beneficial not only in the case of general and theoretical difficulties but also in personal and practical cases. That, as already said, is the basis of my conception of philosophical counseling.

Notes

1. Despite the fact that the term 'hedonism' is derived from the Greek term 'eudaimonia,' its conception of happiness as linked to the pleasure derived from the satisfaction of desires, is very different from the ancient conception, which often demands overcoming desires.

2. The latter ideas are elaborated in Descartes ([1649], 1989).

3. Further elaborations of his ideas: concerning religious toleration (Locke, [1689], 1991), politics (Locke, [1690] 1993) and education (Locke, [1693] 2010).

4. Kant explains his approach and method in Kant ([1787], 1929) and deals there with scientific knowledge, phenomenal determinism and metaphysics; he discusses practical—goal-oriented versus moral judgments and the difference between man as "phenomenon" and as "noumenon" in (Kant, [1788] 2002), where he also implicitly explains what he would expect from a state based on a rational contract, while his realistic doubts are expressed in collections of essays written mainly in the 1790s (Kant, 1991). Aesthetic and teleological judgments are dealt with in Kant ([1790] 2002). His opinions concerning Enlightenment ideals are presented in Kant, [1794] 1999); the "rational religious hope" as well as Kant's pessimism is discussed in Kant ([1793] 2009), and the possibility of "perpetual peace" in Kant ([1795] 2018). His opinions about human (sexual) "animality" and its "humanization" in "relations of alliance" in Kant, 1784–1785 (1997). See also Gruengard (2015).

5. See detailed analysis of the difference in Brook and Wuerth, 2020).

6. My presentation is very simplified and relates only to his conception of philosophy as an endeavor to overcome oppositions. It does not do justice to Hegel's ideas

with regards to many concepts and issues which for him were inseparable from his conception of philosophy.

7. E.g., (Schelling, 2008), (Schopenhauer, 2016), (Nietzsche, 2001).

8. The approaches of philosophical counselors who are more directly inspired by Indian, Buddhist or other East-Asian worldviews are usually very far from Jung's ideas and methods.

9. E.g., (Bergson, 2001, 1992).

10. Mosse deals with German Völkerist trends, but such trends existed in other groups that aspired to "go back" to their allegedly "ethnic roots."

11. There is no place to go into details. Russell, Whitehead, Frege, Wittgenstein, and in some respects also Husserl, were among those who dealt with the philosophy of mathematics and its language, and the appearance of non-Euclidean geometries, the axiomatization of arithmetic and Gödel's theorem in mathematical logic are among the challenging events. The main occurrence in physics was, of course, the emergence of Einstein's theory of relativity, quantum theory and principles such as Heisenberg's principle of uncertainty.

12. It is an imprecise interpretation, as Popper assumes that the belief, that the statement that is considered contradicting evidence, is true is also fallible, and it is a matter of the scientific community's agreement to stop the attempts of falsification and accept it as falsifying evidence.

13. All of them accuse Kuhn with conceptual vagueness. Some of the "Popperians," who deny the possibility to prove empirical truths, insist that one can, with the help of his "revolutionary theory," demonstrate the falsity of the still-dominant theory, and there are methodological limits to the ability of the defenders of the latter to save it with ad hoc hypotheses that are supposed to correct its empirically falsified predictions. However, the fact that the still-dominant theory was falsified does not mean that it was not a genial theory, an advancement that eventually enabled the further advancement by the conception of the "revolutionary theory." Moreover, the fact that it was falsified does not mean that it cannot continue to predict correctly many practically relevant situations. In Einstein's terms, it may be a good approximation to reality, but the new theory, which can make predictions that are not yet falsified, is a better approximation. The "naturalists" or empiricist (Quine et al.) and "realists" or "rationalists" among them (Putnam et al.), do not accept the conclusion that conceptual differences logically justify the claim that the theories are totally incomparable for they refer to the same empirical evidence, and are therefore translatable to one another. All of them criticize the claim that conceptual changes occur only in "revolutionary times" and reject the assumption that they are practically involved with an inability to communicate as they are necessarily based on different ways of conceiving reality. They also do not accept the Kantian position that the presupposed metaphysical and epistemological conceptions are independent of any experience and do not reflect the reality "behind" them. The empiricists among them claim that the real is empirical and philosophical assumptions are abstract and indirect generalizations from the empirical level, while the rationalists argue that if

the human ways of rational elaboration of empirical data had not been adapted to the natural structure of the world the human race would not have survived.

14. From Barthes's interpretation of literature and the study of implicit "mythologies" in society, through Althusser's interpretation of Marx's texts and Foucault's explorations of the "epistemes" of historical epochs to Lacan's revision of Freud's conception of the "unconscious."

15. Being myself a member of several groups of "others," I feel solidarity with such groups, although I am closer to those who want to promote the project of improved and more comprehensive Enlightenment. Moreover, the "other," however oppressed and discriminated against, does not necessarily see himself/herself in the eyes of the oppressor, and I am not sure that members of such groups must agree about their separate identity in their struggle against that oppression. In any case, I do not think that such groups should feel that their "identifying culture" is "appropriated" by, say, a movie actor of a different "identity group" playing the role of a figure from "their" group, as if "white" Olivier did something wrong to the "blacks" by acting the role of Othello. Christianism adopted and reinterpreted Judaic texts and ideas, Islam did the same to both Jewish and Christian ideas. Judaism, despite rabbinical denials, did the same to some "pagan" ideas, and all the three "Abrahamic" religions influenced each other and have some debts to Greco-Roman and Persian legacies. What they "took" was much more important than what Olivier "took" from the "blacks"; yet they did not "appropriate" anything, for neither ideas nor theatrical roles are properties, and the original "owner," if there is any, does not lose his ideas or roles because another "borrows" or "imitates" them. Nor are the "others" "turned into objects" by an outsider who does research about their group. The ancient Israelites described and the "pagans" and explained their behavior, the Christians described and explained the "Jews" and so forth, and some of the descriptions are distorted and some of the explanations are wrong, just like some European descriptions and explanations of "Orientals" and some Arabic, African, Jewish-Orthodox or Indian descriptions and explanations of "Europeans." Yet none of the individuals whose culture was thus misrepresented became thereby an "object" rather than "subject." It is not, unfortunately, needless to add that consistency would require those "identity-protecting others" to avoid such "appropriation" and "objectification" of members of other groups, whether the latter have lower or higher status in their explicit or tacit scales of cultural, social, or political values (or power). Nor is it unnecessary to remind some of them that any intended misrepresentation, even of the supposedly privileged, is unfair.

Appendix C

Philosophical Influences and Presuppositions in Psychotherapy

I deal here with some philosophical influences on psychotherapy and hope to clarify some misunderstandings of some philosophical counselors regarding some psychotherapeutic approaches.

Saying that an approach is inspired by philosophical ideas is sometimes a compliment; in any case, it should not be understood as an underestimation of the originality of the founders of those psychotherapeutic orientations. Interpretation of data is always involved with philosophical assumptions, and the integration of ideas from different sources into a coherent theory is a great achievement. I believe, however, that the part philosophy plays in the formation of the depth-psychologies is very great, while the contribution of empirically tested information is rather small. The clinical evidence that allegedly confirms them is problematic: The reliability of information about patients and occurrences in the clinic is acknowledged as a problem in professional circles and is discussed therein. Philosophers are concerned with the logical circularity, which bothers only some of the professionals. With all due respect to the intelligence, experience and wisdom of the professionals involved, I allow myself to expose some of the comic aspects of that problem.

There are philosophical counselors who agree with some psychotherapists that depth psychology deals with the past of the patient to uncover the *causes* of the patient's current condition. It may be that these misunderstandings arise from Freud's insistence on the scientific nature of his theory, which led some philosophers of science to prove that it is not scientific (Popper, 2002), while others showed that it is scientific but false (Grünbaum, 1985).

According to Jung, his own theory is based on wisdom that is deeper than those intellectuals' understanding, and beyond the scope of their criteria. Therefore, they did not bother to examine its scientific status. Adler was less pretentious than both were. He had a skeptic's attitude regarding scientific theories in general, and he was more concerned with the patients' future than their past, as was Freud. Even so, he had some assumptions about causal connections (some of which fitted the methodological criteria of scientific explanations better than Freud's). In any case, many depth psychologists today acknowledge that they are offering interpretations and not causal explanations (Schafer, 1976; Spence, 1982).

In consequence, some psychotherapists with a background in depth psychology claimed that what matters is the efficiency and effectivity of an interpretation, and therefore there is room for considering their replacement by alternative, non-causal but effective approaches, which are less painful, perhaps also less harmful, and surely less costly. Some propose to explore the problematic situations of the patients in the present, instead of looking for their alleged sources in the past. Others suggest that the patient's problem may be due to his place and role in his family or other social system rather than in his personal disturbances. Some maintain that knowing the causes for a problem does not guarantee its solution. Others claim that the patient needs to understand the meaning of his problem rather than its causes. Some go further and insist that the real problem is not due to past events but to the patient's present moral or existential confusions, or the confusions of his generation or culture. Others respond that what the patient needs is not the solution of a specific problem or clarification of specific confusions but finding a meaning for his life.

All these claims sound logical, but the depth psychologists, who, in fact, *are* dealing with some of the issues that the alternative approaches propose, do not deal with the patient's past in order to discover the *causes* of his present difficulty. They *already know the cause*; that is, they presuppose it in their theory; not, of course, the specific details of the actual patient, but in general.[1] They assume that something in the developmental process of the patient went wrong or was not completely achieved. The need to *correct the results*, not the difficulties in discovering the causes, is responsible for the length of psychoanalytic treatment. The treatment may sound more medical in the case of Freudian psychoanalysis, more philosophical in the case of Adlerian "personal psychology" and more spiritual in the case of Jungian "analytic psychology," but the three schools take upon themselves the ancient philosophical project of reforming people, or changing their characters, by purging them of their allegedly inadequate beliefs, wishes, emotions and ways of thinking, as part of the project of the education of humanity. The developmental hypotheses at the basis of that project are however far from obvious. I therefore deal with their philosophical roots.

The allegedly inadequate content and process that these approaches attack are not *conscious* or "*preconscious*." They pretend to reveal the *unconscious* material, but do not do this by logical exploration but rather by processes that resemble, to my mind, a deciphering of encoded information that the psychotherapist can observe. Although some of them assume that the patient may be conscious of what the psychologist perceives, they share with the others the conviction that the patient is not aware of it *as a signifier of something beyond itself*, and therefore misinterpret it. Such pretensions justify a discussion of their conception of the "unconscious."

For depth psychologists, the patient is like a prisoner in Plato's cave, unable to see what stands behind the silhouettes of objects lit by fire. By descending to the depth of the unconscious, they are out of the cave and see the real things in the bright light of the true sun, even when there are some clouds in the sky. They also pretend to know which values and principles should guide the cave prisoners, and this is a reason for a non-Platonic philosopher to discuss their moral conceptions.

Developmental Blueprint

The Positivist Story and Its Critics

The positivist story is reflected in Piaget's theory of intellectual development (Piaget and Inhelder, 1958) and Kohlberg's theory of moral growth (Kohlberg, 1976). Therefore, despite the apparent anachronism, I rely on these theories in my description of the positivistic background of earlier psychoanalytic theories. The story is based on the positivist conception of historical and personal evolution:[2] Intelligence, sociability, and morality, which have evolved through crises in the history of the species, develop in the same order in the life of the individual, but it also contains some Kantian elements. The assumption that the newborn thinks associatively, perhaps in a dreamlike state of mind (Lévi-Bruhl, 2015),[3] unable to identify objects, distinguish between his sensations and reality, himself and others, or think in terms of time, space or causality (Freud's "primary process"), originated, perhaps, in the speculations of the old empiricists. The modern orthodox positivists, who did not believe in the possibility of exploring individual minds, started the story by guessing, considering the modern explorer's difficulties to understand the behaviors, rituals and myths of primitive *groups*, the nature of their assumed shared mentality. The old empiricists' newborn, especially if one follows Hobbes rather than Locke, is totally egocentric, egoistic, and hedonistic (Freud's "pleasure principle"). The modern positivist assumes that his intellectual tools (Freud's "secondary process"), social understanding and moral thinking evolve in stages, through his growing ability to interact with his environment (Freud's "reality principle"). The evolution is, however, not the way empiricists would see it; instead, at each developmental stage, the child is supposed to develop a priori tools for processing information, forming ideals and projects, making judgments and decisions. The passage from stage to stage occurs through crises when difficulties cannot be overcome by the existing mental tools. What is supposed to be specific to mature persons is the ability to think coherently in general and abstract terms and in the objective manner that enables one to study mathematics and science, and to think independently of others, and yet conceive of himself and his group as one among many. Although he is aware that everyone perceives himself and others from a subjective perspective, he understands that they can exchange perspectives and constitute together an intersubjective world and form social alliances that are based on mutual agreements. (Kant would love it, although there are no "transcendental ego" and "noumena" in the story). The child's morality is first influenced by parental prescriptions, threats and rewards, with legends or religious myths reinforcing the message; later, pair-group interactions become more relevant. Finally, the mature adult is supposed to be able to adopt autonomous moral principles, which take the non-egocentric understanding into account, and are therefore never purely egotistic and hedonistic. He is also supposed to be able to overcome parental and social influences and autonomously choose political positions that take into consideration the point of view, interests and rights of other persons and other groups. In brief, the mature adult can realize Enlightenment ideals, with some degree of freedom between utilitarian considerations in Mill's style and Kantian ideals of human dignity, fairness, and justice.

Failures to overcome developmental crises, due to lack of the necessary natural and social conditions, might leave traces, which find expression in mental disabilities or psychological difficulties in later stages. Moreover, many positivist sociologists, psychiatrists and psychologists believe that even in modern societies or adult minds there are residues from former periods. They find expression culturally, in myths, religious beliefs and rituals, and psychologically in states of mind that are less than full wakefulness, such as dreaming, dozing, hallucinating, or being under the influence of hypnosis, drugs or fever. Some positivists maintain that in times of stress even well-developed individuals or societies might regress to former developmental stages.

This story, whose sources are more speculative than factual, was taken for granted by many modern thinkers, but is challenged nowadays from a variety of perspectives:

Some research psychologists empirically exploring children's cognitive and social development disagree with the positivists' factual statements. Others reject the theories more fully. The empiricists among them use new terms (for example, "connectivity") and tools (computer simulations and statistical probabilities) but assume, like their predecessors, that the newborn is a tabula rasa, without prior concepts, rules or patterns of thinking and assume that the same mechanism that explains animal or human acquisition of knowledge in general is sufficient for the explanation of the child's development (Elman *et al.*1997). The rationalists in this group, or rather their nativist inheritors—Chomsky, Fodor, and others (Fodor, 1983)—assume that the child is born with specific inherited capacities. They do not share the classical belief in the nonmaterial nature of a priori knowledge and speak instead of species-specific and function-specific cerebral capacities, which developed in the process of evolution. They are not discoverable by introspective explorations as they are supposed to be operating nonconsciously, like the "deep grammar" in Chomsky's generative linguistics. Hypotheses about them should have empirical testable implications or be demonstrable by computer simulations. The assumed *capacities* exist from birth. What develops is the child's *ability to perform* accordingly. Researchers of intelligence and animal behavior claim that the abilities to communicate, learn from the experience of others, plan actions and use tools which, according to the positivist story, evolve only in human societies, as well as tendencies that are supposed to evolve only in later stages, such as altruism, cooperation, and solidarity, are found in nonhuman species (Andrews and Monsó, 2021).

Anthropologists and researchers of myth and religion, who nowadays study so called "primitive" cultures from perspectives which are different than those of their positivist predecessors, also call the positivist story into question. They claim that the worlds of the "primitives" are not less intelligent than those of the positivists or their modern Western models (Lévi-Strauss, 1966); archaeologists are now joining them in claiming that recent discoveries from prehistoric times undermine the idea of primitive minds.

The positivist story is also challenged by ideological groups: feminists, who claim that it does not give due respect to feminine capacities; conservatives, who accuse it of failing to understand religious beliefs, values, and behavior; members of cultural, ethnic, or other groups of "others" which are presented by it as not fully developed.

Counter-Positivist Voices

When psychiatrists like Freud and his peers, both friends and rivals, started to apply their "talk therapies" to normal "neurotics" and develop general theories about the developmental roots of "psychiatric illnesses," "personal disturbances" and the difficulties of sane people in dealing with their life problems, the challenges to the positivist developmental story came from other directions. Marxists, on the one hand, claimed that the story stopped before the end and represented bourgeois society. It ignored the exploited majority and the values that would be cherished in the more advanced stages of history. Nietzsche, on the other hand, claimed that it was the story of the majority, but a majority of "slaves." Counter-Enlightenment thinkers believed that the development of Enlightenment ideals involved the forgetfulness of deeper ideals, and was the result of the oppression of primordial, perhaps unconscious, ethnic or racial legacies. This oppression was at the hands of "foreigners," who illegitimately assumed dominance, and/or mediocre local rulers or masses, who were afraid and envious of outstanding heroes and other "master" types. Nietzsche rejected the conservative, religious, and nationalistic tendencies of both these groups. His myth of human development, which is supposed to change with the advent of the "over-man," is a variation, or a parody, of the positivistic Hegelian story. It presents Enlightenment heroes, the partisans of rationality and liberal democracy (and a *fortiori* but implicitly the socialists), as the inheritors of "slaves," who accepted ancestral and later religious authority out of fear, and now unite under the ideals of the Enlightenment in a resentful and envious struggle against the minority, the masters, the noble individuals. They are hypocritical, speaking of equality but eager to rule others instead of striving, like the "overman," for self-overcoming; they care for the poor, but do so out of contemptuous pity rather than a generous will to share. It is a self-deceptive story of slaves whose morality is just obedience to the prohibitions of tyrannical fathers, and whose rationality is just an adaptation to one-sided "Apollonian" values and suppression of the "Dionysian" aspects of life. Their quest for knowledge or any other apparent excellence is a quest for power. It is also a story of the denial of instinctual desires, whose suppression may find expression in alleged "sublime" kinds of love for "sublime" objects but is just a deceptive "sublimation" of sexual wishes. It is the story of the repression of traits and wishes that are shameful according to prevailing norms, and their projection onto others. It is also the story of people who fail to follow their person-specific "instincts" and thus fail to develop according to them (Wicks, 2021).

The Reflection of Those Challenges in Depth Psychologists' Developmental Theories

The reactions of the founders of depth psychology to the Marxist challenge were simple: Freud agreed that while there are many social problems that should be addressed, communism was based on illusion, as the abolition of private property and sexual restriction would not abolish instinctual aggressivity and sexuality and would not eliminate personal drives or the threats that untamed drives might pose to civilization[4] (Freud, 2002). Adler introduced some socialist ideals—although not in their Marxist version—into his developmental story (Adler, 1938); Jung never bothered about so-called "materialistic" concerns.

Their reactions to the Nietzschean challenge were much more complicated. Freud, who admired Nietzsche for his self-understanding and sincerity, agreed with his counter-version to the religious story (the degradation of the primordial love of God and his creatures after the Fall to merely carnal desire), and introduced primordial sexuality to his positivistic version of human development. Yet he did not share Nietzsche's conception of slave morality, nor accept the values underlying the call to "re-evaluate all values." Needless to add, he did not share the politically and historically incorrect opinions that Nietzsche expressed about the Jewish contribution to the European "degeneration" into "ascetic Christianity.[5] As I try to show later on, the idea of the Oedipal drama as the origin of morality is (also) an answer to Nietzsche.

Adler seems to have been indifferent to these provocations and to Nietzsche's interest in the instincts, but he borrowed from him the idea of the "will to power" (Adler, 2003). His developmental story starts with the inferiority feelings of the dependent child, and deals with the relative power of children in the family. He believes that people unconsciously develop "styles of life" for coping with the inferiority complex. Only one of the six possible styles that occurred to him fits a mature and sane adult: solidarity rather than rivalry with other people.

Jung, in contrast to both, saw himself as a Nietzschean, and missed, to my mind, the ironic tone in his master's voice, and the latter's attitude to the other teachers of the Swiss psychiatrist, from German Idealists to East Asian gurus with some theosophic ideas in the fusion. Like Freud, Jung admired Nietzsche's self-knowledge. However, what most impressed him was not the sincerity,[6] but what seemed to be a holistic self-acceptance which included not only the "positive" aspects, of which one is conscious, but also those that are considered "negative" or nonconventional and are "repressed" as "shadow" in the "unconscious." That holistic acceptance is, however, a German-Idealistic ideal, which makes sense only when one is a pantheist whose concern is to write a theodicean treaty.[7] Jung also owes to Nietzsche the idea of the "self" as different and more reliable than the "ego," but while the Nietzschean Self is biological and despites its individualist identity is as "instinctual" as the Freudian "id," the Jungian Self is "biological-spiritual" and is wiser than the Freudian "ego" while his inner conscience is more moral than any exogenous "superego." Moreover, Jung, apparently inspired by Nietzsche, liked myths about the heroic overcoming of obstacles. But while Nietzsche was aware of internal weaknesses as well as external obstacles in life, and spoke of accepting *fate*, self-*overcoming* and realizing one's personal "instinct," Jung's hero was searching for his "true self" and accepting the "shadow." He interpreted Nietzsche's criticism of the Apollonian tendencies as a biased and conventionalist intellectualism. While Nietzsche spoke of the insufficiency of logic and the need for imaginative empathy, Jung criticized the disrespect for intuition and other messages that, he supposed, arrive from the unconscious sphere. Jung's developmental story is about the socialization of the child by his submission to conventional norms and parental ambitions, the formation of the conscious ego and the self-presenting "persona," the split from the "shadow" and the unconscious "self," and the possible "individuation" by gradual "self-conscious" return, in a version of German Idealism, to "wholeness" through re-connection not only to one's unconscious personal aspects and divine messages, but also to common "archetypes." At least until the end of World War II, the latter included, besides the universal, ethnic ones.[8]

The Interfering "Residues"

All three school-founders presuppose that past developmental failures are responsible for present difficulties in coping with life problems.

According to the psychoanalysts, there are two sorts of developmental failures. The serious ones, which are responsible for "psychoses" and very problematic "personality disorders" like "narcissism" and "borderline," are said to be due to the failure to constitute basic structures such as the "ego" and its "functions," in the proper stage, most of them in very early childhood. Some of them are due to deprivation rather than conflicts. Although such an assumption seems to be supported by nonpsychiatric examples (failures to develop perceptive or linguistic abilities), many psychiatrists disagree with the claim that it is also the cause for the mental disorders that psychoanalysts call "psychoses," and seek genetic factors and physiological or environmental causes. Some of Freud's more rebellious followers added some pre-Oedipal dramas or deprivations to the Freudian story.[9] They believed that thanks to long and patient treatment, in which events analogous to the childhood events at the stage where the developmental hindrance occurred are re-enacted and experienced under conditions that, unlike the original ones, are beneficial. They believe the missing "structures" can be formed in the "psychotic" patient and this will enable him to become more "integrated."

Freud, who thought that psychoanalysis is inapplicable to "psychoses" and to other conditions in which the patient is unable to transfer his ancient unsolved issues to the analyst, is known thanks to his interest in the other kind of developmental failures, which are supposed to be responsible for "neuroses" (that is, the state of relatively sane people, without psychotic relapses, yet not completely mature: the regular state of every "normal" person). That kind of failure is supposed to leave the evolving person with traces of childhood traumas that fix him to a past developmental conflict that was not resolved completely and left, like the famous Oedipal conflict, traces that may be reevoked (Freud, 2015a). It is supposed to be an associative complex of contradicting wish-thoughts, anxieties, emotions and, most important, *ways of thinking* that were typical of the developmental stage in which an original "trauma", or series of traumas, occurred. The patient, who has repressed the trauma or traumas because of the anxiety they raise, does not remember it, but he is unconsciously reminded of it by a present traumatic experience. Its present intervention in the person's attempt to deal with his actual problems, without awareness that he is also reliving an old trauma, obstructs that attempt, and reevokes irrelevant emotions and inadequate, childish ways of thinking (McLeod, 2019).

Adler's "personal psychology" assumes that the obstructive intervention is by inadequate and unconscious "styles of life" that the patient has developed in prior stages to cope with his complex of inferiority and related difficulties.

Jung's "analytic psychology" does not look for causes of neuroses in childhood. He believed that psychological problems occur in reaction to actual difficulties, which may be due to a variety of causes, and may have occurred at any time in the person's life. The "neurosis," which occurs in crises and is relatively rare, is a defensive reaction: "one shrinks from the difficulties which life brings and thus finds oneself back in the world of the infant" (Jung, 1970 para. 473). The difficulty in coping is due to what Jung calls "disunity with oneself" (Sharp, 2001) which means obstructively intervening factors, such as denied or suppressed aspects of the patient's personality, the unconscious impact of "archetypical poles," (such as the perception of a woman as either a holy virgin or a whore), an exaggerated attention to the conscious and the intellectual, inattention to "intuitions" and other messages from the personal and collective unconscious, tendencies to conventionalism and failure to listen to one's personal self—all of which are supposed to be the residues of stages that are prior to the final stage of wholeness and individuation, stages where adaptation to parental prohibitions, conventional norms, and dominant current beliefs or ideals seem more important than authenticity, and there is a dissociation between what the person "is" and what he "ought" to be (Jung, ibid.).

The Unconscious

Philosophical and Scientific Sources

Plato has already observed that some past learning may exist "in the soul" without us being aware of it (Plato, 1997, Meno). His indirect influence still lives on in religious beliefs about the presence of God in each individual's soul. As Leibniz has already noted, we are not always aware of what we see, and his "petites perceptions" are not just Descartes's "unclear" and "indistinct" ideas or the phenomenologists' "non-thematic noema": they are "subliminal" contents that escape our notice altogether (Leibnitz, 1982). In addition, even though past philosophers would argue that the idea of nonconscious consciousness is contradictory, the empiricists assumed nonconscious laws of association (Locke, 1975), and Kant assumed a nonconscious "schematism" that processes our "blind" sensations before we become aware of them as perception (Kant, 2003). Since the advent of biology some philosophers, including Schelling in his later period (Schelling, 2008), Schopenhauer (Schopenhauer, 1969), and Nietzsche (Wicks, 2022), began to speak of "life energy," "drives," and "instincts" that are somehow relevant to our conscious lives, but of which we are not directly aware. They did not wait for Freud to speculate about hidden aggression and unconscious sexual wishes, or the repression of conventionally condemnable wishes and emotions. Nietzsche added to the assumed unconscious sexuality the assumed "forgetfulness" of shameful acts. Also, he talked about instincts as if they were specific to each individual and encouraged people to heed them (a position that echoes, despite the biological term, a religious or romantic belief in the unconscious "call" every person has, and his personal duty to discover and fulfill it). Herder assumed a nonconscious transmission of ethnic heritage, which some later German philosophers interpreted as a mission of which the whole "Volk" should become aware, and fulfill it for the benefit of humanity (Forster, 2007). In another vein, Bergson described memory of ideas and experiences as the *nonconscious* part of the spiritual "consciousness," in contrast to the "memory of the actions," which is stored in the material brain (Bergson, 1994). Bergson was referring to medical studies concerning the relationship between brain lesions and aphasia, which showed that nouns were easier to recall than verbs. Finally, Freud began his psychoanalytic career by explaining patients' difficulties in retrieving from their memory forgotten traumatic events (Jones, 1964).

Experimental psychologists today agree that much of our knowledge is "stored" in our "memory" rather than appearing on our consciousness screen. Many of our sensations, they agree, are overlooked, or just at the margin of our attention. They explore the brain mechanisms that process and store memories and perhaps also erase some of them.

In their view, the processing of memories, as well as present mental performances that appear simple and explorable by introspection, are, in fact, the result of complex unconscious elaborations. In this context, they differentiate between the 'intuitive' and the 'logical,' and some speculate that sometimes the 'intuitive,' resulting from unconscious patterns or processes, may be preferable to the more precise but slower 'intellectual.' As Freud would put it, they agree that there is a "nonconscious" and a "preconscious."

However, they disagree about the "unconscious." No one, as far as I know, refers to intuition in the Jungian sense, that is, to attain spiritual insights that are beyond the intellect.[10] They disagree whether there are defensive repressions or unconscious defensive mechanisms functioning in the way Freud described them. However, they agree that they do not possess experimental tools to test the validity of what psychoanalysts claim about the unconscious thoughts of babies in their first months. Dreams and hallucinations are examined, but the unconscious meaning of these experiences is not assumed. Those researchers are concerned with mental exhaustion or a lack of motivation, but not with nonconscious "drives," "life energy," or "instincts."

Yet there are other aspects to the notion of the "unconscious" and need to explore additional philosophical sources. The German Idealists (Horstmann, 2021) proposed that dream imagery, religious imagery, folktales, poetry, and visual arts communicate unconscious truths that become fully explicit and conscious when they are expressed adequately in philosophical concepts. Due to that explanation, and our understanding of the role of the *Geist* in history, God—*sive natura* (*et cultura*)—finally becomes totally "conscious.," i.e, "self-conscious."

The German term 'Unbewusst' may indeed refer to a content hidden in an unconscious part of the mind, but it may also mean something that "appears on the monitor of consciousness," but one is *not aware of its significance*: Myths, religious beliefs, poetry, and historical events, for instance, can be *misinterpreted*. Following Hegel, Marx talked about misinterpretations of implicit messages on an ideological level, which entails *failing to recognize one's—or one's group's—role and responsibility for the creation of the implicit messages*. Marx's followers translated this into the notion of "class false consciousness" in which members of a rising social class are still *unaware of their power* and contribution to the common wealth, and members of the still dominant class are *unaware of their responsibility* for the exploitation of the "real contributors"—or *deceive themselves* with regard to it.

'Self-consciousness' [*Selbsbewusstsein*] means the "acknowledgement of authority or responsibility" (Lukács,1972). By referring to the projection onto others of our denied and repressed desires, or the accusation of acts we would have committed if we had been self-aware, Nietzsche speaks of the failure of our "self-consciousness" in such a sense.

Depth psychologists, who expect their patients to understand that they are *the authors of their lives and must take responsibility for their troubles*, write variations on the theme of *misinterpretation*, although they also hint at hidden secrets in closed drawers.[11] So philosophers, suspicious of unjustified claims to knowledge, have to decide when to suspect the depth psychologists' claim to know contents that are supposed to be *forgotten forever*, such as unretrievable memories of the worlds of authors of prehistoric myths, and when to wonder why they are so sure that *the patient misinterprets* and that they themselves know the right meaning.

In Freud's "topographic" model, the unconscious is where nonconscious parts of the personality reside, whatever is the cause for their not being conscious (Sandler *et al.*, 1997). The unconscious in its specific Freudian meaning, is both a special "defense *mechanism*" which operates unconsciously, and the *contents*, which it hides or simulates. Freud assumes that the "primary process," which continues to be active when the person is aware of secondary process thinking or when he is sleeping, operates automatically according to the "pleasure principle." It satisfies wishes by associating them with memories of things that satisfied such wishes in the past or by fantasies that are associated with such memories. It causes forgetfulness of painful (thoughts about) events by replacing (parts of those thoughts about) them with non-painful associates, and therefore we often do not remember such events yet react unconsciously to their associates. However, the unconscious, in its very specific sense, defends from *anxiety*-raising and not just painful events, and the anxiety, as in the case of Nietzsche's repression, is related to something that is involved with shame or guilt, that is, wishes or deeds that the repressing person conceives of as *bad* because they are *forbidden* by others. In contrast to Nietzsche, Freud does not consider the repressing person a hypocrite: the ego that represses still does not understand that other persons are not reading his thoughts, and still does not understand that bad thoughts do not cause real bad events. Thus, the anxious ego, which lets the primary process deceive the others, fantasized by him as very dangerous, is actually *self-deceiving* because the processes of simulation obstruct his own ability to recall the hiding activity and the hidden dangerous thoughts (Freud, 2015a). The ego that does the original repression is the ego of a three- to six-year-old. The repressions that occur at later ages happen when events that "unconsciously remind" the subject of the original repressed thoughts, cause unconscious regression to the childish anxieties *and the ways of thinking* of the childish ego.

Although Freud spoke of the interaction between the "ego" and the "censor" (Freud, 2015a), the functioning of this mechanism can be compared to a dialogue in a comedy between a silly thief suspected by a stupid policeman. The thief tries to give excuses for his presence by lying, but the policeman remains suspicious; the anxious thief corrects his lies, contradicts himself, adds fictitious details, confuses himself with the policeman or another person, past with future and so on. Finally, he speaks nonsense and does senseless things. I guess that Freud's conception of the defensive process and its comical tactics was also inspired by the analyses of his teacher, Brentano, of what might happen to intentional speech if it were the product of merely associative rather than logical and grammatical thinking[12]. I do not assume, however, that Brentano used as an example a chain of intentional statements like the following "I want to do a to A, but if I do it, B will do b to me. It will be horrible if B does b to me, therefore I shall do c to B," which is Freud's original contribution. The "defense mechanism" causes the original intentional thoughts to become, in the relatively sane case, another, false, intentional thought: like "I do not want to do a to A . . . ," D wants to do a to A . . . ," | " All the E's want to do b to me . . . " , or "B did a to A in order to induce A to do b to C" and so on, but, when the "ego" is very anxious, it can also become linguistically and logically nonsense. Moreover, as the primary process does not distinguish between words and things that can be associated with them, it can be "acted out" as an action, or "converted" to a stomachache, while the originally associated emotions can change even to their opposites.

The purpose of the analysis is to retranslate the apparently incomprehensible results to a sensible *intentional thought* similar to the (assumed) original and enable the patient to make adult judgments about it, and thus accept its possible recurrence with an *adult attitude*. The possible recurrence is explained by the fact that the original wish cannot be fully satisfied by any real or imagined associated substitute and "the energy that was not discharged" is charged, as extra energy, to other associatively similar wishes.

If one takes the so-called "economic model" (Sandler *et al.*, 1997) seriously, one can ask what happens to that energy in the "economy" between the two events. But the big question is different: If the length of the chain of associative changes is as long and as wild as Freud describes it, how can

Freud, or any analyst, find the way back to the original thoughts, and how can he know that he has arrived at the original thoughts if the patient cannot recall them, and nobody besides him knew at the time what he was fantasizing? The official answer is: the recurrence of "clusters" or "complexes" of ideas reminiscent of the original in the process of free associations or in the interactions in the transference. I suspect that the more precise answer is, as some dynamic psychologists who do not know much about Freud, spontaneously answer: "Everybody knows: the Oedipal thoughts. All the little boys think of them and all the myths talk about them." (It does not occur to them that the boys' behaviors and the myths can be interpreted independently of Freud's assumption that little boys think according to his interpretation of myths.)

Jung did not think that all the myths talk about them. He also did not think that Freud's interpretations were always correct, although they were understandable, according to Jung, if one takes into consideration Freud's patriarchal cultural heritage (Freud, 1994). Jung had another collection of myths, which talk about "great mothers" and "heroes overcoming obstacles," which he interpreted in an *equally circular way*. Each of the two had his favored collection, each abducted from it the kind of prehistoric society that allegedly created such myths, and inferred from the imagined structure or history of that society the themes that are reflected in the myths and their meaning. Both assumed that the prehistoric dramas are reflected unconsciously in the biographies of their alleged inheritors and that the analyses of the patients' unconscious corroborated the myths and the imagined sociological story (or vice versa). The only difference was between Freud's Enlightenment belief in universal human heritage and Jung's conviction that "matriarchal societies," cultures, and individuals are forever different from "patriarchal societies," cultures, and individuals, as the ethnic unconscious transmittance continues forever from one generation to the next.[13]

The Freudian unconscious is not busy only with deceptions. It is also supposed to enable the relevant drive to "charge the extra energy" of the forbidden desires to desires that get their energy from other drives: Thus, if one is pleased to work, knowing that it is a means to earning one's living, but also enjoys *the activity of working* itself, that extra pleasure comes from the sex drive (Freud, 2015a). Some interpreters connect Freud's assumptions about energy to the Aristotelian concept of ἐνέργειᾰ [energeia], as one of its meanings. At least according to Arendt, it is an activity that is done for its own sake (Arendt, 1958). Sexual activity (in its strict sense) is often performed for its own sake, irrespective of purposes or consequences. Yet one can survive without engaging in it, and that is one of the reasons Freud thinks that the "free energy" that comes from the "sex drive," unlike the energy from the "ego drives," is "not bound" to specific kinds of objects (Freud, ibid.). But if that is the case, then the object-changing Platonic eros, the Neo-Platonic idea of the changing-object love, and the Kantian moral and esthetic ideals of doing the good without considerations of utility or the disinterested nature of esthetic enjoyment, could also have inspired Freud. His theory of wit however, was about the *tension discharged* in laughter and not the intellectual activity of finding something funny (Freud, 2015b),[14] which shows that the meaning of "energy" for Freud was connected to the physiological model of homeostasis.

Jung's unconscious (Jung, 2002) has room for repression, as he assumes that social conventions cause us to suppress to the "shadow" the "bad" and "strange" aspects of our personalities. The mechanism of that suppression is different from Freud's because Jung's cognitive assumptions are different. But the main difference is Jung's assumption that the unconscious, as it allegedly appears in dreams, myths, and free associations, is not a mirror of primitive and infantile ways of thinking that reflect the "residues" of our prior stupidity, but rather a source of intuitive wisdom and "biological-spiritual" energy. It also reflects, in archetypes that are allegedly inherited from primordial times, the experiences of former generations, and shows us when we are drawn to mistakes or frustrations and despair by thinking of the opposite poles as separate, unconsciously conceiving, say, woman as the evil, old and ugly witch *or* the good, young, and pretty fairy. Yet we can also be "spiritually inspired" by their interaction and by understanding the double nature of the "great mother" as, say, both Lilith and Eve. The latter example could remind us of Hegel's claim (and Klein's interpretation) that the baby and the (eternal) Jew tend to identify self and other as either Satan or God, and therefore their moods change between envy and spite, gratefulness and anger, instead of accepting themselves and others as "integrated" beings who are sometimes good and sometimes less good. The baby, or the narcissistic patient, has to understand that the satanic and the godly are his still non-integrated "internal objects" (Klein, 1975), and the "Jew" has still to acknowledge that the Divine is immanent in the world and in the soul (Hegel, 2018). But Jung is not precisely there. He insisted in his 1934 paper, "The State of Psychotherapy Today" (Jung, 1970), that Jews have psyches which are different from those of Germans and Slavs and therefore should not pretend, as Freud or Adler do, that their theories may have universal validity.

Freud claims to identify the unconscious "encoded" in facts of which the patients are conscious, but, as with Marx's "false consciousness," they are not conscious of their meaning. It is the analyst who knows how to decipher the code. Jung, in contrast, invites patients to participate in interpretation, especially of their dreams, and listen to their unconscious selves (Sharp, 2001). It sounds much more liberal and inspiring than the Freudian way: Playing with associations may be enjoyable and foster imagination and creativity. But if one remembers how missionaries can manipulate people in search for support to "find their true selves" in their dreams or in the secrets of holy texts until they find their "true selves" precisely in the "true religion" as the missionary sees it, one might wish to be more cautious. The patients may feel "whole" and "individuated" thanks to taking part in the interpretation; but as the process is guided by the non-neutral Jungian therapist, *one should, philosophically, worry about the possible weakening of the patient's power of judgment, the possible uncritical adoption of debatable beliefs and questionable values, their unawareness of other possible interpretations—and choices in life*. It is the place to stress that I do not think that all the Jungian analysts share all Jung's convictions. My "resistance" to the method does not depend on the specific convictions of the interpreter, and it started before I knew anything about its founder besides his interpretative method.

Biographers say that Freud disrespected Adler. I guess that if this is true, it was because Adler did not go as deeply as he or Jung into unconscious matters. Adler assumed that the child feels inferior and may deny his inferiority by illusions or self-presentations of superiority. This leads him to follow, without being aware of it, "styles of life" in which he seeks to compete with others, or alternatively, avoid competition altogether. Such assumed schemes are not conscious; yet they belong to the easy-to-retrieve "preconscious" rather than the unretrievable "unconscious." They are presuppositions and not simulated wish-thoughts. What the Adlerian is doing is similar to what philosophical counselors are supposed to do—not deciphering codes but revealing presuppositions by logical dialogues. But there are at least two differences: Adlerian, like Gestalt therapy, is not necessarily interested in the *philosophical* presuppositions of their clients, and their presenting their philosophical view of the adequate "style of life" as "the" appropriate one rather than one possibility among others, and the patient is invited to accept it, not to explore it.

Moral Development

Freud's Version

According to Freud, the Oedipal crisis is the beginning of the child's evolving morality. The importance he attributed to that issue is demonstrated by the fact that he dedicated two books to the subject: an invented myth about the birth of the morality of a whole tribe (Freud, 2017) and a historical analysis about the origin of the morality of a nation (Freud, 1967). The issue was also important to Brentano and Nietzsche, but Freud accepts neither the former's conviction that there is an innate capacity for an objective recognition of the good (Brentano, 1969), nor the latter's idea, according to which the super ego represents an irrationally obeyed "slave" morality (Nietzsche, 1994). He seems to follow the Biblical myth which links the knowledge of good and evil to eating the fruit of the tree of knowledge and connects it to what the Bible sometimes refers to eponymously, as "knowledge": sexual intercourse. Yet he changes the order of events: First little Adam (that is, the child, fantasizing that he was formerly in paradise) realizes that when he is naked, he is slightly different from the naked daughters of Eve, and is afraid of losing that advantage and the recently discovered "zone of erotic pleasure." When associations remind him of snakes, he starts to *fantasize* "eating" the forbidden fruit (the mother) and being threatened by the rival (the father) with punishment (castration). The fantasies are supposed to echo the actual traumatic experiences of his prehistoric ancestors—a reinterpretation of the myth of the original sin. The reiterated sin drives little Adam away, forever, from the prenatal paradise for which he was still longing. No more actual feelings of eudaimonia, no more real "oceanic" experiences of being in the mother's womb (which some authors, like Romain Rolland, fool themselves into interpreting as being one with God or the cosmos (Freud, 2002)): Although little Adam, in his "anal" stage, has already experienced some clashes with civilization, only the "genital" fantasies introduce him to the world of moral conflicts. But it is not the eating of the fruit that gives him the knowledge of good and evil; it is the list of instructions of what one should do and what one should not do). Little Adam, however, does not know any such list before he hears the instructing father (the moral knowledge is not innate in the heart, one should, as a start, obey to an imposed Torah). He does not accept it before the reevoking the allegedly real experience of his ancestors—the prehistoric brothers who wanted women and had to murder their tyrannical polygamic father in order to get them—the *fantasy* of killing the father, *and the consequent feeling of remorse*. One may wonder what all the Oedipal fantasies might mean to a three- to six-year-old child; but what matters for the explanation of the origin of his morality is only what *reminds* him of his patricidal intentions. If I understand Freud correctly, anything that the child conceived as bad for the father may be equivalent, in his childish mind, to the father's death, and if he sees himself as its cause, that "death" means to him that he is guilty of "patricide." If he indeed thinks as a child is supposed to think, according to Freud, he might experience feeling guilty of that "atrocity" whenever he is angry with the father about something that concerns the mother and something bad happens to the father. That is not an infrequent experience, and although it is less traumatic than the original experience of his murderous ancestors, the emotional ambivalence toward the father, as well as the remorse for the "murder"—is the same. Remorse leads him, as it allegedly led them, to identify with the father and internalize his instructions in the emerging "superego."

The origin of morality is therefore not the fear of oppressive fathers and "slavish" obedience, but the moral feelings of remorse and guilt of the sons who revolted. This is far from being just an untestable assumption about male children. It is the answer to Nietzsche and Christian thinkers from Saint-Paul through Saint-Augustine and from Hegel to Brentano, who believed in an alliance "of love" which is innate "in the heart" rather than an external alliance and a transcendent Law transmitted through others. It is the answer to Plato, who believed in being "reminded" of the beloved "Agathon"—the Good—while all that one can be "reminded" of are traces of an infantile or primitive "bad" past. It is an answer to friends, perplexed secular Jews, like he himself was. It is, above all, an answer to Jung, who, before his quarrel with Freud began, hoped to mobilize psychoanalysis for the "renewed morality" of Pagan Christianity (Freud, 1994). Morality starts with the remorseful acceptance of the father's Torah [Hebrew: Instruction], or, in other words, tradition is transmitted through the parents to *revolting* sons. It is, therefore, *reinterpreted with every new generation* and may gradually develop, as civilization itself did, and hopefully, as little Adam will do. He will grow toward the limited ability that is possible for humans, whose common father, according to the Freudian version of the Genesis story, *did not* eat the forbidden fruit of the tree of knowledge of good and evil. His descendants have no absolute, Platonic, moral knowledge, but they are searching for it, just as the grown-up children of Eve, somewhat neurotic, seek constantly for a satisfying substitute for the lost object of the primordial love. Their ability is that of the more rational but not very strong "ego" to redirect biological drives, restrain the cruelty of a rigid super ego, choose their own ideals, select from the tradition what is worth preserving, and,—unlike the "barbarian Christians misinterpreting Saint Paul" (Freud, 1969), find new ways to realize the old ideal common to monotheistic cultures and enlightened pagans: a golden path between Law and Love, Justice and Compassion, Need and Duty and Pleasure. The strong ego should have the ability to laugh at itself and use irony, the wisest and most moral way of redirecting anger and aggression toward oppressors whom one cannot fight and opponents whom one cannot convince. (Freud, 2015b). (Freud learned it from Heine, one of his most important hidden teachers.)

Philosophically, the Oedipal story is the story of an ego searching his way between "nature" and "culture," "id," and "superego." What Freuds tells his patients is that the "repressed" will keep on "returning" when the analysis is terminated, and that the uncritically internalized instructions will also occasionally pop up: "Sin—and the feeling of guilt—are crouching at your door; they still desire to have you; and you should rule over it—and you are able to rule logically over your mind although the childish way of thinking crouches at its door."[15] I think that it is an interesting philosophical attitude to morality and life—but the treatment is not fully philosophical as it is Freud's and not the patient's opinion, and alternatives are not discussed.

Jung's Version

Jung is interested in the development toward "individuation," a lifelong process in which one realizes himself as an individual, that is, realizes Jung's versions of the ideals of "wholeness" and "authenticity." The morality of those ideals, which sometimes clash with other ideals, is a matter of debate. But Jung, unlike Freud, is not interested in interpersonal moral debates; the only conflict that seems morally relevant to him is intrapersonal—between one's conscious side, which represents the conventional, and one's unconscious side, where one can find the personal. He therefore has no specific theory of moral development, and, as far as I know, he refers to moral issues only in some marginal remarks in his later writings.

He seems to take the slave morality for granted: the dependent child is obedient to the parent; the adult is obedient to conventions. Yet one may, finally, listen to the unconscious "inner voice," the Vox Dei within the self (Jung, 1970).

Nietzsche did not listen to divine voices, but he seems to have felt free to hate the voices of liberal democracy and nationalists at times, and when, as the old little woman recommended (Nietzsche, 2006, 50), he went to the woman with a whip, he despised the yells of a female chorus. One may, however, wonder what "the" conventional opinion could mean to an adult of Jung's generation, living between two world wars, when the clashes between liberals and Fascists, communists and Nazis, Universalists and racists were even louder, and each was challenging some conventions of the other. Yet it seems that the only moral conflict that occurs to Jung in his late remarks is between the conscious "moral conscience" of the conventionalist ego and the unconscious "ethical conscience," within the Self.

Conflicts motivate moral deliberations and lead to moral knowledge (Rozuel, 2010). In Jung's opinion, they are neither rational analyses of opposing criteria or rules nor explorations of opposing philosophical conceptions of morality. According to him, "there is great and justified uncertainty in this regard." However, precisely because of this, one "needs unusual courage or, to put it another way, unshakable faith . . . in order simply to follow his own conscience" (Jung, 1970, para. 835). One has to be aware of the "ego's tricks" and consciously integrate the contents of one's "shadow" in order to possess such courage, or faith. Hence, a moral person should listen to his inner *Self* rather than his *Ego*, and let it guide him to the relevant archetypes in his "collective unconscious," which connect him to humanity as a whole. Their conscious integration with his "shadow "contents, should enable one to imagine moral options, true to one's Self, of which one was initially unaware (Jung, 1970).

Some psychoanalysts (Merkurs and Mills, 2017) and ethical counselors (Rozuel, ibid.) are impressed by the religious and spiritual aura of that approach. I do not know whether they are aware that at least between 1914 and 1945 Jung held the opinion that different ethnic groups have different collective unconsciousness, and since 1933, and possibly earlier, he thought that they should live separately[16]—and his horizon did not seem to include any universal human collective. In any case, suspicious philosophers might wonder how one can know that the inner voice is God's and not that of a deceptive demon, or an internalized Vox Populi; how one can be sure that there can be no conflict within the "ethical conscience"; how associative processes that allegedly evoke the relevant archetypes and aspects of the "shadow" can help *resolve contradictions* in the "inner voice" when they are capable, at most, of "reminding" one of additional moral options; and finally, how one can know whether one's decision is beneficial or harmful to *others* when one excludes the opinions of *concrete* contemporary others, which are based on their different perspectives, and listens only to what are supposed to be echoes of voices from an allegedly collective but remote ethnic past.

Adler's Version

Adler did not have a general theory of moral development; he maintained, like Vaihinger (1935), that both scientific theories and self-knowledge are fictions, and believed that everyone develops in his own way. More importantly, he distinguished between what one is and what one should be, and thus separated moral questions from apparently factual issues of "maturity" and "sanity." He conceived of psychotherapy as changing fictions not only to more helpful fictions, but also to more moral ones, which gives more room in one's "style of life" to solidarity with others, belonging to a community, equality and freedom (Marková, et al., 2016). Those ideals, however, do not guarantee absence of moral conflicts, and I am not sure that I understand which abilities or criteria an Adlerian "graduate" should have in order to deal with them.

Notes

1. I hope that the psychologists that may read this text will excuse my audacity to sum up in few phrases, with imprecise terminology, the wisdom that took them years to acquire; I do not pretend to be precise, underestimate their efforts, or take their place, I just try to protect them from the false accusation with inadequate dwelling on causes.

2. Piaget's and Kohlberg's specific claims have been tested, but both empiricists and rationalists disagree about the interpretation of the results. . . . What has not been tested, was dominant and nowadays is contested, is the positivistic developmental view.

3. It is not clear to me whether Lévi-Bruhl attributed that mentality to ritual and mythic representations or to everyday life as well.

4. Some of Freud's followers and interpreters were Marxists and some contemporary sociologists read his remarks about civilization (as well as Nietzsche's onslaughts) as a critic of capitalism. I did not find in his writings any hint for such a position. He certainly did not believe, as did the neo-Marxist Herbert Marcuse, that removal of sexual tabus would end wars.

5. See Jones (1964) with regards to his admiration for Nietzsche's psychological understanding. The rest is my analysis.

6. Some researchers accuse Jung, Freud's nemesis (and vice versa), with worse than insincerity. See Kaufmann (1980) with regards to his relations with Freud, (amuels (1997) with regard to his antisemitism and Noll (1997) with regards to his Pan-Germanism and mysticism. However, there are others who claim that he was misunderstood.

7. The German Idealists' cosmic-history, a "Spinozist" version of Neo-Platonism, starts with the "absolute I," God, projecting himself onto the "non-I" matter. That "alienation" is gradually overcome when He recognizes the world as Himself. The divine "self-consciousness" is enabled through the human individual and universal "self-consciousness" and the understanding that the world and God are one.

8. Information based on Noll (1997), the interpretations are mine.

9. Klein, Kohut, Lacan, and Green are salient in that group. They claim to have revealed the causes of some severe "disturbances" in conflicts or deprivations that babies experience not only far ahead of the ability to inform others about it, but also before having acquired, according to the positivist and the Freudian developmental story, the necessary intellectual capacities for having such conflicts. The Kleinian drama of the suckling's ambivalent and opposites feelings while comparing himself to the "good" and "bad" breast (Klein, 1975), and the Lacanian drama of the pre-toddler comparing his "objective" image in the looking glass to his "subjective" contrary self-feeling (Lacan, 1997), reminds me of the dialectical dramas of babies and Jews according to Hegel. Hegel, as his critics have noticed, was not bothered about the epistemological difficulty of attributing unconscious logical conflicts to pre-logical creatures; he made such attributions even to unthinking beings. Lacan and probably also Klein have read, or indirectly heard about, Hegel's "unhappy consciousness"

(Hegel, 2018). The two other psychoanalysts added, without Hegelian help, and on the basis of more direct experience and observation pre-Oedipal "deprivations": Kohut assumed the absence of an admiring and admired father (Kohut, 1971), and Green assumed the absence of attention by the "dead" mother (Modell, 1999).

10. Structuralist analyses of myths apparently corroborate Jung's assumption of unconscious archetypes by pointing to the frequency of bipolar symbols, but, as Lévi-Strauss has shown, (Lévi-Strauss, 1963b) they are explainable by entirely different assumptions, with no need to assume inherited unconscious, universal (or ethnic) types or beliefs in specific internal dramas.

11. It is the issue of one of the most important controversies between Freud and some of his rebellious followers, who claim that the patients' recollections or associations mean that their troubles are due to their actual sexual abuse by their parents rather than their own Oedipal fantasies.

12. Freud does not say that; he just says that the unconscious has a special logic, which does not distinguish between negation and affirmation, subject and object, cause, and effect, before and after and so no. (Freud, 2015), which amounts to the same thing. Lacan, whose basis of thinking was neither positivistic legends nor Brentano's conception of intentional thinking and grammar, offered instead a theory of unconscious functioning that is based on structural linguistics and sociology. That theory, interwoven with Hegelian and Heideggerian ideas, not only transplanted psychoanalysis onto a new conceptual scheme; it changed diagnoses, prognoses, aims and practices.

13. Anthropologists nowadays do not make such distinctions. They prefer the distinction between societies where relatives on the side of the father are dominant and societies where relatives on the side of the mother have the main influence on the life of the person or the married couple. (Lévi-Strauss, 1958). I do not know whether Jung was informed about that change. He stopped writing about his distinctions after World War II but for other reasons.

14. The experiment in which students, under different conditions, had to appreciate how funny some jokes are (Kelling, 1971), is an example of empirical testing that is based on a misreading of Freud.

15. Many psychoanalysts prefer nowadays to deal with shame rather than guilt. But they do not treat it as the origin of morality.

16. Neuman, 1991.

Bibliography

Achenbach, G. B. (1987). *Philosophische Praxis [Philosophical Practice]*. Köln: Jürgen Dinter.

Achenbach, G. B. (2010). *Das kleine Buch der inneren Ruhe [The Little Book of Inner Peacefulness]*. Freiburg: Herder.

Adler, A. (1938). *Social Interest: A Challenge to Mankind*. (J. L. Vaughan, trans.) London: Faber and Faber LTD.

Adler, A. (2003). *The Neurotic Character [1907]. The Collected Clinical Works of Alfred Adler* (Vol. 1). (C. K. 1927), Classical Adlerian Translation Project.

Adorno, T. W., Frenkel–Brunswik, E., Levinson, D. J., & Sanford, R. N. (1950). *The Authoritarian Personality*. New York: Harper and Row.

Alt, J. A. (1982). *Die Frühschriften Poppers—Der Weg Poppers von der Pädagogie und der Psychologie zur Spätphilosophie*. [The Early Writings of Popper—Popper's Way from Education and Psychology to His Late Philosophy]. Frankfurt–am–Main und Bern: Peter Lang.

Amir, L. (2018). *Taking Philosophy Seriously*. Cambridge: Cambridge Scholars Publishing.

Amir, L. (2019). *Philosophy, Humor, and the Human Condition: Taking Ridicule Seriously*. London: Palgrave Macmillan. (Electronic edition, 2020).

Andrews, K., & Monsó, S. (2021). *"Animal Cognition" in Stanford Encyclopedia of Philosophy*. Retrieved February 9, 2022, from https://plato.stanford.edu/entries/cognitionaninal.

Aristotle. (1984). *Nicomachean Ethics* (Vol. II). In Barnes.

Aristotle. (1984). *Poethics* (Vol. II). In Barnes.

Aristotle. (1984). *Rhetoric* (Vol. II). In Barnes.

Arendt, H. (1958). *The Human Condition*. Chicago: University of Chicago Press.

Augustine. (2006). *Confessions. 2nd Ed.* (F. Sheed, trans.) Indianapolis: Hackett Publishing Company.

Austin, J. L. (1952). *Sense and Sensibila.* Edited by J. G. Warnock. Oxford: Oxford University Press.

Austin, J. L. (1972). How to Do Things with Words. In *The William James Lectures Delivered at Harvard University 1955.* Edited by J. U. Sbisà. New York: Oxford University Press.

Ayer, A. J. (1952). *Language, Truth and Logic [1936], (2nd Ed. [1946]).* New York: Dover Publication.

Ayer, A. J. (1973). *The Central Questions of Philosophy.* London: Weidenfeld & Nicolson.

Bachofen, J. J. (1967). *Myth, Religion and Mother Right, Selected Papers [1861].* Translated by R. Manheim. Bollington: Princeton Press.

Bacon, F. (2000). *The Advancement of Learning* [1605]. Edited by M. Kiernan in *The Oxford Francis Bacon, Vol. IV.* Oxford: Oxford University Press.

Bacon, F. (2004). *Novum organon [1620].* In *The Oxford Francis Bacon.* Edited by G. Rees and M. Wakely. Upper Saddle River, NJ: Pearson Prentice Hall.

Baltzly, D. (2018). *"Stoicism" in Stanford Encyclopedia of Philosophy.* Retrieved March 3, 2022, from Stanford Encyclopedia of Philosophy: https://plato.stanford.edu/entries/stoicism.

Barnes, J. (1984). *The Complete Works of Aristotle: The Revised Oxford Translation. Vol. I and II.* Princeton: Princeton University Press.

Barrett, L. F. (2017). *How Emotions Are Made: The Secret Life of the Brain.* Boston: Houghton Mifflin Harcourt.

Barrientos-Rastrojo, J. (2006). "Philosophical Counseling as Poietic Philosophy." *Philosophical Practice,* 2(1), 17–27.

Barrientos-Rastrojo, J. (2021). *Experiential Philosophical Practice: Beyond Philosophical Posturing. Translated* by T. MacFarlance. Retrieved December 30, 2021, from https://www.amazon.com/–/es/Jos%C3%A9–Barrientos–Rastrojo/dp/B09BGN6VJG?asin=B09BGN6VJG&revisionId=&format=4&depth=1.

Bateson, G., D. D. Jackson, J. Haley, & J. Weakland. (1956). "Toward a Theory of Schizophrenia." *Behavioral Science,* I(4), 251–64. doi:10.1002/bs3830010402.

Bergson, H. (1992). *The Creative Mind: An Introduction to Metaphysics [La Pensée et le Mouvant 1934].* Translated by M. L. Andison. New York: The Citadel Press.

Bergson, H. (1994). *Matter and Memory* [1896]. Translated by N.M. Paul and W.S. Palmer. New York: Zone Books.

Bergson, H. (2001). *Time and Free Will: An Essay on the Immediate Data of Consciousness [1889].* Translated by F. Pogson. Dover Publications.

Bergson, H. (2005). *Laughter—An Essay on the Meaning of the Comic* [1911]. Translated by F. Rothwell. Mineola, NY: Dover Publications.

Biderman, S. (1980). *The Basic Principles of Indian Philosophy [in Hebrew].* Tel Aviv: Misrad Habitachon.

Bird, A. (2018). "Thomas Kuhn" in Stanford Encyclopedia of Philosophy. Retrieved May 18, 2021, from Stanford Encyclopedia of Philosophy: https://plato.stanford.edu/entries/thomas-kuhn

Bishop, M. (1936). *Pascal: The Life of Genius*. New York: Reynal & Hitchcock.

Borisov, S. (2020). The Birth of "Deep Philosophy" from the "Spirit of on to Designing." In S. Borisov, *Philosophical Practice for Self–Knowledge by Means of Intellectual Creativity: Collection of Writings of the Online Conference on Philosophical Practice*, pp. 124–29. Chelyabinsk: Russian Presidential Academy of National Economy and Public Administration.

Bourdeau, M. (2006). *Les Trois États: Science, Théologie et Métaphysique chez Auguste Comte* [The Three States: Science, Theology and Metaphysics in Auguste Comte]. Paris: Cerf.

Brenifier, O. (2010). "Oscar Brenifier in Philosophical Counseling with Carmen." *Philosophical Practice* 27 July 2010. Retrieved May 29, 2021, from https://vimeo.com/13668633

Brenifier, O. (2015). *The Practice of Philosophy with Children Paris: Institute of Philosophical Practices*. Retrieved January 29, 2021, from http://www.pratiques-philosophiques.fr/wp-content/uploads/2015/07/The-practice-of-philosophy-with-children-ORIGINAL-1.pdf

Brenifier, O. (2017). *"The Socratic Pact" [Last Edit]*. Retrieved June 7, 2021, from https://rafaelrobles.com/filo/index.php?title=The_ten_agreements_of_the_Socratic_Pact

Brenifier, O. (2018). *"Oscar Brenifier in a Live Broadcast."* Retrieved June 7, 2021, from https://m.facebook.com/story.php?story_fbid=705506973163069&id=100011113183557

Brenifier, O. (2019). *Philosophical Consultation*. Retrieved December 30, 2021, from Paris: Institute of Philosophical Practice.

Brenifier, O. (2020, June). *The Art of Philosophical Practice*. Retrieved June 18, 2021, from Paris: Institute of Philosophical Practice: http://www.pratiques–philosophiques.fr/wpcontent/uploads/2020/06/artpp.pdf

Brentano, F. (1969). *The Origin of Our Knowledge of Right and Wrong* [1902]. Translated by R. C. Schneewind. London: Routledge.

Brentano, F. (1973). *Psychology from an Empirical Standpoint*. Translated by A.C. Rancurello, and D. B. Terrell. London.

Brook, A. (2020). "Kant's View of the Mind and Consciousness of Self." Retrieved January 8, 2022, from Stanford Encyclopedia of Philosophy: https://plato.stanford.edu/entries/kant-mind.

Camus, A. (1991). *The Plague* [1947]. Translated by S. Gilbert. New York: Vintage.

Camus, A. (1992). *The Rebel: An Essay on Man in Revolt* [1951]. Translated by A. Bower. London: Vintage.

Camus, A. (2012). *The Outsider* [1942, *L'Etranger*]. Translated by S. Smith. New York: Penguin.

Camus, A. (2018). *The Myth of Sisyphus* [1942]. Translated by J. O'Brien. New York: Vintage.

Carnap, R. (2003). *The Logical Structure of the World and Pseudo-problems in Philosophy* [1928]. Translated by R. A. George. Chicago: Open Court.

Cohen, E. D. (1988). *Dew Rational Therapy: Thinking Your Way to Serenity, Success, and Profound Happiness*. Lanham, MD: Rowman & Littlefield Publishers.

Cohen, E. D. (1994). *Caution: Faulty Thinking Can Be Harmful to Your Happiness*. Fort Pierce: Trace-Wil Co Publishers.

Cohen, E. D. (2016). "In Memoriam" in *International Journal of Philosophical Practice*. Retrieved January 15, 2021, from https://www.google.com/search?q=in+memoriam%3A+renowned+israeli+philosophical+counselor+dr.+shlomit+c.+schuster+dies+at+64&oq=&aqs=chrome.0.69i59i45018.415777589j0j15&sourceid=chrome&ie=UTF-8.

Comte, A. (1961). *The Positive Philosophy of Auguste Comte* [*Cours de philosophie positive*, 1830–1842]. Translated by H. Martineau. London: Parsons.

Davis, B. W. (2009). *Will and Gelassenheit Martin Heidegger*. Retrieved May 19, 2021, from Cambridge Core—Chap. 12, 168–82: https://www.cambridge.org/core/books/martin–heidegger/will–andgelassenheit/52C3B6B12EA46AEEA9B3432FD2735051].

De Haas, L. (2012). "Situational Philosophy—Towards a Theory of Philosophical Practice." *Official Journal of the Korean Society of Philosophical Practice*, 3, 1–15.

Deleuze, G., & F. Guattari. (1994). *What Is Philosophy?* Translated by H. T. Burchell. New York: Columbia UP.

Descartes, R. (1989). *Passions of the Soul* [1649]. Translated by S. H. Voss. Indianapolis: Hackett.

Descartes, R. (1999). *Discourse on Method [1637] and Related Writings*. Translated by M. Clarke. London: Penguin.

Dewey, J. (1929). "Philosophy's search for the Immutable." In *The Quest for Certainty*, pp. 28–49. Retrieved June 25, 2021, from https://www.cambridge.org/core/journals/philosophy/article/abs/quest-for–certainty-studyof.

Dilthey, W. (2002). "The Formation of the Historical World." In *The Human Sciences, Selected Works* (Vol. 3). Edited by R. M. Modi. Princeton, NJ: Princeton University Press.

Ellis, A. (1994). *Reason and Emotion in Psychotherapy*. Secaucus, NJ: Carol Publishing Group.

Ellis, A. (1998). *How to Control Your Anxiety*. New York: Citadel Press.

Elman, J. L., E. A. Bates, M. H. Johnson, A. Karmiloff-Smith, D. Parisi, & K. Plunkett. (1997). *Rethinking Innateness: A Connectivist Perspective on Development*. Cambridge, MA: MIT Press.

Farr, J. (2008). "Locke, Natural Law, and New World Slavery." *Political Theory*, 36(4), 495–522.

Fayerabend, P. (1975). *Against Method*. London: Verso.

Fodor, J. A. (1983). *The Modularity of Mind: An Essay in Faculty Psychology*. Cambridge MA: The MIT Press.

Foster, M. (2007). "Johann Gottfried von Herder." In *Stanford Encyclopedia of Philosophy*. Retrieved January 1, 2021, from https://meinong.stanford.edu/entries/herder.

Foucault, M. (1973). *The Order of Things* [*Les mots et les choses*, 1966]. Translated by A. Sheridan. New York: Vintage.

Foucault, M. (1978). The Will to Knowledge [*La volonté de savoir*, 1978]. In *History of Sexuality* Vol. 1, translated by R. Hurley. New York: Pantheon.

Foucault, M. (2001). *Fearless Speech*. Edited by J. Pearson. Semiotext(e).

Frankl, V. E. (2006). *Man's Search for Meaning [1946]*. Boston: Beacon Press.

Frazer, M. (2006). "The Compassion of Zarathustra: Nietzsche on Sympathy and Strength." *Review of Politics*, 68(1), 49–78. Retrieved July 8, 2021, from https://dash.harvard.edu/handle/1/3350069.

Freud, S. (1957). "Mourning and Melancholy" [1915]. In *The Standard Edition of the Complete Psychological Works of Sigmund Freud Vol. XIV [1914–1916]*, translated by J. Strachey, pp. 343–56. pp. 343–56). London: The Hogarth Press: The Institute of Psycho-Analysis.

Freud, S. (1967). *Moses and Monotheism* [1939]. Translated by J. Strachey. New York: Random House.

Freud, S. (1990). "Analysis of a phobia of a five–year old boy" [1909]. In *The Penguin Freud Library—Case Histories I: 'Dora' and 'Little Hans,'* translated by J. Strachey. London: Pelican.

Freud, S. (1992). *The Letters of Sigmund Freud to Eduard Silberstein, 1871–1881*. Edited by W. Bochlich, translated by A. Pomerance. Cambridge, MA: Harvard University Press.

Freud, S. (1994). *The Freud/Jung Letters: The Correspondence between Sigmund Freud and C. G. Jung Abridged Paperback Edition*. Edited by W. McGuire, translated by R. M. Hall. Princeton: Princeton University Press.

Freud, S. (2002). *Civilization and Its Discontents [1930]*. Translated by D. McLintock. London: Penguin.

Freud, S. (2015a). *The Interpretation of Dreams [1900]*. Translated by J. Strachey. Mineola, NY: Basic Books, Dover Publications.

Freud, S. (2015b). *Wit and Its Relation to the Unconscious [1905]*. Translated by A. A. Brill. Mineola, NY: Dover Publications.

Freud, S. (2017). Totem and Taboo [1912–1913]. In *Complete Psychological Works of Sigmund Freud* Vol. 13, translated by J. Strachey. New York: W.W. Norton.

Gadamer, H.-G. (1989). *Truth and Method, 2nd rev. revised edition*. Translated by J. W. Marshall. New York: Crossroad.

Gilligan, C. (1982). *In a Different Voice*. Cambridge, MA: Harvard University Press.

Goodman, M. (2015). *Maimonides and the Book That Changed Judaism: Secrets of the Guide for the Perplexed*. Philadelphia: Jewish Publication Society.

Grimes, P., and Uliana, R. L. (1998). *Philosophical Midwifery: A New Paradigm for Understanding Human Problems*. Coast Mesa CA: Hyparxis Press.

Gruengard, O. (1998). "Introverted, Extroverted and Perverted Controversy: Jung against Freud." *Science in Context*, *11*(2), 255–90.

Gruengard, O. (2006). "Freud-Jung Controversy: A Failed Intercultural Dialogue. *Kulturen: Konflikt-Analyse-Dialog, Beiträge des 29. Internationalen Wittgenstein Symposiums—6–12.*" *XIV*, pp. 108–12. Kirchberg am Wechsel: Wang-Stefan.

Gruengard, O. (2015). "An Unwritten Philosophical Autobiography." *International Journal of Philosophical Practice*, *4*(2), 1–14.

Gruengard, O. (2015). "The Need to Be Needed." In *Women in Philosophical Counseling*, pp. 99–120, edited by L. d. Paula and P. Raabe.. New York: Lexington Book.

Gruengard, O. (2018). "Philosophical Biography: Its Relevance to Philosophical Practice." *Philosophical Practice, Journal of the APPA*, *13*(3), 2213–21.

Grünbaum, A. (1985). *The Foundations of Psychoanalysis: A Philosophical Critique*. University of California Press.

Gutting, G., and J. Oksala. (2018). "Michel Foucault Stanford Encyclopedia of Philosophy." In *Stanford Encyclopedia of Philosophy*. Retrieved May 18, 2021, from https://plato.stanford.edu/entries/foucault.

Hadot, P. (1974). "Exercices spirituels." *Annuaire de lécole pratique des hautes études, Section des sciences religieuses*, *84*, 25–70.

Hadot, P. (1981). "Exercices spirituels et philosophie antique." *Collection des études Augustiniens, Série antiquité*, *88*.

Hadot, P. (1995). *Philosophy as a Way of Life*. Translated by M. Chase. Oxford: Blackwell.

Hadot, P. (2002). *What Is Ancient Philosophy?* Translated by M. Chase. Cambridge, MA: Harvard University Press.

Hadot, P. (2005). "There are Nowadays Professors of Philosophy, but Not Philosophers." *The Journal of Speculative Philosophy*, *19*(3), 229–37.

Harteloh, P. (2010). "On the Competence of Philosophical Practitioners," 2010. 36–47. *Journal of Practical Philosophy*, *10*, 36–47.

Harteloh, P. (2013). "The Diagnosis in Philosophical Practice." *Journal Humanities Therapy*, *4*, 67–82.

Harteloh, P. (2018). "The Role of Erasmus' Philosophy in Peace Building Social Philosophy." *Proceedings of the XXIII World Congress of Philosophy*, *72—Social Philosophy*, pp. 41–46. Retrieved January 21, 2021, from https://www.pdcnet.org/wcp23/content/wcp23_2018_0072_0041_0046.

Heckman, G. (2018). "Das sokratische Gespräch." [The Socratic Conversation] 3 Aufgabe. In *Sokratischen Philosophieren Schriftenreihe der PPA und GSP* (Vol. XVI), edited by D. Krohn, B. Neißer, and N. Walter. Berlin: Lit Verlag.

Hegel, G. W. (2004). *The Philosophy of History*. [Lectures, ed. by Karl Ludwig Michele, 1833, rev. 1842]. Translated by E. Haldane and J. S. Mineola, NY: Dover.

Hegel, G. W. (2018). *The Phenomenology of Spirit [1807]*. Translated by M. Inwood. Oxford: Oxford University Press.

Heidegger, M. (2010). *Being and Time [1927]*. Translated by J. Stambaugh. Albany: SUNY Press.

Heidegger, M. (2010). *Leviathan: Or the Matter, Form, and Power of a Commonwealth Ecclesiastical and Civil.* Translated by I. Shapiro. New Haven and London: Yale University Press.

Heidegger, M. (2013). "The Question Concerning Technology [1949]." In *The Question Concerning Technology and Other Essays*, translated by W. Lovitt. New York: Harper Perennial.

Heidegger, M. (2014). *Introduction to Metaphysics (1953)* (2nd ed.). Translated by R. Manheim. New Haven & London: Yale University Press.

Hempel, C. G. (1965). *Aspects of Scientific Explanation.* New York: Free Press.

Hobbes, T. (1981). *De Corpore [1655]. Part I.* Translated by A. Martinech. New York: Abaris Books.

Homi, B. (2004). *The Other Question: Stereotype, Discrimination and the Discourse of Colonialism: The Location of Culture.* London and New York: Routledge.

Honneth, A., MacCarthy, T., Offe, K., & Wellmer, A. (1992). *Philosophical Interventions in the Unfinished Project of Enlightenment.* Boston: MIT Press.

Horikoshi, Y., & Kono, T. (2020). Philosophical Practices in Japan from School to Business Consultancy. *Philosophical Practice and Counseling, 10*, 5–33. Retrieved January 4, 2022, from https://kiss.kstudy.com/thesis/thesis–view.asp?key=385050.

Horstmann, R.-P. (2021). "Idealism." In *Stanford Encyclopedia of Philosophy.* Retrieved December 23, 2021, from https://plato.stanford.edu/entries/idealism.

Humberto Dias, J. (2015). "From the happiness paradigm in Marías to the application of the PROJECT@ method in a case of philosophical consultation." *Journal of Humanities Therapy*, 6, 93–130.

Hume, D. (1930). *A Treatise of Human Nature* [1739–40]. London: Everyman Library.

Hursthouse, R., & Pettigrove, G. (2016). *Virtue Ethics.* In *Stanford Encyclopedia of Philosophy.* Retrieved May 18, 2021, from https://plato.stanford.edu/entries/ethics-virtue

Husserl, E. (1965). "Philosophy as Rigorous Science [1910]." In *Phenomenology and the Crisis of Philosophy. Philosophy as a Rigorous Science and Philosophy and the crisis of European Man*, translated by Q. Lauer. New York: Harper.

Husserl, E. (1982). *Ideas: General Introduction to Pure Phenomenology. First Book: General Introduction to a Pure Phenomenology* [1913]. Translated by F. Kersten. The Hague: Nijhoff.

Hylton, P., & Gary, K. (2019). *Willard Van Orman Quine.* In *Stanford Encyclopedia of Philosophy.* Retrieved May 4, 2021, from https://plato.stanford.edu/entries/quine.

James, W. (2012). *The Varieties of Religious Experience: A Study of Human Nature* [1902]. Edited by B. Mathiew. Oxford: Oxford University Press.

Jones, E. (1964). *The Life and Work of Sigmund Freud.* Edited by L. Trilling and S. Marcus. Harmondsworth: Penguin.

Jones, E. (1976). *Hamlet and Oedipus.* New York: Norton.

Jung, C. (1970). "Civilization in Transition." In *The Collected Works of C.G. Jung* 2 ed, Vol. 10, translated by R. Hull. Princeton: Princeton University Press.

Jung, C. (1983). Alchemical Studies. In R. Hull, *The Collected Works of C.G . Jung* (Vol. 13). Princeton: Princeton University Press.

Jung, C. (2002). *Psychology of the Unconscious [1912]*. Translated by B. M. Hinkle. Mineola, NY: Dover Publications.

Kant, I. (1885). *Kant's Introduction to Logic*. Translated by T. K. Abbott. London: Longmans. Green & C. Retrieved January 23, 2022, from https://archive.org/stream/kantsintroductio00kantuoft/kantsintroductio00kantuoft_djvu.txt.

Kant, I. (1930). "Moral philosophy: Collin's lecture notes" [1784–1785]. In *Lectures on Ethics*, translated by P. Heath. Cambridge: Cambridge UP.

Kant, I. (1974). *Anthropology from a Pragmatic Point of View [1798]*. Translated by M. Gregor. The Hague: Martinius Nijhoff.

Kant, I. (1991). *Political Writings* (2 ed.). Edited by H. Reiss, translated by H. B. Nisbet. Cambridge: Cambridge University Press.

Kant,I. (1999a). Critique of Pure Reason (2 ed.) [1787]. Translated by P. Guyer and A. W. Wood. Cambridge: CUP.

Kant, I. (1999b). "An Answer to the Question What Is Enlightenment" [1784]. In *Practical Philosophy*, translated by M. C. Smith. Cambridge: Cambridge UP.

Kant, I. (2002a). *Critique of Practical Reason [1788]*. Translated by W. S. Pluhar. Indianapolis: Hackett.

Kant, I. (2002b). *Critic of the Power of Judgment* [1790]. Edited by P. Guyer, translated by E. Matthiews. Cambridge: Cambridge UP.

Kant, I. (2009). *Religion within Bounds of Bare Reason* [1793]. Translated by W. S. Pluhar. Indianapolis: Hackett.

Kant, I. (2018a). In *Critique of Pure Reason* (1 ed.) [1781]. Translated by M. Meiklejohn. Digireads. Retrieved July 29, 2021, from https://www.gutenberg.org/files/4280/4280-h/4280-h.htm.

Kant, I. C. (2018b). *Perpetual Peace: A Philosophical Essay* [1795]. Translated by M. C. Smith. Createspace Independent Publishing Platform.

Kasher, A. (2002). *A Little Book on the Meaning of Life [in Hebrew]*. Tel Aviv: Hakibbutz Hameuchad and Yehoraz Association.

Kaufmann, W. (1980). *Freud, Adler, and Jung: Discovering the Mind* (Vol. 3). New York: McGrow-Hill.

Kelling, G. W. (1971). "An empirical investigation of Freud's theory of jokes." *Psychoanalytic Review*, 58(3), 473–85.

Kierkegaard, S. (1982). *Either/Or: A Fragment of Life [1843]*. Edited by V. Eremita, translated by A. Hannay. London: Penguin.

Kierkegaard, S. (2004). *The Sickness unto Death: A Christian Psychological Exposition for Edification and Wakening by Anti–Climacus [1849]*. Translated by A. Hannay. London: Penguin.

Kierkegaard, S. (2014). *The Concept of Anxiety* [1844]. (A. Hannay, ed., & A. Hannay, trans.) New York: Norton and Company.

Klein, M. (1975). *Envy and Gratitude [1957]*. New York: The Free Press.

Kohlberg, L. (1976). Moral Stages and Moralization: The Cognitive-Developmental Approach. In *Moral Development and Behavior: Theory, Research and Social Issues, edited by T. Lickona*. New York: Holt, Rinehart & Winston.

Kohut, H. (1971). *The Analysis of the Self: A Systematic Approach to the Psychoanalytic Treatment of Narcissistic Personality Disorders*. New York: International University Press.

Konstan, D. (2018). "Epicurus." In *Stanford Encyclopedia of Philosophy*. Retrieved March 3, 2022, from https://plato.stanford.edu/entries/epicurus.

Krantz, S. (1990). "Brentano on 'Unconscious Consciousness.'" *Philosophy and Phenomenological Research, 1*(4).

Kuhn, T. S. (1962). *The Structure of Scientific Revolutions*. Chicago: University of Chicago Press.

Lacan, J. (1977). "The Mirror Stage as Formative of the Function of the I as Revealed in Psychoanalytic Experience." In *Écrits: A Selection*, translated by A. Sheridan. New York: Norton. Retrieved December 25, 2021, from https://english.hawaii.edu

Lahav, R. (2021). *What Is Deep Philosophy—Philosophy from Our Inner Depth*. Hardwick, VT: Loyev Books.

Laing, R. D. (1983). *The Voice of Experience*. New York: Pantheon.

Lakatos, I. (1970). "Falsification and the Methodology of Scientific Research Programs." In *Criticism and the Growth of Knowledge*, edited by I. Lakatos and A. Musgrave. Cambridge: Cambridge University Press.

Leibnitz, G. W. (1976). Principles of Nature and Grace, Based on Reason [1714]. In *Philosophical Papers and Letters*, translated by L. E. Loemker. Dordrecht, Holland & Boston: D. Reidel Pub. Co.

Leibnitz, G. W. (1982). *New Essays on Human Understandings*. Edited by P. Remnant and J. Bennett, translated by P. Remnant and A. J. Bennett. Cambridge: Cambridge UP.

Lévi-Bruhl, L. (2015). *How Natives Think [1910 Les fonctions mentales dans les sociétés inférieures [The Mental Functions in Inferior Societies]*. Translated by L. A. Clare. Eastford, CT: Martino Fine Book.

Lévi-Strauss, C. (1963). *Structural Anthropology [1958]*. Translated by C. Jacobson and B. G. Schoepf. London: Hatchett.

Lévi-Strauss, C. (1963). The Structural Study of Myth. In *Lévi-Strauss*.

Lévi-Strauss, C. (1966). *The Savage Mind* [*La pensée sauvage, 1962]*. Translated by D. Weightman and J. Weightman. Chicago: University of Chicago Press.

Lipman, M. (2003). *Thinking in Education* (2 ed.). New York: Cambridge University Press.

Lipman, M., Sharp, A. M., & Oscanyan, F. S. (1980). *Philosophy in the Classroom* (2 ed.). Philadelphia: Temple University.

Locke, J. (1975). *An Essay Concerning Human Undemanding* [1670]. Edited by H. Nidditch. Oxford: Clarendon. Retrieved March 31, 2021, from https://enlightenment.supersaturated.com/johnlocke/BOOKIIChapterXXXIII.html.

Locke, J. (1991). *A Letter Concerning Toleration* [1689]. Edited by J. Hortus and S. Mendus. London: Routledge.

Locke, J. (1993). *Two Treatises of Government* [1690]. Translated by M. Goldie. London: Everyman.

Locke, J. (2010). "Some Thoughts Concerning Education" [1693]. In *The Educational Writings of John Locke*, edited by J. W. Adamson. Cambridge: Cambridge UP.

Lorenz, K. (1966). *On Aggression* [1963]. Translated by M. K. Wilson. London: Harcourt Brace & Company.

Lukács, G. (1972). *History and Class Consciousness* [1923]. Translated by R. Livingstone. Boston: MIT Press.

Lyotard, J. F. (1984). *The Postmodern Condition: A Report on Knowledge [La condition postmoderne: Rapport sur le savoir 1979].* Translated by G. Bennington & B. Massumi. Minneapolis, MN: University of Minnesota Press.

Margolis, E., & Laurence, S. (n.d.). "Concepts." In *The Standford Encyclopedia of Philosophy*, translated by E. N. Zalta. Retrieved May 13, 2021, from https://plato.stanford.edu/archives/spr2021/entries/concepts.

Marías, J. (1997). *Persona* [Person]. Madrid: Alianza Editorial.

Marías, J. (2005). *La felicidad humana* [Human Happiness]. Madrid: Alianza Editorial.

Marinoff, L. (1999). *Plato, Not Prozac! Applying Eternal Wisdom to Everyday Problems*. New York: Harper.

Marinoff, L. (2001). *Philosophical Practice*. San Diego, CA: Academic Press.

Marinoff, L., & Engels, F. E. (2012a). *The German Ideology—A new abridgement*. (T. Whyman, ed.) Penguin Random House.

Marková, D., Čechová, D., Adriana, S., & Shearmann, D. J. (2016). *Adlerian Ethic – Applications in Counseling and Psychotherapy*. London: Adlerian Society UK.

Marx, K. (2000). *Selected Writings Part 2* [texts written 1844–1847]. (D. McLellan, ed.) Oxford: Oxford University Press.

Matthews, G. (1984). *Dialogues with Children*. Cambridge, MA: Harvard University Press.

McLeod, S. (2019). *Psychoanalysis*. Retrieved February 12, 2022, from Simply Psychology: https://www.simplypsychology.org/psychoanalysis.html

Merleau-Ponty, M. (2012). *Phenomenology of Perception* [1945]. Translated by D. A. Landes.

Merkur, D., & Mills, J. (2017). *Jung's Ethics: Moral Psychology and His Cure of Souls – A New Abridgement*. London: Routledge.

Mill, J. S. (2015). *Auguste Conte and Positivism [1865]*. Cambridge: Cambridge University Press.

Modell, A. H. (1999). "The Dead Mother Syndrome and the Reconstruction of a Trauma." In *The Dead Mother: The Works of André Green*, edited by G. Kohon. London: Routledge.

Mosse, G. L. (1966). *The Crisis of German Ideology: Intellectual Origins of the Third Reich*. London: Weidenfeld & Nicolson.

Nardin, T. (2015). "Michael Walser, Just and Unjust Wars." In Oxford Handbook Online, edited by J. T. Levy. Retrieved December 30, 2021, https://www.oxfordhandbooks.com/view/10.1093/oxfordhb/9780198717133.001.0001/oxfordhb9780198717133-e-26.

Nelson, L. (1970). Die Sokratische Methode [The Socratic Dialogues]. In *Gesammelteschriften. Bd. 1: Die Schule der kritischen Philosophie und ihre Methode [The School of Critical Philosophy and its Method]*. Hamburg: Meiner Verlag.

Nelson, L. (1975). *Vom Selbstvertrauen der Vernunft* [On the Self–Confidence of Reason]. Hamburg: Felix Meiner.

Nelson, L. (2016). *The Relationship between C.G. Jung and Erich Neumann Based on their Correspondence*. Asheville, NC: Chiron Publications.

Neuman, M. (1991). "A Propos Jung's Antisemitism [in Hebrew]." *Sichot, 5*(3).

Nietzsche, F. (1954). *The Antichrist [1895]*. Translated by W. Kaufmann. New York: Viking.

Nietzsche, F. (1966). *Beyond Good and Evil* [1886]. Translated by W. Kaufmann. New York: Vintage.

Nietzsche, F. (1968). *The Will to Power*. Edited by W. Kaufmann. Translated by W. Kaufmann and R. J. Holingdale. New York: Random House.

Nietzsche, F. (1994). *The Genealogy of Morality*. [1887]. Edited by K. A. Pearson. Translated by C. Diethe. Cambridge: Cambridge University Press.

Nietzsche, F. (1999). *The Antichrist* [1888, published 1895]. Translated by H. L. Meneken. Tuscon, AZ: Sea Sharp Press.

Nietzsche, F. (2001). *The Gay Science* [1882]. Edited by B. Williams. Translated by J. Nauekhoff. Cambridge: Cambridge University Press.

Noll, R. (1997). *The Jung Cult: The Origins of a Charismatic Movement*. New York: Simon & Schuster.

Nuesbaum, M. (2001). *Upheavals of Thought*. Cambridge University Press. Retrieved December 30, 2021, https://www.cambridge.org/core/books/upheavals-ofthought/3FF62D25B63C90964FF9BC72D6C38459

P.L.E. (2022). *The Principle of Charity*. Retrieved September 3, 2022, from P.L.E: https://philosophy.lander.edu/intro/charity.shtml.

Pascal, B. (1901). The Thoughts of Blaise Pascal – Translated from the text of M. Auguste Molinier. Translated by C. K. Paul. London: George Bell and Sons. Retrieved September 23, 2022, from https://oll–resources.s3.us–east–2.amazonaws.com/oll3/store/titles/2407/Pascal_1409_EBk_v6.0.pdf.

Pascal, B. (n.d.). "Preface to the Treaty on Vacuum." In *Blaise Pascal, part III, Minor Works* pp. 444–51, edited by C. W. Eliot, translated by O. W. Wright. New York: P.F. Collier & Son. Retrieved from Blaise Pascal: https://en.wikisource.org/wiki/Index:Blaise_Pascal_works.djvu.

Peirce, C. S. (1935). *Collected Papers of Charles Sanders Peirce* (Vol. V). Edited by C. Hartshorne, P. Weiss, and A. Burks. Cambridge, MA: Harvard University Press.

Piaget, J., & Inhelder, B. (1958). *The Growth of Logical Thinking from Childhood to Adolescence*. New York: Basic Books.

Plato. (1977). *Complete Works*. Edited by J. Cooper and D. S. Hutchinson. Indianapolis: Hackett.

Plato. (1977). Meno. In *Plato*, pp. 870–97, translated by G. Grube.

Plato. (1977). Republic. In *Plato*, pp. 971–1223, translated by G. Grube and C. Reeve.

Plato. (1977). Sophist. In *Plato*, pp. 234–93, translated by N. P. White.

Plato. (1977). Symposium. In *Plato*, pp. 457–505, translated by A. Nehamas and P. Woodruff.

Plato. (1977). Theaetetus. In *Plato*, pp. 157–234, translated by M. J. Levett and M. Burnyeat.

Plato. (1997). Protagoras. In *Plato*, pp. 746–90, translated by S. Lombardo and K. Bell.

Popper, K. (1957). *The Poverty of Historicism*. Boston: Beacon Press.

Popper, K. R. (1928). "Zur Methodenfrage der Denk Psychologie." Vienna: Doctoral dissertation. Mentioned in Alt, 1982.

Popper, K. R. (1959). *The Logic of Scientific Discovery*. London: Hutchinson.

Popper, K. R. (1982). *Unended Quest*. La Salle, IL: Open Court.

Popper, K. R. (1983). "The Rationality Principle [1967]." In *A Pocket Popper* , edited by D. Miller. London: Fontana.

Popper, K. R. (2002). *Conjectures and Refutations*. London & New York: Routledge Classic.

Popper, K. R. (2020). *The Open Society and Its Enemies* [1945]. Princeton: Princeton University Press.

Raabe, P. (2001). *Philosophical Counseling Theory and Practice*. London: Praeger Publisher.

Raabe, P. P. (n.d.). *Philosophical Counseling Theory and Practice*. London: Praeger Publisher.

Rorty, R. (1979). *Philosophy and the Mirror of Nature*. Princeton: Princeton University Press.

Rossem, K. V. (2017). "Socrates in Orison: Socratic Dialogues with Prisoners." *Philosophical Practice, 12*(3), 1980–1991.

Rousseau, J. (1979). *Emile, or On Education*. Translated by Allan Bloom. New York: Basic Books.

Rousseau, J. (1997). "The Social Contract [1762]." In *The Social Contract and Other Later Political Writings*, translated by V. Gourevitch. Cambridge: Cambridge University Press.

Rozuel, C. (2010). "Moral Tension in the Psyche: A Jungian Interpretation of Managers' Moral Experiences." *EJBO Electronic Journal of Business Ethics and Organization Studies, (15, 1)*. Retrieved February 4, 2022, from http://ejbo.jyu.fi/pdf/ejbo_vol15_no1_pages_36-43.pdf.

Russell, B. (1948). *Transcript of the Russell/Copleston Radio Debate* [in BBC, 1948]. Retrieved March 3, 2021, from http://www.scandalon.co.uk/philosophy/cosmo logical_radio.htm.

Samuels, A. (1997). *Jung and Antisemitism*. Retrieved February 15, 2022, from Institute of Social Research – University of London: Https://sasspace.sas.ac.uk/4412/1/Jung_And_Antisemitism_by_Andrew_Samuels___Institute_of_Historical_Research.pdf.

Sandler, J., Holder, A., Dare, C., Drehe, A., Usrsula, W., & S, R. (1997). *Freud's Models of the Mind*. London: Routledge.

Sandler, J., Holder, A., Dare, C., Dreher, A. U., & Wallenstein, R. S. (1997). *Freud's Models of the Mind*. London: Routledge.

Sartre, J.–P.(1948). *Antisemite and Jew* [*Réflexions sur la question juive*, 1946]. Translated by G. J. Becker New York: Schocken Books Inc.

Sartre, J.-P. (1993). *Being and Nothingness* [1948]. Translated by H. E. Barnes. New York: Washington Square Press.

Sautet, M. (1995). *Un cafe pour Socrate* [One Cup of Coffee for Socrates]. Paris: Laffont.

Schafer, R. (1976). *A New Language for Psychoanalysis*. New Haven and London: Yale University. Retrieved January 24, 2021, from Yale University: http://www.radpsynet.org/journal/vol1–1/vonMorstein.

Schelling, F. W. (2008). *The Grounding of Positive Philosophy: The Berlin Lectures [1830–1833]*. Translated by B. Matthew. Albany: SUNY Press.

Schopenhauer, A. (1969). *The World as Will and Representation* (Vol. I and II). Translated by E. F. Payne. New York: Dover Publications.

Schopenhauer, A. (2016). "Transcendent Speculation on the Apparent Deliberateness in the Fate of the Individual." In *Parerga and Paralipomena: Short Philosophical Essays*, pp. 177–97. Edited by S. Roehr and C. Janaway. Cambridge: Cambridge UP.

Schuster, S. C. (1999). *Philosophical Practice: An Alternative to Counseling and Psychotherapy*. Westport and London: Praeger.

Schuster, S. C. (2003). *The Philosopher's Autobiography: A Qualitative Study*. Westport: Praege.

Schuster, S. C. (2010). "Life, Happiness and Desert Reflections." *Journal of Humanities Therapy*, *1*, 1–16.

Schutz, A. (1967). *The Phenomenology of the Social World* [1932]. Translated by G. Walsh and F. Lenhert. Evanston, IL: Northwestern University Press.

Shakespeare, W. (1993). *The Complete Works of William Shakespeare*. Retrieved October 8, 2021, from Shakespeare Web's first edition: http://shakespeare.mit.edu.

Shakespeare, W. (1993a). *Hamlet*. In *Shakespeare*.

Shakespeare, W. (1993b). *Macbeth*. In *Shakespeare*.

Shakespeare, W. (1993c). *Richard III*. In *Shakespeare*.

Sharp, D. (2001). *Digesting Jung: Food for a Journey*. Toronto: Inner City Books.

Skinner, B. (1948). *Walden Two*. Indianapolis: Hackett Publishing Company.

Smith, P., & West, B. (2008). "Cultural Studies, Overview: section on structuralism. In *Encyclopedia of Violence, Peace, & Conflict (2nd Edition)* (pp. 528–40). Edited by L. Kurtz.Cambridge, MA: Academic Press.

Sorel, G. (1999). *Reflections on Violence [1908]*. Edited by J. Jennings. Translated by E. Hulme and J. Roth. Cambridge: Cambridge University Press.

Spence, D. P. (1982). *Narrative Truth and Historical Truth: Meaning and Interpretation in Psychoanalytic Theory*. New York: W. W. Norton.

Spengler, O. (2013). *The Decline of the West [1918–1923] – Abridged Edition*. Edited by H. Verner and A. Helps. Translated by C. F. Atkinson. Oxford: Oxford Paperbacks.

Spinoza, B. d. (1954). *Ethics [1677]*. Edited by J. Gutman (1883). Translated by Amelia Hutchinson Stirling (1894). New York. Retrieved May 6, 2021, from https://download.tuxfamily.org/openmathdep/epistemology/Ethics–Spinoza.pdf.

Spinoza, B. d. (1955). *On the Improvement of the Understanding [1661]*. Translated by R. H. Elwes. New York: Dover Publications.

Sternhell, Z. (2006). *Les anti–Lumières—Une tradition du XVIIIe siècle a la guerre froide* [Opponents of the Enlightenment—A tradition from the 18th century to the Cold War]. Paris: Librairie Arthème Fayard.

Strawson, P. (1959). *Individuals: An Essay in Descriptive Metaphysics*. London: Methuen.

Vaihinger, H. (1935). *The Philosophy of 'As if': A System of the Theoretical, Practical and Religious Fictions of Mankind* [1924] (2 Ed.). Translated by C. Ogden. London: Routledge and Kegan Paul.

Veening, E. P. (1987). "Monoloog, Dialoog en Metaloog" [Monologue, Dialogue and Metalogue]. *Filosofische Praktijk, 2*, 9–25.

Veening, E. P. (1994). *Denkwerk* [Thought–Work]. Culemborg: Phaedon.

Vogt, K. (2018). "Ancient Skepticism." Retrieved March 3, 2022, from *Stanford Encyclopedia of Philosophy*: https://plato.stanford.edu/entries/skepticism-ancient/.

von Morstein, P. (1991). "Anxiety and Depression: A Philosophical Investigation." *Radical Psychology, 1*.

von Morstein, P. (1994). "Wittgenstein on Philosophical Methods sä Therapies." *Zeitschrift für Philosophische Praxis, 2*, 3–19.

Weber, M. (2010). "The Foundations of Understanding Sociology" [Part I of Wirtschaft und Gesellschaft 1922]. In *The Theory of Social and Economic Organization*. Translated by T. Parsons. New York: Free Press.

Whitehead, A. N. (1978). *Process and Reality [1929]*. Edited by D. R. Griffin, & D. W. Sherburne. New York: Free Press.

Whitehead, A. N. (1997a). *Science and the Modern World [1925]*. New York: Free Press.

Whitehead, A. N. (1997b). *The Function of Reason* [1929]. Boston: Beacon Press.

Wicks, R. (2001). Nietzsche's Life and Works. Retrieved February 12, 2022, from *Stanford Encyclopedia of Philosophy*: https://plato.stanford.edu/entries/nietzsche–life–works.

Wisdom, J. (1952). "Other Minds." In *Other Minds* (pp. 206–29). Oxford: Blackwell.

Wittgenstein, L. (1922). *Tractatus Logico–Philosophicus*. Translated by C. K. Ogden. London: Routledge & Kegan Paul.

Wittgenstein, L. (1958). *Philosophical Investigation* (2 ed.). Translated by Anscombe. Oxford: Basil Blackwell.

Yaguri, T. (2018). *Unraveling Life's Riddle*. Cambridge: Cambridge Scholars Publishing.

Index

About the Author

Dr. Ora Gruengard studied philosophy in Israel and France and received her PhD in philosophy from the Hebrew University in Jerusalem. She also holds an MA in economics from that university. In addition, she studied cognitive psychology and family therapy. She taught philosophy at the Hebrew University in Jerusalem, Tel Aviv University, and at various other institutes, mainly in Israel. She was last affiliated with Shenkar College. She is a member of several international groups discussing philosophical controversies. She has been practicing philosophical counseling since 1992, with the conviction that philosophy provides a richer arsenal of tools than clinical psychology and a wider range of theories that are relevant to the understanding of conflicts and dilemmas and the ability to cope with them.

Her central theme of interest is self, and other persons' knowledge, its social and social-scientific relevance, and its cultural context. For example, in her work "Introverted, Extroverted and Perverted Controversy: Jung against Freud," she explored all those aspects with regards to various psychoanalytic approaches, while her introduction to the book *Knowledge and Politics*, edited by her and Marcelo Dascal, examines relations between Popper's epistemological and political views.

Among her writings relevant to philosophical counseling, we find: "Catastrophes and Dialogues"; "The Virtues and Vices of Philosophical Counseling: Irony and Clean Hands"; "Dialectical Ways of Coping with Dilemmas"; "Tolerance and Ignorance"; "Conversion and Conversation";

"To die alone or grow older together: Schutz' response to the Heideggerian challenge"; "The need to be needed"; "Philosophical and Cultural pluralism"; "Knowledge and Understanding of Self and Others"; "Philosophical Biography".

www.ingramcontent.com/pod-product-compliance
Ingram Content Group UK Ltd.
Pitfield, Milton Keynes, MK11 3LW, UK
UKHW041835031026
15587UKWH00002B/788

9 781793 649096